THE STEAMBOAT ERA

in the

MUSKOKAS

VOLUME I — *To the Golden Years*

THE STEAMBOAT ERA
in the
MUSKOKAS

VOLUME I – *To the Golden Years*

Richard Tatley

A History of Steam Navigation
in the districts of
Muskoka and Parry Sound
1866–1905

Stoddart

A BOSTON MILLS PRESS BOOK

Canadian Cataloguing in Publication Data

Tatley, Richard
  The Steamboat Era in the Muskokas

Contents: v. 1. 1866-1905.
Bibliography: p.
Includes index.
ISBN 0-919822-50-9 (v. 1)

1. Steam-navigation - Ontario - Muskoka - History.
2. Steamboats - Ontario - Muskoka - History. 3. Inland
water transportation - Ontario - Muskoka - History.
I. Title.

VM627.05T37   386'.5'0971316   C83-098606-5

Published by
Stoddart Publishing Co. Limited
34 Lesmill Road
Toronto, Ontario
M3B 2T6
(416) 445-3333

A BOSTON MILLS PRESS BOOK
The Boston Mills Press
132 Main Street
Erin, Ontario
N0B 1T0

3rd printing 1995

Typeset by Speed River Graphics, Guelph, Ontario
Printed in Canada

The publisher gratefully acknowledges the support of the
Canada Council, Ministry of Culture, Tourism and Recreation,
Ontario Arts Council and Ontario Publishing Centre in the
development of writing and publishing in Canada.

Steamers at Port Carling. Circa 1902.
S.S. "Medora" (rear) and S.S. "Islander" (original version), locking through.

The yacht "Flyer" and S.S."Nipissing" on Lake Muskoka.
Painting by Thomas Sinclair of Sharon, Ontario — 1983.

Thomas Sinclair is an illustrator of historical transportation machinery, having for many years painted aircraft and automobiles as well as railway scenes. His work has been exhibited in a number of Ontario galleries.

A commercial artist by profession, he lives in the country north of Toronto.

FOREWORD

This writer's interest in steamboats, and in particular those on the Muskoka Lakes, began in 1952 at the highly impressionable age of ten, when his family obtained a cottage on Lake Muskoka and began summering there. That same season he took his first of many 100 Mile Cruises aboard the lordly *Sagamo*, which was then nearing the end of her dignified career. To the author, the "Sag" seemed like a miniature ocean liner — and sounded like one too! His imagination was fired from that day on. It became a part of every summer day during those years to watch for the black plume of smoke among the islands, announcing that "The steamboat's coming!" Whenever possible, it was customary to hop into one's motorboat and scuttle out to meet the big ships on their runs, and to chase them as far as possible. Thus the writer was privileged to witness the last remnants of a gracious, charming era. We cherished the lake steamers because they were haughty, graceful and large, and because we realized that they were a vanishing breed whose days were numbered. We missed them very much when they were gone.

It did not take long for the writer to sense that the lake steamers had a long history behind them. Having a passion for history generally, he soon began to delve into the past; trying to find out more about the boats. Little did he imagine that it would turn into a 30-year search, eventually involving thousands of hours of wading through pictures, books, manuscripts, newspapers and documents. Best of all were the scores of interviews, many with people no longer with us, in an effort to piece together a gigantic mosaic of a million inlays, of which at least 950,000 were missing. In spite of the enormous complexity of the subject matter, however, it has been an exciting quest; an attempt to salvage some of the lore of the past. This book, and its sequel, are the results of those efforts.

The author wishes to thank all those who, in diverse ways, have helped to make this book possible, and to apologize for any errors or omissions which will inevitably be found in it. For these and all other defects he assumes full responsibility. If the text seems too long and cumbersome, the writer can only shrug helplessly and beg to remind the reader that it would have been much longer still, had a lot more information not been deleted from it. If at times the author has plagiarized a bit from some of his earlier writings, he can only reply that sometimes he was unable to think of a better way to express his ideas. And if perceptive readers notice discrepancies between this book and any others by this writer, let him freely admit that additional research has sometimes thrown a new light on things and induced him to alter some of his earlier impressions. At the very least, he hopes and believes that most of his information and conclusions are correct. As to his biases, which may become obvious to the reader, the author is proud to acknowledge them. What could be more monotonous than unbiased history?

If this book and its future partner (Volume II) prove to be of some interest, and help to arouse a deeper awareness and appreciation of the lake steamers of old, the author will consider his efforts amply rewarded.

Three Grand Old Ladies in their Heyday.
Crammed with passengers, the S.S. "Medora" (left), "Muskoka" and "Nipissing" leave the port of Gravenhurst in concert, around 1904.

Str. "Rosseau"

CONTENTS

S.S. "Oriole" on the Muskoka River.
Courtesy of the late Mr. Lester Turnbull, Dundas.

S.S. "Kenozha" (Third Version) at Port Carling.

The Navigation Company Fleet at Gravenhurst, 1908.
The boats are now liveried in white! Shown above (from left) are the S.S. "Nipissing", "Muskoka", "Oriole", "Medora" and "Kenozha" on the marine railway. The Company houseboat "Victoria" appears at the right.

Regatta at Port Sandfield, 1898.
The S.S. "Medora" and the tug "Queen of the Isles" are in attendance, both in the canal. Prospect House is in the background.

Crew of the S.S. "Muskoka", Circa 1900.
Captain C.E. Jackson appears in the back row, third from the left.

INTRODUCTION

Where the mighty, majestic Canadian Shield spreads its wrinkled Precambrian crust into Southern Ontario, there lies, directly east of Georgian Bay and north of the Severn River, a large tract of land, totalling 5,921 square miles. This tract, extending north to Lake Nipissing and east to Algonquin Park and the Haliburton highlands, is divided into two sections: the District Municipality of Muskoka to the south (totalling some 1,585 square miles), and the much larger District of Parry Sound to the north. It is these two districts that form the setting for our story.

Most Canadians are well aware of the nature of the Shield. Some know it as a vast expanse of rolling, sterile granite stretching from Labrador to Alberta and the Arctic wastes. Carelessly splattered with thousands of lakes and swamps and dressed with millions of acres of birch, pine and hardwoods, it subsists precariously on a thin layer of acidic black soil, through which the gray rocks protrude in all directions. To many, the Shield is the great barrier, hindering and obstructing transport and communications across the nation. To others it is the gigantic storehouse of lumber, pulpwood and mineral ores (not to mention furs), which now gives employment to thousands of people and provides the lifeblood of countless communities and corporations — and helps make Canada one of the luckiest and most affluent countries on Earth. To many the Shield is the ideal untamed recreation area, challenging the fortitude of the canoe-tripper, the resourcefulness of the hunter, and the patient dexterity of the angler. And finally, for thousands of city-dwellers weary of the noise, the constrictions and the frantic pace of urban life, the Shield is the lovely sylvan setting for their cottages and summer homes, amid the pine-scented air of the northern forests, close to a placid lake or stream. For better and for worse, much of Canada 'is' the Canadian Shield.

In some respects the Districts of Muskoka and Parry Sound are typical of the Shield country, whereas, in others they are unique and distinct even from each other. Geographically, the two districts lie almost entirely within the watershed of Georgian Bay, into which almost all their lakes and rivers flow, in contrast with the adjoining District of Nipissing, which lies mostly within the embrace of the Ottawa River system, and the County of Haliburton, whose waters empty southwards into the Kawartha Lakes. Climatically, Muskoka and Parry Sound share the warm short summers and cold bracing winters characteristic of the Shield, though a combination of southern latitudes and the warming influences of the Great Lakes help to moderate the severity of the cold season. Agriculturally, the two districts contain a rather unusual amount of land suitable for farming. Despite fires, erosion and the ice ages that relentlessly scoured the region, there are still numerous pockets of clay soil scattered here and there, allowing a few farmers to scrape a marginal living raising cattle or cultivating hay or root crops. As a result the area supports a denser permanent population than most other portions of the Shield. Mineralogically, the region is almost barren of the immense mineral resources characteristic of more northerly areas such as the Sudbury basin and the Porcupine.

Other accidents of geography have had profound effects on Muskoka and Parry Sound within the space of recorded history. Unlike most other parts of the Shield, the two districts lie relatively close to large metropolitan centres, Toronto in particular. All of the major arteries of transport and communications between Toronto and the mines and mills of the central Shield pass directly through the Muskokas. As a result, Muskoka and Parry Sound are served by three railway lines and a network of excellent roads, which together go a long way towards eliminating the problem of isolation and remoteness dogging so many other portions of the Shield country.

It would be misleading, however, to suggest that the extensive transportation facilities in the Muskokas are solely a by-product of commercial exploitation of the mines and forests of Northern Ontario. Historically, they are a refinement and expansion of the amenities already provided by Nature, which means, of course, the waterways. Since the days of the Indian and the fur trader, travel northward from Toronto has been immensely simplified by the navigable lakes and rivers. As early as 1615 Étienne Brulé, in making his exploratory trek from Georgian Bay to what is now the capital of Ontatio, took advantage of the forty-mile expanse of Lake Simcoe. This lake also helped to attract traffic moving east and west across the province, in conjunction with the Trent River system. In due course the Muskoka Lakes were also to prove both destinations and points of passage in the lengthening transport route north from Toronto.

No doubt the lakes are the most distinctive feature of Muskoka. All portions of the Shield are well watered with lakes and rivers, but few regions can match Muskoka with respect to lengthy, navigable waterways that lead somewhere. Essentially there are two separate lake chains in the district, which between them provide access to seventeen of Muskoka's twenty-one townships, plus two more in the Parry Sound District. The principal chain, of course, is composed of Lake Muskoka, Lake Rosseau, and Lake Joseph, whose shorelines total abour 140 miles. Of the three, Lake Muskoka is the largest and most southerly, extending about sixteen miles from the Town of Gravenhurst, at its southernmost tip, to the Indian River, a short three-mile stream which flows from Lake Rosseau. On the river stands the village of Port Carling, popularly and fittingly known as the "hub of the lakes". Beyond Port Carling lies Lake Rosseau, which stretches another fourteen miles northward. Immediately to the west of Lake Rosseau is its twin, Lake Joseph, the smallest, and some would say, the loveliest, of the three Muskoka Lakes. All three are exceedingly irregular in shape, and studded with hundreds of rocky islands large and small, but those on Lake Joseph have the steepest shorelines, and hence the grandest scenery. The two upper lakes are maintained at the same level (742 feet above the sea), and they are connected naturally by the Joseph River, and artificially by a short canal at the tiny village of Port Sandfield. Both lakes are about three feet higher than Lake Muskoka, and both drain into it. The former rapids on the Indian River have long since been tamed by the construction of locks and a dam at Port Carling.

Lake Muskoka also receives the waters of the North Muskoka lakes, often called the Huntsville lakes, which empty into the east side of Lake Muskoka by way of the two branches of the Muskoka River. The river itself is navigable for a distance of six miles from Lake Muskoka, as far as the Town of Bracebridge. About thirteen miles north of Bracebridge lies Mary Lake, on the west branch of the Muskoka River, where stands the charming village of Port Sydney. Eight miles northeast of Port Sydney, Mary Lake contracts and gives way to the sinuous upper portion of the river, flowing down from Fairy Lake, at the west end of which lies the Town of Huntsville. Except for the branch to Port Sydney, the Huntsville lake system forms an essentially east-west water route, extending about ten miles northwest of Huntsville by way of Vernon Lake, and twelve miles east across Fairy and Peninsula Lakes. All three are at the same elevation, and are linked by short streams. Mary Lake, by contrast, is eight feet lower, but again a lock on the upper Muskoka River allows boats to navigate between them without portaging.

Immediately to the east of the Huntsville lakes is the Lake of Bays, the source of the east branch of the Muskoka River, which joins its westerly twin at Bracebridge. From its outlet, at the village of Baysville, the Lake of Bays extends two long arms; one spreading northwards about fourteen miles to the little hamlet of Dwight, and the other about eighteen miles northeastward to the small village of Dorset. Six townships are watered by the Lake of Bays, and five more by the neighbouring Huntsville lakes. The north arm of the Lake of Bays, in fact, comes to within a mile of the Huntsville lakes, but there is no connection between them. Notwithstanding, they have always been lumped together, traditionally, historically and commercially, with the Town of Huntsville serving as the focal point for the whole.

The North Muskoka lakes, except Mary Lake, are maintained at a level of 931 feet above sea level, and the Lake of Bays at 1,036 feet. Both chains are of course fed by numerous small lakes and rivers flowing southwards from the Almaguin Highlands of the Parry Sound District and Algonquin Park. All of these empty into Lake Muskoka, which itself drains westward into Georgian Bay by way of the Moon and Musquash Rivers. The outlet is at the little town of Bala.

On the average map the Muskoka Lakes usually look very tiny — quite a misleading impression. Being right in the heart of Ontario's most popular resort and cottage-country the lakes are used today almost exclusively for recreation, and on any pleasant summer day, they are certain to be teeming with pleasure craft. This being so, it is difficult for the modern observer to understand that these same lakes were once used very intensively for the much more serious pursuits of travel, trade and commerce. Distances of eight, ten, twenty or even forty miles seem inconsequential to the man with a motorboat or an automobile. To the man with only a canoe or rowboat, or a horse and wagon, or perhaps only his own two feet, however, a distance of ten miles becomes something to reckon with, especially if it happens to be through sparsely-populated bush country. For this reason, the existence of the Muskoka Lakes was welcomed by travellers and forwarders alike, especially if the only alternatives were muddy, stumpy trails. (This state of affairs did not change markedly until the 1930s.) Historically, then, the Muskoka Lakes must be seen as former transport routes and commerce-carriers, the importance of which once transcended the immediate areas which they served. Besides that, practically all the more important communities in the District owe their very existence to the waterways, and in many cases entire industries did as well.

If the growth and development of the Muskoka District was influenced enormously by its waterways, the same cannot be said of such neighbouring regions as Haliburton and Parry Sound. Haliburton County is liberally sprinkled with lakes and drained by large rivers, often flowing in convenient directions. But the lakes of Haliburton are mostly rather small, and the rivers much interspersed with rapids and waterfalls. Thus the people of Haliburton, throughout their history, have been forced to rely primarily on land transportation, a serious handicap in the days when railways were few and roads wretched. This was undoubtedly one of the main reasons why the growth of the settlement in Haliburton, even in the best of times, always lagged behind that of Muskoka. Only the lumber trade was ever able to derive much advantage from the Haliburton waterways: to the lumberman, small lakes and fast-flowing streams were often a positive advantage in the moving of logs.

The Parry Sound District resembles Haliburton, and differs from Muskoka, in that its lakes are quite small (Lake Nipissing excepted), and its rivers frequently fast flowing. Furthermore, the rivers all move in a westerly direction toward Georgian Bay. All this was quite satisfactory to the lumbermen, who, during the last century, were engaged in cutting primarily for the American market across the Great Lakes, but it was not very helpful to incoming settlers moving mostly northwards with their goods and chattels, or to forwarders trying to transport provisions. With only meandering roads to link the scattered settlements together, the sprawling Parry Sound District has always lacked cohesion, and today there are clear indications that the eastern portion, usually called the Almaguin Highlands, is starting to split off from the rest of the district.

Excepting canoe routes, only three portions of the Parry Sound District are blessed with extensively navigable waterways. One of these is the region of Lake Nipissing. The second is the Pickerel River area, south of the French River, between Port Loring and Lost Channel. The third is the central section of the Magnetawan River, between the village of Burks Falls and the hamlet of Ahmic Harbour, about thirty-five miles west. Both of the latter two systems encompass a string of local lakes, and both tended to serve as feeder routes to the main, north-south movement of traffic. Besides these, several small lakes in Parry Sound have been used for navigation on a severely limited and local scale.

There is very little evidence that the waterways of either Muskoka or Parry Sound were ever utilized to any extent as east-west corridors except by the Indians and perhaps a few nameless fur traders. As an artery between Georgian Bay and the Ottawa River, the celebrated voyageur route by way of Lake Nipissing and the French River has always stood unrivalled. The Georgian Bay coastline has a number of good harbours (that of the Town of Parry Sound itself being one of the best on the Great Lakes!), but the rocky forested hinterland is far too poor to allow any coastal community to develop very much. The actual Town of Parry Sound has only about 6,000 permanent residents. An effort was made to develop its hinterland in 1896, by building a railway from Ottawa and Arnprior to Depot Harbour. Significantly, however, the railway failed to pay for itself once the pineries were depleted, and not surprisingly it has been largely dismantled since. Georgian Bay will play only a modest role in our story.

As transport routes for large vessels, the interior waterways of Parry Sound were unsuited for anything but occasional feeders to the major north-south avenues of commerce. Not so the Muskoka Lakes. Once settlement was under way and steamboats were in service, the Muskoka systems provided (for a time) vital links in a transport network extending as far north as Lake Nipissing. Initially, traffic went by stage up Yonge Street from Toronto to Lake Simcoe, where steamers and schooners took over. Then, as "civilization" crept northwards, Lake Couchiching, that long narrow finger appended to the north end of Lake Simcoe and pointing straight north to Muskoka, was added to the boat route. By 1860 a "road" of sorts was opened across the fifteen-mile gap between Washago, at the head of Lake Couchiching, and Gravenhurst on Lake Muskoka. From here travellers could take one of three routes further north. One way was by boat to Bracebridge on the Muskoka River, then overland about eleven miles to Port Sydney, and continuing another nine miles by boat up Mary Lake to Huntsville, then resuming the trek overland. Or they could proceed by boat from Gravenhurst to Port Carling and on to Rosseau, then overland another 67 miles to Lake Nipissing. Or they could veer west to Port Sandfield by boat, continue to the head of Lake Joseph, a distance of fourteen miles, and trek overland another eighteen miles to Parry Sound.

As the years went by, the routes were improved. In order to open up and exploit its hinterland, the City of Toronto in 1853 supplemented Yonge Street by building a railway to Lake Simcoe. As a result, local outposts such as Barrie and Orillia developed as transshipping points and distribution centres along the route. Later, as these communities grew and became small commercial entrepôts in their own right, they strove to expand their own hinterlands by opening new roads north and west. One of these, the Muskoka Road, extended the corridor from Washago up to Lake Muskoka and places further north. Gravenhurst emerged where the Muskoka Road reached Lake Muskoka, and with the advent of steamboating it, too, became a major transshipping point as cargoes were unloaded from stages onto steamers heading for Bracebridge and Port Carling. Since the steamers were unable to proceed past Bracebridge falls, that town became the chief distribution centre for Muskoka. Port Carling likewise sprang up where the boats had to meet and exchange cargoes around its rapids, while the village of Rosseau became the unloading point from the boats to the stages of the Nipissing Road, which crossed the interior of the Parry Sound District. The Muskoka communities thus began as dependencies of Orillia, just as Orillia and Barrie were satellites of Toronto. Naturally, all of them supported the extension of the railway from Barrie to Gravenhurst in 1871-75.

The same pattern was repeated further north. Port Sydney emerged as another transfer point from stages to steamers, and Huntsville as the hub of the north Muskoka Lakes, beyond which commodities had to be unloaded onto stages proceeding up the Muskoka Road. Wherever the road crossed a major river, as at Burks Falls and South River, or tapped a major lake, as at Sundridge and Callander, a town or village was born. On and on, the tentacles of trade and transport uncoiled, ultimately as far as Moosonee.

Every so often patterns could be altered. For example, stage lines sometimes lost their business to steamboats during the navigating season, as water transport supplanted land travel. Steamboats occasionally caused the decline of promising inland communities not accessible by boat. Railway extensions often had momentous consequences, shifting trade routes and bringing prosperity to the towns in their path — and stagnation to those they bypassed. The railways reasserted the basic primacay of land travel, as modern highways are continuing to do today, and it goes almost without saying that whenever boat services were put into direct competition with railways, the railways sooner or later won. Some of the inland boat services managed to survive the advent of the railway era, but only sightseeing craft, at best, could co-exist with the automobile.

These are some of the themes of our story: the role played by steamboats and their interactions with other forces and agencies in the historical evolution of the Muskoka and Parry Sound Districts from the 1860s to modern times. Our heroes — if historians are still entitled to have heroes — will be the men who planned, built, launched and ran the steamers. The villains will be all those persons and agencies that tried to prevent steamers from sailing. And our heroines will be the boats themselves.

Lake Muskoka
From *Picturesque Spots of the North*, by G.M. Grant, Chicago, 1899.
Courtesy, Metropolitan Toronto Library

CHAPTER 1
Pre-Steamboat Days in Muskoka
(to 1866)

One fine day during the autumn of 1865, when the first chill breath of the north wind was adding splashes of gold and crimson to the forests around the shores of Muskoka Bay, a small party of axemen and carpenters gathered with their meagre provisions to begin an unusual task, laying the keel of the first steam powered craft ever to ply within the boundaries of Muskoka and Parry Sound. From that rudimentary beginning would emerge the proudest fleet of steam vessels ever to sail on any of Canada's minor inland waters, encompassing a tradition that would span the course of 92 years and more. To understand that beginning, however, we must look back well before 1865, to perceive something of the setting that called steamboats into being in Muskoka and Parry Sound.

The early history of the region is very obscure. No one knows when human beings first set foot on its rolling rocky ridges or floated some crude contrivance on its placid waters. Undoubtedly nomadic groups of Indian hunters wandered through the Muskoka forests in pursuit of game for thousands of years, but all-consuming Time and his allies fire, snow and the underbrush have eradicated almost all trace of those silent centuries. Every so often, a chance excavation near a lake or stream turns up a few burins, or arrowheads, or potsherds, or the ashes of an ancient campsite, but these are the only indications that people dwelt in Muskoka ever since the glaciers receded nearly 10,000 years ago.

The first recorded history begins during the seventeenth century, with the early French explorers from the St. Lawrence valley. In 1615 Samuel de Champlain, following in the footsteps of Étienne Brulé and Father Joseph Le Caron, paddled across Lake Nipissing and down the French River to Georgian Bay; then in late July he turned southward past the island studded shorelines of the Bay and up the Severn River to Lake Simcoe. In the years following, the Jesuit and Recollet fathers opened up a number of mission stations in what is now the Midland area to convert the Huron Indians to Christianity. However, the Jesuits never set up any outposts to the east of Georgian Bay, probably because the Indian population there was scanty and on the move. Consequently, their records tell us little about the region northeast of Huronia.

The sequel to these events is well known. In 1648-49 a thousand Iroquois warriors from what is now New York State took to the warpath, invaded Huronia by way of the Trent-Kawartha Lakes, and almost exterminated the Huron people. The surviving missionaries and their flocks withdrew to the St. Lawrence, abandoning the entire region as far as Lake Nipissing to the Iroquois. For nearly two more centuries, the darkness of illiteracy again settled over the wilds of Muskoka. No doubt the occasional fur trader ventured into the region after the Iroquois wave subsided, but no records of their activities have survived. Only Lake Nipissing and the French River were still frequented by white men, as adventurous voyageurs and 'coureurs de bois' paddled farther and farther west in the pursuit of furs.

The coming of the British in 1760 heralded a new period in Canadian history, but this made little difference to the Muskokas, which remained almost undisturbed for another century. In 1783 Yonge Street was cut through the bush from Toronto to the Holland River by the British Army, and during the War of 1812 there was some movement of troops and provisions to the northwest by way of Lake Simcoe. Also during the war, an Ojibwa chief by the name of Mesqua-Ukee, or Yellowhead, distinguished himself as an ally of the British, aiding in the defence of Little York (Toronto) against the Americans in 1813. Mesqua-Ukee afterwards settled with his people near Lake Couchiching, and during his lifetime that whole area, including the Muskoka River region, was recognized as his exclusive hunting grounds. It is likely that his name still lives on, somewhat corrupted, in the modern name "Muskoka".

During the uneasy period following the War of 1812, the British authorities, worried about the vulnerability of the St. Lawrence waterway to American guns, began sending a series of military expeditions inland to look for alternate water routes to the Ottawa River. One of these parties was commanded by Lieutenant Henry Briscoe of the Royal Engineers, who afterwards worked on the Rideau Canal, under Colonel By. In the summer of 1826, Briscoe and his men paddled up to Lake Muskoka, following the old Indian portage route by way of Sparrow and Muldrew Lakes. From here they went on to the Lake of Bays by way of the Muskoka River, and wended their way east to the Ottawa through lakes and streams of the Madawaska Valley. Lt. Briscoe thus became the first white man known to have crossed the heart of the Muskoka District, but, as he had failed to find a water route suitable for military purposes, his report was buried in the Public Records Office in London, England, and forgotten, until recent times.

Three years later, another exploratory expedition pushed into Muskoka from the opposite direction. Canal construction was then proceeding rapidly, especially south of the border, and chagrined Canadians were finding the produce of the Great Lakes region, formerly bound for Montreal and the St. Lawrence, now disappearing south to New York City by way of the Erie Canal. Consequently, interest revived in a possible waterway between Georgian Bay and the Ottawa, this time for commercial reasons. In the autumn of 1829, Alexander Shirreff of Fitzroy Harbour organized a party of six to investigate the waterways of the Ontario highlands, and also to see if the country was suitable for settlement. By way of the Petawawa system and a long series of portages, Shirreff's party reached the Lake of Bays, the Muskoka River, and Lake Muskoka. They crossed Lake Muskoka, paddled down the Moon River to Georgian Bay, and finally reached Penetanguishene. On the return trip they took the same route, except that they followed the Severn River to Sparrow Lake and portaged to Lake Muskoka. The expedition inevitably convinced Shirreff that there was no satisfactory route to Georgian Bay from the Ottawa except by way of Lake Nipissing. Unluckily, it also convinced him that there was good soil in the Ontario highlands, largely because of the magnificent stands of hardwood he had observed in passing. Thus Shirreff helped to found the myth of Shield-country fertility, a myth that did not die out until the 1880s. (His report, incidentally, was deposited with the Literary and Historical Society of Quebec, where it did little to increase public awareness of Muskoka.)

The same fate befell a number of other expeditions sent out in the 1830s. Still interested in a practical water route between Georgian Bay and the Ottawa, the Government of Upper Canada despatched more teams to prepare maps and amass information. One of these, commanded by Lieutenants John Carthew of the Royal Navy, and F.H. Baddeley of the Royal Engineers, pushed nearly eighty miles into the heart of what is now Muskoka and Parry Sound in 1835, compiling a great deal of geological and botanical information and mapping several lakes for the first time. Their report was ignored. In 1837, David Thompson, the now famous explorer of the Thompson River in British Columbia, was engaged to map the waterways east of the Georgian. Setting out from Penetanguishene, Thompson's expedition ascended the Moon River to Lake Muskoka, which Thompson called Ground Swamp Lake. From here they completed a rapid survey of all three of the Muskoka Lakes, before proceeding to the Lake of Bays, which they called Forked Lake, and on to the Ottawa. Thompson submitted a voluminous report to the government, complete with maps that were the first to depict the Muskoka Lakes with a fair degree of accuracy. His work, too, was filed away and forgotten until recent times — the usual fate of information not put to use. Years later Alexander Murray, a geologist who made a rough map of part of Lake Muskoka in 1854, was quite unaware that anyone had preceded him, while in 1862 an early settler of Gravenhurst was to speak of the recent "discovery" of Lake Joseph, "not before known to white men". Map makers continued to rely on their imaginations regarding Muskoka; some indicating a group of three lakes, some two and some only one.

Was Muskoka otherwise ignored by white men during this period? Not quite. Around the year 1862, when the "Muskoka Club" was starting to explore Lake Joseph, its members were intrigued to discover the ruins of a fair sized house with a collapsed roof on Yoho

Island. Sizeable trees were growing within the house, while nearby were found the remains of a garden. Traces of early cabins were also reported on Chief's Island, Lake Joseph. Similarly, the remnants of a stone fireplace, as well as arrowheads and tomahawks, were uncovered near Alport on the Muskoka River during clearings. The trees overhead had been standing for at least a hundred years. Other such remains were found at Norway Point, on the Lake of Bays. Clearly there had once been white men residing in Muskoka, but who were they?

Many tend to regard such finds as the vestiges of early fur trading posts, and there is still a persistent tradition in Bracebridge of a Hudson's Bay Company fort on the Muskoka River below town, or on the Lake of Bays, which was long known as Trading Lake. It is just as likely, however, that these "forts" were merely trappers' shanties, used strictly temporarily and abandoned whenever they outlived their usefulness. Mysterious though most of these habitations are, there seems at least to be an explanation for the Yoho Island house. We are informed that it was built by a prominent fur merchant named William B. Robinson, of the firm of Robinson, Borland and Rowe, which was engaged in bartering with the Indians from Newmarket and Penetanguishene around the 1820s. The bookkeeper for the firm was a French Canadian trader from Montreal, Jean-Baptiste Rousseau, who came to Penetanguishene after 1825. Not too much is known of Rousseau, but he was undoubtedly familiar with the Muskoka Lakes, having explored them before Robinson and his men arrived. Carthew and Baddeley, in their journals of 1835, refer to Lake Rosseau as "Rousseau lake", which no doubt explains the origin of the name. Lake Joseph is presumed to have been named by Rousseau in honour of his father, Joseph Rousseau of Montreal, while Alexander Murray was the first to apply the modern names to Mary Lake, Fairy Lake, Peninsula Lake and the Lake of Bays.

Islands on Lake Joseph.
Charcoal Sketch by Seymour Penson, 1878.
From the *Atlas of Muskoka & Parry Sound*, 1879.

As the fur trade gradually petered out, new currents of change converged on Muskoka in the form of colonization and lumbering.

The idea of colonizing the Ottawa-Huron Tract, as the region between Georgian Bay and the Ottawa River was known, was conceived and nurtured by the Canadian Government around the middle of the last century. Cynics might argue that only politicians and bureaucrats could possibly have entertained such a notion, but this is to argue from the wisdom of hindsight. Few people knew much about the Tract then, except that it was covered with excellent timber and well watered with lakes. In those days it was practically taken for granted that wherever there was good timber, there must be good soil underneath. If so, the country could be colonized. All that was necessary was to advertise the area and build access roads. Settlers would clear the land, barter timber or potash for implements, horses and cattle, and soon be the proud owners of prosperous farms. So argued the government of the day. We must also remember that the frowning gray rocks that one sees everywhere in the Shield today were far less obvious before the protective mantle of the forest was cut or burned away, allowing rain to wash away the fragile leaf-mould soil. Critics objected to the idea from the very start, protesting that the land was worthless. Some even advised that the whole of Muskoka and Parry Sound should be turned into an enormous Indian reservation. But the government did not want to hear such protests, and the plan went ahead.

Why were the authorities so keen on the colonization scheme? In part, because of pressing economic considerations. By the late 1840s most of the good land in the Southern Ontario peninsula was taken up, and though immigration to Canada was brisk at the time, emigration to the greener pastures of the United States was just as brisk. Economic stagnation was looming. In those pre-Confederation days, of course, the prairies were still out of reach, locked in the grip of the Hudson's Bay Company. If Canada were to have any future, she would have to find a new frontier, and the only lands then available lay to the north, in the Ottawa-Huron Tract.

In 1850 overriding all objections, the government obtained from the Ojibwas (who had displaced the Iroquois about seventy years earlier) the cession of most of the Tract, and began an ambitious network of "colonization roads" to open it up. Over fifteen such roads were planned, mostly running north from existing settlements. Roads were the key to the north, and it was hoped they would reverse the exodus of Canadians across the border and provide supply routes for settlers. That they might also benefit the lumber companies was played down. That was not their purpose.

Some of these colonization roads, like the Muskoka Road, were completed in full. Others, like the Bobcaygeon Road, were started but discontinued when the country became too rough for road building. Others, like the Peterson Road, were completed, but soon reverted to the bush for lack of use. Still others were never built at all. The most successful roads were generally those that led to reasonably good farming land.

Building roads in the Shield is not easy. The country is generally so rough and hilly and laced with muskeg that straight roads like those in the south usually proved impossible. Creeks had to be bridged, swamps required causeways, labour was scarce and wages were low, even for the times. Surveys were often conducted hastily and contractors frequently proved unreliable, in that they submitted unrealistic bids and ended up asking for more money or surrendering their contracts. Very often, too, all they did was chop a trail through the bush and throw logs across the swampy sections. That was their idea of a "road".

Even when the roads were opened, the government's problems were far from solved. Originally it was expected that the local settlers would keep the roads maintained, but as a rule the settlers had enough to do without spending a lot of time and effort on the highways. Besides that, the roads went through some areas that were totally unfit for settlement, which meant that there were no settlers to keep them open. Sometimes the roads became casualties of their own success. If they attracted a lot of traffic, they deteriorated rapidly, not having been built to withstand a lot of wear and tear. The results were a never-ending flow of repair bills, in an age when governments ordinarily did not look after roads.

Several colonization roads contributed to the development of Muskoka and Parry Sound. One was the Bobcaygeon Road, which was started in 1861 at the Village of Bobcaygeon and continued north through Kinmount, Minden, and on to the eastern tip of the Lake of Bays, a spot now known as Dorset. The road was supposed to continue north to Mattawa, but beyond the Oxtongue River it was deflected west after 1863 to connect with the Muskoka Road at Huntsville.

The Muskoka Road was more successful. Starting at the little lumber village of Washago, at the head of Lake Couchiching, this road, which approximated the modern Highway 411, became the main artery into Muskoka and Parry Sound, and as such it determined the location of many towns and villages and the movement of men and materials for decades. It first received a government grant of £500 in 1857, with larger sums being voted over the next six years. Work began in 1858, and by 1860 it was open as far as the present site of Gravenhurst. By the following year it had progressed as far as the South Falls of the Muskoka River, a total distance of twenty-six miles. Steadily work continued, until by 1863 the Muskoka Road had been extended another twenty-seven miles to the vicinity of Fairy and Vernon Lakes, though it did not reach the future site of Huntsville until 1870. Eventually it was to reach Lake Nipissing.

In 1861, meanwhile, the government decided to build a new road to link the Muskoka Road with the rising port of Parry Sound. After several initial surveys, work was started in 1863 at the little hamlet of Falkenburg, some four miles north of Bracebridge. The Parry Sound Road was twenty-six miles in length, and about midpoint it wandered past the head of Lake Rosseau, where the Village of Rosseau now stands. By 1865 the road was reported passable by wagons, although stumping operations continued until 1867.

In the meantime the government was busy publicizing its plans. In 1853 it passed the Public Lands Act, which empowered it to "appropriate as free grants and Public lands in this Province to actual settlers, upon or in the vicinity of any Public Roads in any new settlements which shall be or may be opened through the Lands of the Crown". The act also limited each grant of land to 100 acres and set the prices at fixed rates. Meanwhile, pamphlets were circulated in the British Isles, France, Prussia, the German states and Norway, painting a rosy picture of the prospects of life in the Canadian bush, where a man could, with thrift and industry, rise from a mere farm labourer to the proud owner of a farm of his own. Among other things, the pamphleteers assured their readers that the new Eden abounded in fish, game, wild fruit and maple sugar: in fact, nearly everything except the proverbial milk and honey. Less was said about mosquitoes, blackflies, and long cold winters. Such propaganda had a definite appeal for European peasants who were working under the thumb of a landlord and yearning for something better. The records were to show that most of the early settlers who moved to Muskoka during the 1860s came from Ireland, Scotland, England, Germany, France and the United States. Not many were Canadians. Perhaps the native born had a clearer idea of what the Shield country was really like.

Upon arrival, the newcomers were frequently advised to select their lots in September, build a shanty as quickly as possible, and utilize the winter for chopping and clearing, so as to have some space ready for planting crops in the spring. They were further advised to bring a little capital, to pay for the help of some local Canadian axemen in erecting the shanty. Wives and children were best left back at the front settlements until the spring, in order to spare them the full rigours of that first winter in the bush.

The early shanties were usually rectangular affairs, built of logs chinked with moss and covered by a flat, sloping roof. In time they would give way to more substantial squared log houses, measuring about twenty feet by eighteen, with a high peaked roof. Windows were few, wooden floors rare, and fireplaces almost unknown.

Crops planted in the black, loaf mould soil and sometimes fertilized with ashes, often did quite well at first, especially root crops like potatoes and turnips. The emphasis, however, soon shifted to grain. Livestock was scarce owing to the problems of feeding and stabling them over the winters. Oxen were the usual beasts of burden until the 1870s, when they began to give way to horses.

Settler's Farm, near Port Sydney
(Now the property of Mrs. Alex Hughes.)

26

Settler's Shanties, Dorset, Ontario.
Courtesy, Mr. Brad Robinson, Dorset

Settlers and their Ox-Team, Port Sydney.
To the right is Edward Jenner, whose family founded the Clyffe House resort on Mary Lake.
Courtesy, Mr. George Johnson, Port Sydney

Settler's Home and "Fort" at Gibraltar, Ontario.
Located on the Muskoka Road about seven miles south of Gravenhurst, Gibraltar was the home of "Governor" James Cuthbert, a colourful, eccentric Scottish boot and shoemaker. His friend the Hon. John Carling, M.P.P. and Minister of Public Works, eventually donated a genuine three-pounder cannon to Cuthbert's "fort" on Gibraltar rock (right rear), around 1870. Cuthbert would usually fire the gun on special occasions. Both the fort and the cannon have long since disappeared.

The settler's lot has invariably been a hard one, and in Muskoka unusually so. Things were especially bad for the poor "greenhorns" from Europe, who came out to the bush knowing nothing of the conditions they were soon to face. Most of them had never handled an axe before in their lives. The winters were long and bitterly cold, the snows deep, and in some cases settlers had to go to bed fully dressed, wearing overcoats and comforters to boot. In the summertime, bush fires posed a constant threat, while mosquitoes and blackflies were another scourge, especially aggravating to those not inured to their attacks. Oxen were few, and many a settler's crop was ruined by frosts while he waited to borrow his neighbour's beasts. Most tragic of all were the countless cases of hopeful immigrants who spent months or years trying to clear some land, only to find rock and more rock just below the surface of the ground. Today, hundreds of abandoned homesteads along the back roads of the Canadian Shield bear mute testimony to shattered hopes and broken dreams. In addition, there were no doctors in Muskoka prior to the seventies, and no stores, except a few bush stores at Gravenhurst, Bracebridge and Muskokaville. That meant practically all staples had to be brought in from the front, by the settlers themselves, since there were no transport facilities until 1866. There are accounts of settlers having to walk as far as Orillia, or even Barrie, just to buy a sack of flour or mail a letter, and then carry commodities home on their backs over wretched roads. Small wonder that so many of them became discouraged and left.

Numerous abuses compounded these problems. Settlers who purchased lots on an instalment basis had great difficulty paying for them, since for years their labours were unremunerative. Speculators acquired land but left it uncleared, hoping to sell it at inflated prices, thus blocking the way for serious settlers. Others bought land solely for the pine, which they cut and sold as quickly as possible. Then they abandoned their lots. In 1865 the

Simcoe County Council, to whose jurisdiction the Muskoka townships were originally assigned, sent a memorial to the Governor-General, pointing out several of the above problems and recommending free grants (rather than sales) of lands with stringent duties of settlement attached. Speculators who were doing nothing with their holdings should not be allowed to keep them. Not until 1868 did the government revise its policies along those lines.

How many people actually moved into Muskoka during those years? In 1859 Mr. Richard Jose Oliver, one of the new locating agents for the Crown lands, met a group of waiting applicants at Severn Bridge and issued seventeen tickets for lots along the newly opened Muskoka Road. By the end of the year he could report 54 locations, and added that some of the settlers were planning to enlarge their holdings by purchasing more land. Already they were asking for a postal service and planning a church and school. The Canadian Sessional Papers for 1860 indicate that 41 actual settlers had cleared a total of 170 acres in Muskoka. By 1861 Mr. Oliver reported 180 people living in the District, a figure which climbed to 281 by the end of 1862, with 743 more on the Crown lands. By that time 275 acres were reported cleared. The first census for Muskoka, taken in 1861, revealed a population of 670. All in all, such returns were very disappointing, especially considering that Muskoka was attracting more immigrants than any other part of the Shield.

As a rule, each new road extension led to a rush of new locations, but usually stagnation followed. In 1864, for example, R.J. Oliver glumly reported only two new locations and thirteen relocations along the Muskoka Road. Obviously the new colony was not doing well. It was not helpful that the terrain immediately north of the Severn is particularly rough and rocky. Travellers journeying up the Muskoka Road during the 1860s noted a string of desolate log huts surrounded by stumps amid rocky outcroppings, and wondered what could have induced anyone to want to live in such wilderness. Defenders of the region insisted that the land was better farther north, but to many a prospective immigrant, one look at the forlorn rocks of Washago or Severn Bridge was enough to turn him away.

It would be misleading to suggest that the Shield colonizing scheme was a tragic and unmitigated failure. The country was opened up, and some settlers were fortunate enough to find pockets of arable land. Others found prosperity in other forms of activity. Nevertheless, the true nature of the region soon became abundantly clear, and by the 1880s the effort to settle it further was quietly abandoned.

Among the most vociferous critics of the idea were, predictably, the lumbermen. During the nineteenth century the timber trade was almost the only large-scale industry in the country; the only one employing hundreds of men, operating over a wide terrain, and transcending the level of the local community. Not that Canada, with its scanty population, had very much need for forest products. The demand came chiefly from Britain and the United States. In Britain the call was for square timber, which meant pine logs expertly squared by skilled axemen for use in ship building, roof rafters and the like. British importers were very choosy about their lumber. The wood had to be perfectly sound, without any trace of rot, and the trees had to be at least twenty-one inches in diameter. Thus, cutting for the British market was an extremely wasteful process, as thousands of fine trees would be cut and left to rot if they weren't quite up to standard. Supplying the British market created other headaches for the lumbermen, who had to face extreme fluctuations in prices and were never paid until the timber had been cut, trimmed, floated to the railheads, hauled to seaports, loaded aboard ships, and finally delivered to the United Kingdom.

Gradually, a new market developed in the United States. By the 1850s the pine forests of Michigan, Wisconsin and even Minnesota were fast retreating before the axe, and in view of the voracious demands of Chicago and New York City for building materials, lumbermen inevitably turned their gaze toward Canada. By 1869 the Americans were buying more Canadian wood than the British, and furthermore, the Americans wanted sawn lumber, not square timber, and were prepared to accept almost anything they could get, regardless of quality. This made for more advantageous cutting and simpler operations by Canadian lumbermen, though the American market, like the British, was somewhat erratic in its demands and prices.

Logs on the Moon River.

Logging near Lake Nipissing.
Courtesy, North Himsworth Museum, Callander

In Canada West (now Ontario) the lumber trade was in full swing by the 1850s, busily depleting the forests of the Kawarthas and the Lake Simcoe basin, and lumbermen began eyeing the pineries of Muskoka and Parry Sound. The region then supported immense stands of cedar, spruce, balsam, tamarack, birch, maple, hemlock and oak as well as pine. The problem was how to export the logs, since the rivers all ran west into Georgian Bay. When the assault began, it came primarily from that direction, notably from the village of Parry Sound itself, where in 1857 the firm of J. and W. Gibson and Company of Willowdale first built a sawmill. In 1863 this mill was sold to J. and W. Beatty, whose family practically owned Parry Sound for many years, and who were intimately associated with its growth. As early as 1856, licences were granted for cutting along the Seguin, Moon and Severn Rivers, but even so the Muskoka Lakes region was virtually untouched until after 1870, largely because neither the Moon nor the Musquash Rivers has a reasonable harbour at its mouth, and it simply was not profitable to drag logs overland from Lake Muskoka to the Severn River.

Thus the lumber industry's interest in the Muskoka forests happened to coincide with the government's interest in Muskoka agriculture. The lumbermen were not very happy about the colonization scheme. They wanted the pineries reserved for themselves, and complained bitterly when they found prime timber limits being ruined and turned into worthless farms. At the very least, the lumber companies tried to have zones set aside for them, but their appeals were not heeded. The government drew a lot of revenue from timber dues and regulated the industry very heavily, while continuing to favour farming, because agriculture was expected to prove permanent while lumbering was viewed as merely a passing concern. Besides, lumbermen at that time were generally credited with an attitude of "public be damned", which some of them certainly deserved, and consequently they had few friends in high places.

In several respects, the settler could be a decided nuisance to the lumberman. He might be trying to farm within the lumberman's timber limits, for which the lumberman paid hard cash for a licence, yet until 1860 the lumberman had no legal right to cut on the settler's land, whereas the settler was under no restrictions as to the cutting and selling of his own timber. Some so-called "settlers" took advantage of this to strip their lots of timber, at a profit, before moving on. Others tried to clear their lots by burning away the bush, and often started forest fires in the process. On the other hand, the settler could, on occasion, be helpful. He raised farm produce, including fodder for oxen, which the lumber camps badly needed, and as the years went by he frequently began working in the camps himself for a little extra cash. In 1860 the Canadian legislature passed an Act permitting the lumbermen to cut anywhere within their limits, whether on private property or not, while settlers were not allowed to sell timber except as a means of paying for their lots. Many a settler must have witnessed lumber crews cutting timber on his property, resentfully aware that he had no authority to make them leave. In practice both sides violated the regulations if they found it in their interests to do so.

Thus by 1865 the settler and the lumberman were both starting to invade the Muskokas, with the former enjoying a temporary head start. But the pace of settlement was slow. As we have seen, transport facilities were haphazard or non-existent. As late as 1865 there was still no mail, stage or boat service in the district, and a quotation from a government superintendent's report on the Muskoka Road in 1861 will help illustrate the reason:

The first two miles [of the road] traverse Orillia Island. This is a generally level, stony bed tolerably passable in the dry season. At the end of this distance the Severn River is crossed by a wooden bridge, supported by log crib piers and three sets of king posts — the piers are weak and ill founded — the King posts and brace beams too ponderous for the foundations — the result is shown in the swerved and sunken condition of the bridge. The Abuttments are likewise very poor — The approaches are not carried out far enough to admit of an easy ascent so that in its present condition a short abrupt hill with a mud hole at its base has to be overcome from each side in order to ascend the bridge. — The road from the Severn bridge for about two miles or more is in a wretched state — Bad mud holes, bad roots, and bad stones abound — indeed nothing but positive ingenuity or invention, — offspring of necessity, avails a traveller to conquer certain impediments of the above nature.

At the time the Muskoka Road was just a few years old!

In 1939 a former settler in Stisted Township, Frederick Dela Fosse by name, described the early roads as he recalled them:

> The roads were . . . abominable — veritable sloughs of despond. The chief motive power was oxen, and wonderful feats the patient beasts performed in drawing the rude vehicles over the treacherous highways. Outfits would at times be almost engulfed in morasses and in passing over corduroyed causeways.

Roads like these, of course, were a terrible handicap for the early settlers. Not only did they make it extremely difficult to bring in even the basic necessities of life, they also helped make isolation and loneliness almost unbearable, and almost nullified any hopes of selling surplus crops. Starting in 1862, the government grudgingly started allocating money to repair the roads, but still no teaming company was prepared to risk its horses and vehicles on them — until 1866. Besides, the meagre population didn't seem to merit the effort.

As commerce stagnated and settlement lagged, so did the newly emerging villages in the district. The oldest community in Muskoka is Severn Bridge, which came to life when the Muskoka Road reached the river in 1859. By 1860 the little hamlet had two or three houses and a store, and the following year it became the site of Muskoka's first post office. By 1865 it also boasted a sawmill, a schoolhouse whose lower storey served as a stable, a tavern and several shops. Nonetheless, despite its water power the community grew slowly, surrounded as it is by frowning cliff-like rocks.

Gravenhurst had much better prospects, but at first nobody noticed them. Two young men who walked up the newly opened Muskoka Road in 1860 found no sign of human habitation anywhere around the south end of Muskoka Bay, save a couple of Indian wigwams close to the beach. When they returned again in 1861 it was to discover a single solitary log dwelling on the west side of the road, about a mile south of the lake. The occupants were an Irishman, James ("Mickey") McCabe and his wife Catherine, who had earlier located, briefly, at Beaver Creek. Their home was a tavern, which they called "The Freemason's Arms Hotel". Mickey McCabe also built a rudimentary dock on Muskoka Bay, and as other settlers moved in the community became known as McCabe's Landing. A post office was opened in the tavern in 1864, with Mickey McCabe doing the honours as postmaster, but the government declined to accept the local name, choosing instead to call it "Gravenhurst". How this name came to be selected is disputed, but the likelihood is that it was borrowed from a book by Washington Irving, called *Bracebridge Hall*, which was popular at the time, in which a fictitious place called "Gravenhurst" is mentioned. Be that as it may, as late as 1865 the new village consisted of only one or two tiny "stores", an unfinished log Anglican church, and a handful of homes. It had no industries, no mills, no organized transport facilities to the front, and no regular mail service. Something was urgently needed to give the languishing little hamlet a boost, and in 1866 it came.

A few more towns and villages emerged in embryonic form during those years. One was the settlement of Alport, on the Muskoka River near its mouth. Here the presiding genius was Augustus J. Alport, a New Zealander who had moved to Muskoka with his family around 1862 to take up a new life as a gentleman farmer. With considerable sagacity Mr. Alport selected a large block of land on the south side of the river, with frontage on both the river and on Lake Muskoka, and being a man of some means he was able to hire help in clearing it. By 1869 he had erected several barns, developed a garden with fruit trees, and constructed an attractive home called "Maple Grove", which soon became a gathering place for the emerging "upper crust" of Muskoka society. His farm, now owned by the Beaumont family, might be considered the finest in the district. Needless to say, "Squire" Alport became very active in local affairs, and served as a justice of the peace. In 1866, his home became another post office, known as "Alport".

By that time only a few people had settled around the lakes north of Alport. As early as 1861 a few families trickled in to the Lake Rosseau region from Parry Sound. Four years later J. Daniel Cockburn paddled from McCabe's Landing up Lake Muskoka to the Baisong ("thunder-lightning") Rapids on the Indian River, where he found a considerable Ojibwa village, mostly hidden among the trees. Directly facing the rapids, Cockburn set up a trading post. Also in 1865 Michael Bailey of Penetanguishene, a man of mixed French and Indian ancestry, took up residence at the rapids. In this way the future village of Port Carling was founded.

In the meantime, activity was stirring at the North Falls of the Muskoka River, about six miles upstream from Lake Muskoka, to which point the Muskoka Road was extended in 1862. A few squatters, attracted by the roar of the cataract, moved to the site even before the road was opened. One of these was Thomas McMurray, a native of Paisley, Scotland, who arrived in 1861. Ten years later McMurray, who was to become one of Muskoka's most vigorous promoters, described the scene at Bracebridge as he first saw it:

> When the writer first arrived . . . there was not a tree cut nor a settler to be found on the present site — all was dense forest; in fact, there was no road to it, and the only means of crossing the River was by walking over a pine log which fortunately spanned the stream, which . . . was a dangerous experiment.

In 1861 R.J. Oliver, the Crown lands agent, braved the risky crossing over this same pine tree to find two lonely squatters with their log huts and attendant potato patches, plus a log house owned by a settler named James Cooper, and a small tavern owned by a Hiram MacDonald. Two years later a gristmill and sawmill were erected at the falls by the energetic Alexander Bailey, a brother of Michael, who had opened a fur trading post near the mouth of the Muskoka River in 1859, where Patterson-Kaye Lodge now stands. Bailey can thus be considered one of Muskoka's first entrepreneurs. In 1864, when a post office called Bracebridge was first established at the falls, Alexander Bailey became postmaster, and presently he also founded a teaming service along the Muskoka Road. By that time a number of settlers had located at the falls, notably Gilman Willson and William Holditch, each of whom opened a bush store at the site. However, by 1865 there were still fewer than 40 residents at North Falls.

Though the men of Bracebridge were an ambitious lot, they had to face the very possibility that their infant community might never rise beyond the level of a small village. A rival hamlet was emerging only four miles away, at the South Falls on the other branch of the Muskoka River.

In several respects, South Falls seemed to be a much better site for a town than Bracebridge. It stood at the junction of two colonization roads, the Muskoka and the Peterson, which crossed the Ontario highlands from the Ottawa Valley. Its water power was the finest in all Muskoka. There was some good agricultural land in its vicinity. And finally, the level plateau above the falls offered a perfect setting for streets and homes, in stark contrast with Bracebridge, most of which is extremely hilly. So attractive were the prospects of South Falls that as early as 1847 a government surveyor, Robert Bell, recommended that it be set aside as a townsite. R.J. Oliver concurred with the idea, writing to his superiors in 1861 that South Falls was likely to become a major centre of transport, business and industry. Already it had a number of families in residence, and in 1861 a post office, the oldest in Muskoka next to Severn Bridge, was opened there. Shortly afterwards one W.R. Deane laid out an entire street-plan for a village, to which he gave the name "Muskokaville". By 1865 Muskokaville could boast a schoolhouse, church, meeting-hall, at least one store, and several private homes, with many additional lots taken up. Some recommended that the community be named county town.

Yet South Falls failed to live up to its potential. Today the little hamlet, renamed Muskoka Falls, contains: one store and garage, one church, a public school, a power generating station, and a number of homes and little more. North Falls, on the other hand,

Lower Chute, South Falls, Muskoka
Charcoal Sketch by Seymour Penson, 1878.
From the *Atlas of Muskoka & Parry Sound*, 1879

Bracebridge Falls, Circa 1872.

has grown into the Town of Bracebridge, now the district seat for Muskoka, with a population of over 3,200 souls. Why did one community fail and the other flourish?

The reason is not far to seek. Bracebridge was a convenient terminus for steamboats, while South Falls was not. Although steamers could reach both places, a trip to the South Falls meant an additional run of three miles southward up a twisting river to the foot of the cataract. In short, South Falls is about nine miles by boat from Lake Muskoka, whereas Bracebridge is only six. As long as most of the traffic through Muskoka went by land, South Falls prospered, but once a steamboat's whistle echoed through the forests at Bracebridge, South Falls had to see its dreams of greatness fade away, as the little community speedily took second place to its neighbour.

In later chapters we will find other examples of inland communities declining while the lakeside communities flourished. For the moment, however, let us pause to note a few young men who came to the lakes during the 1860s. These men are interesting, in that they came neither to open farms nor to cut timber, but simply because they wanted to see the country and take a holiday. In short, they were the first tourists.

The first recreationists to come to Lake Muskoka were probably John Campbell and James Bain, both of Toronto. In 1860, Campbell was twenty and James Bain eighteen. The two were close friends, both employed by a publishing company headed by Campbell's father. John Campbell was later to graduate from the University of Toronto with a brilliant record, become a Presbyterian minister, and finally join the Presbyterian College of Montreal as professor of church history, while Bain was destined to become the first chief librarian at the Toronto Public Library, where his portrait may now be seen. However, all this was far in the future in the summer of 1860, when the pair decided to take a week's holiday in the Muskoka district: then a novel idea!

In July of 1860, Campbell and Bain took a train on the Northern Railway of Canada, from Toronto to Belle Ewart, on the southern arm of Lake Simcoe. Here they boarded the beautiful big sidewheel steamer *Emily May*, which took them to Orillia. Since there was no steamer service on Lake Couchiching, they rowed up to Washago and walked two more miles through the bush to Severn Bridge. Night was falling, and they put up at the hotel at Severn Bridge.

The following day they set off on foot up the newly built Muskoka Road as far as the future site of Gravenhurst. No journal of the trip was kept, but according to a letter written by Bain around 1900, they found absolutely no sign of human activity there, except for two Indian wigwams beside Muskoka Bay.

On August 5, 1861, Campbell and Bain, along with a third youth and a dog, set out again for Muskoka. This time they kept a journal. Travelling again by rail, steamer, rowboat and foot, they spent their first night at Orillia and their second at Severn Bridge, before setting off up the Muskoka Road. They suffered considerably from mosquitoes and blackflies, and also from thirst, since they considered the waters of the local brooks unfit for human consumption. About twelve miles along the road they came upon a peculiar hut, which proved to be Mickey McCabe's tavern. They were hospitably received by the McCabes, especially Mrs. McCabe — Mother McCabe as she preferred to be called. She offered them some "stirabout", which has been described as "a quart of water mixed with a cupful of vinegar and another of molasses stirred with Mother McCabe's pretty little hand and tested several times by a mouth of corresponding beauty and magnitude." While the trio enjoyed (?) this admirable concoction, Mother McCabe plied them with questions about the motive for their trip. She assumed that they were either landseekers or preachers. They tried to explain that they had come purely for the fun of doing so, but this idea was quite beyond her comprehension.

The youths then set off through the woods to Muskoka Bay. Here they found Mickey McCabe's scow, one of the first craft on Lake Muskoka built by a white man. They had only one paddle and a pole cut from the bush, and furthermore, the scow leaked like a sieve, but by bailing frantically they managed to propel themselves across Muskoka Bay and see the main lake for the first time. They were thrilled by its beauty, being mercifully unaware of what fire and axe would soon do. After collecting some botanical specimens they attempted to return to McCabe's, but the wind proved too strong, and they were obliged to spend the

S.S. "Emily May", docked at Orillia.
This fine big sidewheeler was built at Belle Ewart in 1861, and for 23 years she was the Queen of Lake Simcoe.
Courtesy, Archives of Ontario Acc. 2526, No. 20

A scene on Lake Rosseau, 1878.
Charcoal Sketch by Seymour Penson.
From the *Atlas of Muskoka & Parry Sound*, 1879

night on a small island. The next day they reached the tavern, where they were treated to some cakes and some more "stirabout". The young men also took in a walk up to South Falls, where they found three settlers' shanties, in one of which they spent the night, along with two other men, four children, and the settler's wife. Within a few more days the trio had again returned to Severn Bridge.

Summer after summer, accompanied by more and more friends, Campbell and Bain kept returning to Muskoka. In 1862, a party numbering four or five came, bringing with them a small boat and considerable provisions. In their planning they were assisted by Thomas M. Robinson, an English sailor who had made his home on the lofty bluffs overlooking Muskoka Bay in 1860, and who had gained a deserving reputation of being the best guide available for Lake Muskoka. Robinson met them at the Bay and accompanied them on their trip. They crossed Lake Muskoka, found the Indian village at Baisong Rapids, and dragged their boat past the rapids to reach Lake Rosseau. Here they spent some time looking for Lake Joseph, which had been rediscovered by surveyors the year before, but they mistook the mouth of the Joseph River for a dead end bay. Eventually they noticed a stretch of shoreline around the southwest side of Lake Rosseau, where the trees looked thinner, and upon landing and pushing through the bush a few hundred feet, they found the missing lake. For several days they camped at this spot, which they called Sandy Portage (now Port Sandfield), while they explored Lake Joseph.

"From Island to Island like sea birds we roam.
The Lake is our pathway, the forest our home."

So sang the members of the Muskoka Club (founded in 1864) around their campfires at night. Longer became their visits, more careful their planning, more expert their camping. In 1864 a few adventurous ladies began to defy conventional opinion by coming along with the boys, cheerfully sharing all the hardships and discomforts. About 1866 the Club selected Yoho Island on Lake Joseph as their headquarters, and in that same year they were pleased to learn that a steamboat had just been launched on Lake Muskoka, thereby making the trip to Baisong Rapids much faster and more comfortable.

One more topic deserves some consideration before we end this chapter, and that is the efforts made to utilize the Muskoka Lakes for transportation before 1866.

Little is known about the first boats on the lakes, but it seems clear from the records that the early settlers travelled by water whenever they could, and that dug-out canoes were commonly used. However, Lake Muskoka poses definite disadvantages for such craft, because it is a big lake with large expanses of open water, which frequently become rough enough to swamp small boats without engines. One early settler was to recall in later years that men returning to McCabe's Landing with supplies from Orillia were sometimes held up for days by rough weather, which in turn imposed great hardship — not to mention worry — on their families waiting for them up the lake. In 1862 Mr. Robinson, in a letter to James Bain, remarked that "boats are in great demand up here at this time".

In 1861, according to the 'Atlas of Muskoka and Parry Sound', John Beal, one of the first "squatters" at Bracebridge, reached the North Falls by boat, probably an Indian canoe. It is said to have taken him five days to discover the entrance to the river. The first boat on the lake larger than a canoe was a twenty-foot sailboat used by a government survey crew in 1861. The following year James Cooper of Bracebridge imported a sailboat, and in 1863 Mickey McCabe built another sailboat to carry freight and passengers.

Around 1864 we hear of additional boats on Lake Muskoka, but none proved very satisfactory. In that year James Sharpe, a prominent settler at Gravenhurst, launched a sailboat, while his neighbours the Bradley brothers built an expensive sloop, but these vessels were not suitable for large cargoes. Around this time, too, William Holditch, one of the first merchants and landowners at Bracebridge, tried the usual experiment of constructing a large flat-boat propelled by paddle-wheels powered by horses. This boat, which caused quite a stir at the time, was launched at North Falls and completed her maiden voyage to Gravenhurst in about twelve hours, an average speed of one mile per hour. Even a wagon on the Muskoka Road could do better than that, and it is not surprising that the horseboat never returned to Bracebridge. With no stages on the roads, it was obvious that Muskoka's transport facilities could do with some improvements, both by land and water.

To conclude, we can summarize the history and development of the Muskokas before 1866 largely by one word: frustration. The frustration of settlers trying to find and clear good land, to bring in badly needed commodities and export surplus crops. The frustration of lumbermen trying to beat the settlers to the pineries, and then export their logs. The frustration of merchants and forwarders in their efforts to extend commerce. And also, the frustration of government in its attempts to lure in colonists and keep the roads maintained. In short, the entire colony was stagnating, and already there was talk in official circles about discontinuing the entire effort. Something was needed, urgently, to give the struggling settlements a "shot in the arm" and breathe some life and vitality into them.

That stimulant was soon to be provided.

Ox hauling firewood, Muskoka District.
Courtesy, Mr. George Johnson, Port Sydney

Logging scene near Torrance, Muskoka.
Courtesy, Mrs. Gertrude Johnston, Torrance

Alexander Peter Cockburn, M.P.P. (1867)

CHAPTER 2
The Experimental Years of Steamboating
(1866-1874)

Early in the nineteenth century, long before the first work-crews began building sections of the Muskoka Road, a large number of Scottish immigrants were braving the stormy Atlantic in small cramped sailing ships to carve new homes and livelihoods for themselves in the backwoods of Upper Canada. Among them were John Cockburn of Mellerstain, Berwickshire, who arrived in 1815 with his wife and seven children, and soon took up land in Finch Township, Stormont County; then a typical pioneer region. Sometime later some of the boys settled beside the Payne River, and more or less founded the village of Berwick, Ontario. Amid this rustic setting, on April 7, 1837, the second of three sons was born to Peter Cockburn and his wife, Mary McMillan. This boy, who was christened Alexander Peter, spent the first twenty years of his life in Stormont. During that time several factors helped to mould the lad's character: the rigours of pioneer life, the education he received at the local schools, and the austere Calvinist creed he inherited from his parents. Alexander Peter Cockburn grew into a comely youth with a robust constitution inured to fatigue and hard work, and a patient, persevering spirit that enabled him to meet and overcome formidable obstacles and heart-breaking setbacks that would have daunted many a lesser man. In the realm of politics the young man proved a staunch Reformer, and in 1857, before he was twenty years of age, we find him campaigning on behalf of Samuel Ault, the (successful) Reform candidate for Stormont.

By the 1850s, however, Berwick no longer seemed big enough for Peter Cockburn and his family. Besides, Peter was primarily a lumberman, and the local timber was giving out. In addition, there was considerable speculation that the Trent Waterway was soon to be extended from the Kawartha Lakes to Lake Simcoe, and perhaps to Georgian Bay, following the old Indian portage from Balsam Lake to Gamebridge. Right along this route in northern Eldon Township was the emerging village of Kirkfield, which was likely to be on the canal and seemed to have a bright future. In 1857 Peter Cockburn decided to pull up stakes and go into business as a merchant in Kirkfield, with his sons to assist him. The family did fairly well, and soon came to be quite well known in north Victoria County, especially Alex. Ever the most active of the Cockburn clan, "A.P." as he was commonly called, opened his own store in Kirkfield in 1863 and became the village postmaster. In 1864 he was elected Reeve of Eldon, was re-elected in 1865 and just barely missed becoming county warden as well. These early ventures in business and politics proved invaluable: they sharpened his business sense and taught him a great deal about how to deal with people and manage them. Both gifts were to stand him in good stead in the future.

In the meantime, the Trent Canal fizzle had gone flat. It soon became clear that the government had no intention of extending the waterway at that time. Not until 1907 would it finally be completed to Lake Simcoe. This meant that Kirkfield would never amount to anything more than a small village, and soon the Cockburns were looking around for a more promising place to occupy their talents and energies. The rising village of Orillia seemed to have much better prospects than Kirkfield, and in 1864 the family, now incorporated as Cockburn and Co. built a large store there, called the "Montreal": this became the precursor of a similar store at Gravenhurst. Alexander, too, began to spend more time around Lake Simcoe, where he became acquainted with Miss Mary Helen Proctor, the younger daughter of George Proctor, an English entrepreneur who had settled at Beaverton in 1837 and was now the owner of most of the mills and manufacturing plants in town: by 1859 he was by far the wealthiest man in Thorah. The Proctors liked the genial good humour and the restless entrepreneurial spirit of young Alex Cockburn, and in September of 1864 he and Mary were married. Thus Mr Cockburn acquired both a gracious and supportive wife and some invaluable connections to help further his own business career.

Both Orillia and Kirkfield lie fairly close to the Ottawa-Huron Tract, and we may be sure that the Cockburns were listening with keen interest to reports about the new territories. The feedback was contradictory, especially on the question of settlement, ranging from blind optimism to scathing condemnations. The family generally was interested in lumbering, but Alexander's interests were broader. He wished to find out about 'all' aspects of the north-country. Accordingly, in the early autumn of 1865, A.P. Cockburn decided to take a short trip through the unsettled lands between Lake Simcoe and Lake Nipissing to see for himself.

In September of 1865, Mr. Cockburn, along with a few companions, began a three-week trip through what is now Muskoka and Parry Sound. They trekked up the Bobcaygeon Road to Cedar Narrows, now Dorset, whence they crossed the Lake of Bays and the Huntsville lakes to the head of Lake Vernon, apparently by Indian canoe. From here they paddled and portaged over a series of small lakes to the Magnetawan River system, which they partly explored. Throughout their entire trek, the only human beings they encountered were a few trappers, making preparations for the fall catch. As their provisions started to run low, they discontinued their trip and returned to Lake Vernon, where they abandoned their canoe and walked overland about thirty miles down the Muskoka Road to Gravenhurst. The investigation convinced Mr. Cockburn that the forests of the northland were of immense commercial value, and that much of the land underlying the forests was suitable for settlement, particularly around the Magnetawan River.

Putting in at the Freemason's Arms for the night, the travellers received a little "Irish hospitality" from Mother McCabe, who naturally plied them with questions about their outing. She was appalled to hear that they had toured the district without having seen any of the three major Muskoka Lakes. That would never do! They must not return to the front, she insisted, until they had at least seen Lake Muskoka. Deciding that such an injunction was not to be disobeyed, Mr. Cockburn and his friends rented a punt and rowed the full length of the lake, spellbound by its size and beauty. The lands around its northern end were then entirely unsurveyed.

Without any doubt it was well that A.P. Cockburn heeded Mrs. McCabe's advice to see Lake Muskoka. The more northerly lakes had impressed him considerably, but Lake Muskoka now struck him as offering even better prospects for navigation. It was much larger than any of the others he had seen, and it was much closer to the front. Settlement had already started in its environs. Besides that, there were two more interconnected lakes, each said to be fourteen miles long, adjoining Lake Muskoka to the north. Put together, they represented a thirty-to-forty-mile route of access into the heart of Muskoka; provided, of course, that a few obstacles such as the Baisong Rapids could be overcome some way. After a brief return to the front, Mr. Cockburn returned to take a closer look at the rapids, to see if a lock might be feasible. This time he came in James Cooper's sailboat.

As a result of these two trips, the young Eldon entrepreneur became convinced of several things: first, the government's Crown Lands policies left much to be desired; secondly, more land was needed for settlers; thirdly, transport facilities, both by land and water, needed drastic improvements; fourth, a lock at the Indian village was both practical and necessary; and finally, the place to begin operations was Lake Muskoka, not the Lake of Bays. Gravenhurst, rather than Dorset, was the logical gateway to the Muskoka district.

These explorations in 1865 marked the turning point in Alexander P. Cockburn's life. He was satisfied that Muskoka had a future, for settlers, lumbermen and tourists alike. He knew that it needed an entrepreneur to promote and develop that future, and he resolved to 'be' that entrepreneur.

He started immediately by writing an account of his observations, to which he added several practical suggestions for new roads and other improvements, and presented it to the Hon. Thomas D'Arcy McGee, who was then Minister of Agriculture. The report contained a bold proposal: if the government would agree to make the improvements listed, including certain aids to navigation, he, A.P. Cockburn, would undertake to build "a good substantial passenger and freight"steamer for Lake Muskoka.

Mr. Cockburn's report was very warmly received, and McGee returned it to him with the flattering request that it be printed and circulated under a title. When a number of friends seconded the idea, the work was duly published under the title of 'A Few Weeks in the North'. Nor was this all. The government furnished a letter guaranteeing the right of pre-emption for settlers entering the Crown lands and promising new roads, a liberal land policy, and various navigational aids including lighthouses, a lock at the Baisong Rapids, and probably dredging operations as well — in short, about everything A.P. Cockburn asked for.

Encouraged by these assurances, Mr. Cockburn set to work. First he suggested to his father the idea of building a large sawmill on the Musquash River near its mouth on Georgian Bay. Such a venture, selling lumber to the United States, ought to make a good profit, Alexander argued, and it would also tie in with the proposed steamer on Lake Muskoka, which could be used part time to tow logs to the source of the river at Musquash (now Bala) Falls. Having won Peter Cockburn over to his plan, Alexander then leased his premises at Kirkfield and returned to Gravenhurst a third time, apparently accompanied by his father and brothers. Here they immediately erected a large new "Montreal Store", for years the largest emporium in Muskoka. Besides stocking all the basic necessities for any pioneer community, the store served as a "spare parts" depot for the projected new steamer. Meanwhile Peter Cockburn, making Gravenhurst his headquarters, practically inaugurated the timber trade in the area, although several years were to pass before a permanent mill was set up on Muskoka Bay. In 1871 Thomas McMurray of Bracebridge, who was now a newspaper editor, wrote the following comments on this enterprise:

> Messrs. P. Cockburn and Son, commencing lumbering operations in the country during the winter of 1865-'66, gave an impetus to industry and advancement previously unknown; they purchased logs from the settlers and gave them employment during the winter months, soon convincing the inhabitants that pine trees were useful for other purposes than being burnt to ashes.

While the "Montreal Store" was still under construction, A.P. Cockburn was completing arrangements for his new steamer. The idea of building a large steam-driven vessel in a setting as remote as Lake Muskoka may seem somewhat radical to the modern mind, and to some extent it was considered so at the time. There were then comparatively few steamboats on any Ontario waterways removed from the Great Lakes. Lake Simcoe had about six, most of which were lumber tugs. There were about eight more on the Kawartha Lakes, around Lindsay, and perhaps four plying from Rice Lake into Peterborough. None sailed within the Shield, although by coincidence a tiny steamer was being fitted out at Haliburton Village at the same time as Mr. Cockburn was launching his own at Gravenhurst. Much later, Mr. W.E. Hamilton, editor of the 'Atlas of Muskoka and Parry Sound', was to comment that it had become quite commonplace for businessmen to put steamers on any lake or river beckoning business during the 1870s. Not so in 1866: ". . It is," he continues, "with difficulty, therefore, that we . . strive in our imaginations to live under the disadvantages and gloomy prospects which might well have appalled Mr. Cockburn . . in 1865."

What were some of these "disadvantages and gloomy prospects"? The Muskoka Lakes had many assets, including a long season of navigation from late April to early December, an abundance of good harbours, and soft waters assuring freedom from boiler incrustations. But the drawbacks were formidable. Local conditions were primitive. There were no sawmills on the lakes to provide lumber for a steamer, except at Bracebridge. All the machinery and spare parts would have to be imported from places like Toronto or Hamilton. There were few wharves either, and probably none that could handle a steamboat, which in turn did not make transshipping freight any easier. Nor were there any navigating aids, such as lighthouses, which must have made locating elusive channels like the Muskoka River estuary doubly difficult at night. Charts of the lakes were non-existent at that time, and although most of the waters are quite deep, even close to shore, there are still plenty of reefs and shoals and sandbars, sometimes in the most unlikely places. Many were discovered by early mariners the hard way, perhaps at the cost of a broken propeller. As if these were not sufficient headaches, there was then no dam at the Musquash Falls (Bala) to regulate the lake levels, with the result that Lake Muskoka was generally about nine feet higher in the springtime, following the runoffs of the winter snows, than it was in the fall. Channels that were perfectly safe in May could splinter a ship's timbers in October. Finally, to cap the miseries of a vessel that ran aground, no scows were available to drag her off. All in all, then, the inception of steam navigation at so early a date in Muskoka must be considered a risky and uncertain enterprise.

Nor was this all. Between Gravenhurst and Orillia, the head of steam navigation on Lake Simcoe, there was a distance of 25 miles. Since 1864 a small steamer called the *Fairy* had been providing an intermittent service on Lake Couchiching as far as Washago, but that still left thirteen miles overland from Washago. By 1865 there was still no stage service north of Washago, while the Muskoka Road in turn varied from being unpleasant at best to impassable at worst. Moreover, Muskoka still had only a few hundred inhabitants, and immigration was, by 1865, down to a mere trickle. Unless this could be reversed, and quickly, a steamboat could never pay its way. And finally, there was the problem of economics. A steamboat is an expensive proposition, and Mr. Cockburn was not a rich man. Where was he to find the money?

The last problem did not detain him long. Originally Mr. Cockburn seems to have planned to run his new ship hand-in-hand with his family's lumbering enterprises, and apparently he expected them to help pay for it. Very soon, however, he dropped that idea and decided to operate entirely on his own. Not wishing to borrow from any of his friends in the lumber trade, he arranged a considerable loan, probably exceeding $10,000 in total, for an indefinite period from his father-in-law, George Proctor. All of this went into steamboat construction.

The keel of the new steamer was laid during the autumn of 1865, somewhere along the shores of Muskoka Bay, perhaps close to the modern Ontario Fire College property. The craft was a small, flat-bottomed sidewheeler, with a length of 80.5 feet at the waterline and a beam of 15 feet, though she compensated a bit for this in that her decks, which enclosed the paddle wheels, protruded over the water on both sides and at the fantail of the stern, giving her an overall length of 87 feet and a total beam of 26.5. She drew only 6.3 feet of water, a wise precaution on little-known lakes, and grossed 102 tons, though she was listed at a mere 62. She was powered by a noisy, single cylinder high-pressure engine that gave her a speed of about ten miles per hour — not bad for the times. The best local timber went into her construction, and for lack of a sawmill the planks had to be laboriously cut by whip-sawing. Mr. Cockburn was fortunate to secure the services of two Sparrow Lake residents, Henry Heidman and William Grant, to supervise the building of his boat. Heidman was an old German shipbuilder and sea captain, while Grant was a Scot who had spent many years in British shipyards. Both were experienced mechanics and proud of their calling.

Work continued over the winter, and the following spring, shortly after the ice broke up, the launching took place. A considerable number of people, including practically the entire population of Gravenhurst village, gathered in their best attire to witness the event. Sliding the vessel into the water was tricky, but no complications ensued, and after a few more weeks of additional work the new steamer was far enough advanced to complete her trials. Thomas Robinson, the Gravenhurst sailor who had been helping the members of the Muskoka Club with their outings, was invited to command the vessel, but the affable Englishman declined to do any more than pilot the craft on her first few trips, leaving Mr. Cockburn to find a wheelsman elsewhere. He eventually engaged Captain Finley McKay of Oro Township, a popular and well known steamboat man from Lake Simcoe.

Captain McKay's new command was a rather stubby, quaint-looking craft with two full length decks and a rounded stern. She had very little superstructure at first, except a tiny wheelhouse and a tall slender smokestack, and her only concessions to aesthetics were a little trim on the paddleboxes and a pagoda style dome on the pilothouse, which may have been an afterthought. Compared to her successors she was an ungainly boat, but she was not built for beauty but for hard work. Her colour was white, with her name painted across the bottom of the paddleboxes. Since Mrs. Cockburn had just given birth to her first child, Mary, the steamer was called the *Wenonah*, which in Ojibiwa means "first-born daughter".

As the day grew near for the 'Wenonah' to make her *début*, a wave of excitement swept through the region. A steamboat on Lake Muskoka! Surely this meant great things to come. So sensed the people who gathered from far and near to see her off. Bright and early one June morning, a shrill blast erupted from the little steamer's whistle as the *Wenonah*, amid the cheers and waving of the assembled company, backed slowly away from the shore and chugged her way up the bay, through the Narrows and out into the open waters of Lake Muskoka for the first time. Of course, her proud proprietor was along for the ride. The

R. TATLEY

S.S. "Wenonah".
Possible Appearance of the Vessel during her Maiden Season of 1866. The aft cabin on the promenade deck at this time is not confirmed.

small sidewheeler soon reached the delta at the estuary of the Muskoka River and entered it, weaving past a sandbar which nearly straddled the opening, and worked her way up the stream to the North Falls. Her coming was no surprise to the villagers, who were then so few in number that no more than twenty people were on hand to welcome her. Gingerly swerving to avoid another sandbar which partly clogged the neck of the basin below the falls, the *Wenonah* drew up close to the south bank of the river. She was greeted with cheers, especially for the enterprising Mr. Cockburn. Did those early residents of Bracebridge realize what the *Wenonah*'s arrival heralded for their tiny settlement? Could they guess that she had certified the growth of their little backwoods borough into a thriving town to which she would henceforth deliver most of the freight and passengers passing through the district? If not, they were soon to find out.

The *Wenonah* soon resumed her maiden voyage by plying up to the Baisong Rapids on the Indian River, which was then as far north as she could go. At the Indian village those on board were kindly received by the aging Chief Begahmegahbow, while Mr. Cockburn explained the plan of building a lock there to give the steamer access to Lake Rosseau.[1]

Meanwhile Mr. Cockburn had not been neglecting the overland portion of the new transport service. On July 7, 1866, the following advertisement appeared in the Toronto 'Globe':

COCKBURN'S ROYAL MAIL LINE
(Established June 1866)
The only expeditious and reliable route between Washago,
head of Lake Simcoe, and

LAKE ROSSEAU
Comfortable stages connect (daily) at Washago, (head of Lake Simcoe navigation) running to Gravenhurst (foot of Muskoka navigation) overland (route 14 miles) and on Muskoka Lake (also upon the Indian and Muskoka Rivers), the fine new side wheel steamer

"WENONAH"
33 HORSEPOWER
Makes regular trips, calling at Alport, Bracebridge, Indian Village, and intermediate places . . . The Wenonah also connects at the Indian Village, on Mondays, Wednesdays and Fridays, with an open boat which plies upon Lake Rosseau.
    The new region now attracting the attention of business men and farmers, and for pleasure-seekers, tourists and sportsmen, it is quite unsurpassed in Upper Canada, the trout fishing is this season (as usual) most excellent.
    Charges very moderate . . .

Though detailed information about Wenonah's early years is scarce, there is no doubt that she was immensely beneficial to the Muskoka community. Freight rates dropped dramatically, from $1.00 per hundredweight to a mere 40¢ from Washago to Bracebridge. 'The Atlas of Muskoka' (1879) remarks that the price of salt at Bracebridge fell from $4.00 a barrel to just $1.35 per barrel, and that a keg of nails that used to cost $7.00 cost only $3.50 after the steamer appeared. And the Wenonah carried everything: lumber, cement, lime, bricks, tools, machinery, grain, groceries, dry goods, furniture, fodder, even livestock, all on the lower deck. Passengers travelled aloft. Rates ranged from four cents for a bushel of barley to $3.00 for a ton of loose hay.[2] She also carried the mail, which was now delivered to Bracebridge three or more times a week instead of merely once a week: Bracebridge now supplanted South Falls as the distribution centre for the Royal Mail. On the Muskoka Road south of Gravenhurst, six stages, or buckboard wagons, were required to handle the inflow of goods, while the number of new settlement locations jumped from sixteen in 1865 to 44 in 1866. Since no corresponding increase was felt on any of the other colonization roads, it seems reasonable to attribute this growth to the steamer and the new stage service.
    To the villages of Gravenhurst and Bracebridge, the enterprise of A.P. Cockburn proved a godsend. Neither community had been prospering before 1866. The coming of the Wenonah set both of them on the way to becoming important towns. To quote from the Orillia 'Expositor' (May 7, 1867),

    . . It is wonderful to note the change that five years have wrought in this place [Gravenhurst], chiefly through the energy . . of Mr. A.P. Cockburn. There are at present two hotels with ample accommodation, and one large store owned by A.P. Cockburn & Co. . . This company has also put a beautiful steamer on Lake Muskoka, which plies daily between Gravenhurst . . and Bracebridge.

Bracebridge was doing even better. Its population jumped from a mere forty in 1865 to 300 in 1871 and 750 by 1875, when it was incorporated as a village. Four years later it had reached 1,200. By that time Bracebridge had completely supplanted Orillia as the main commercial entrepôt for Muskoka. Under such conditions the town also became the

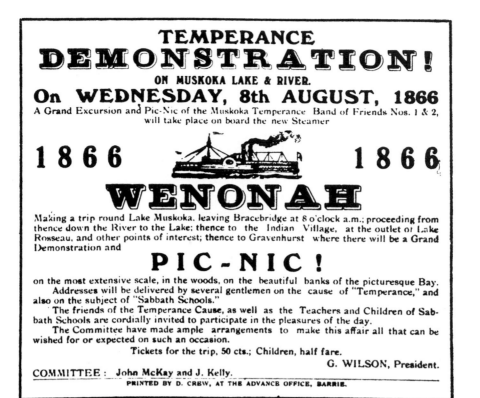

Passengers of the S.S. "Wenonah", Circa 1870.
Alexander Bailey of Bracebridge stands, centre rear, with his son George at his left.
Courtesy, Mrs. Allen Fraser, Bracebridge

administrative, cultural and manufacturing centre of the district. All of this, in the initial stages, it owed to the vigor of its citizens, the water power of her falls, and the *Wenonah*.

The work of the *Wenonah*'s crews must have been characterized largely by monotony, fatigue, cold nights in the spring and fall, ceaseless loading and unloading, long hours and sleepless nights. The steamer ran both day and night, seven days a week when business was good, never taking an intermission except when she piled up on another undiscovered shoal. For her owner, the venture caused many a day and night of anxiety and discouragement, as word would come in that the *Wenonah* had grounded on a rock somewhere or broken a paddle wheel. This in turn would entail more time lost and another explanation to irritated patrons that the boat would be out of service for the rest of the week. For the skipper, Captain McKay, there was the perplexing task of relearning the channels every week as the lake levels fell. Pioneer steamboating was no picnic!

Certain early settlers would later recall standing close by the rocky shores of the lake on a calm, clear night when, aside from the whisper of the wind through the trees, the only sound to disturb the silence might be a distant puffing and chugging noise confirming that the *Wenonah* was busy that night. Even from afar, it was said, one might see the glow of her coal oil lanterns and perhaps a spray of sparks escaping from her tall thin smokestack. On at least one occasion in 1866 this exhaust caused the steamer's proprietor a lot of embarrassment. While cruising down the Muskoka River near Alport, a woman passenger standing on the afterdeck had her dress burned by flying sparks from the funnel. Mr. Cockburn promptly recompensed her for the damages, but, to guard against another incident, he had a hurricane deck added to the *Wenonah* over the following winter. This not only protected the passengers and crew from the elements and exhaust, but also added greatly to the impressiveness of the vessel.

The *Wenonah* was also a part-time excursion steamer. Her owner, by no means insensitive to the beauties of nature, was one of the first to realize that this great land of lakes and forests might also become a tourist mecca, and from the very start he strove to make his boat inviting to the general public. Even in 1866 he had a steward on board to provide refreshments and to prepare sleeping berths for the passengers. In 1867 Peter Savard, a well known caterer from Lindsay performed this service and was touted as "A No. 1".

What was it like to take a cruise on the *Wenonah*? Descriptions in the early Lindsay and Orillia newspapers generally sound very much alike. The same places are visited, the same beauty spots extolled, the participants are lively with enthusiasm, and every cruise ends with cheers and applause for Mr. Cockburn. Typical is the following account, which appeared in the Lindsay 'Canadian Post' on July 6, 1866:

> We are informed that this Excursion was a very successful affair. It took place on the 21st. ult., on Muskoka Lake. A number of Barrionians and Orillians likewise attended it. They were conveyed from Orillia to the Severn Landing by the little steamer Fairy, the polite commander of which did his best to accommodate all parties . . . Arrived at this point the excursionists were conveyed by stages to the big Bay of Muskoka. On their arrival they found good accommodations at Mrs. McCabe's "Freemason's Arms" and at Mr. Cannell's "Gravenhurst Hotel," but had barely sufficient time to refresh themselves, as the "trim little craft Wenonah" was blowing off steam at a fearful rate. All embarked on board, putting themselves under the protection of its always urbane commander, Captain McKay . . "All on board" being repeatedly shouted, we steamed at last out into the Bay, and in an incredibly short space of time were out on this picturesque and beautiful Lake . . passing along a very large island, the property of A.P. Cockburn, Esq. We proceeded eastward, and passed up the Muskoka River some 7 or 8 miles, stopping at different places on our route. Mr. Alport has the principal farm along the river. This gentleman has a fine house and nicely laid out grounds attached, at a point which was once the site of an old Indian trading post. There are other farms probably equally as good in point of soil, but the improvements are rather backward. We at last arrived at the North

Falls. Here a village is rapidly growing up called Bracebridge, where the green pines waved but a few short years ago . . Many of the excursionists visited their old friend McDonald at his hotel, and having been plentifully regaled with the "one thing needful," returned to the boat; and after taking a number of passengers on board, the Wenonah proceeded on her way down the river to Lake Rosseau. Running up the Indian River a short distance, we arrived at the Rapids, where a lock is required to unite the waters of Muskoka with Rosseau Lake. At this point there is really some enchanting and lovely views. We noticed a number of canoes, this river being but a short distance from the Indian village. We saw some Indians, squaws and a few papooses, peeping through the leafy branches which in many places dropped to the water's edge . . So lazy looking and impassive were they, that more than once some of our party asked if they were statues.

We steamed out once more on to this romantic lake, studded in some places so thickly with islands, that one would almost, if it were not for its dark waters, be led to imagine it the "Lake of the Thousand Islands" on the St. Lawrence. At last, after *too short a time*, so the young people exclaimed as they desisted from dancing, which was kept up with lively spirit during the afternoon, to the music of a violin and occasionally the accompaniment of a big drum, Tommy Cooper put the violin in his bag, saying, "Enough, we are at the wharf," which, by the way, extends about 100 feet out into the lake and is a fine structure.

The entourage concluded by retiring to Mr. Cannell's hotel for the night, but not before several of the gentlemen moved a vote of thanks to Mr. Cockburn for his courtesy and thoughtfulness in arranging the cruise. "The people of the North," concluded the correspondent, "appear to fully appreciate the worth of Mr. A.P. Cockburn, and only wish that a few more gentlemen of his enterprising calibre would come amongst them."

Despite Cockburn's enterprise, growth in the district remained slow. The inflow of settlers, though a little more rapid than in 1865, was still sluggish. Whether Peter Cockburn was able to complete his sawmill on the lower Musquash before 1867 is uncertain, although it was definitely in business by June of that year. Hence we cannot be sure that the *Wenonah* did much log towing during her maiden season: her schedule, featuring daily trips, suggests not. When one considers also the time lost through accidents, it is not surprising that her owner found himself considerably in the red by the end of the year. Another source of disappointment was the failure of the government to take any action towards building a lock at the Baisong Rapids. However, Mr. Cockburn persevered. Probably he did not expect the *Wenonah* to be an overnight success. In October he shifted his residence from Kirkfield to Orillia, and began to plan a new house in Gravenhurst.

Meanwhile a new year, 1867, was on the horizon, and with it an increasing certainty that the Province of Canada would soon be united with at least two of the maritime colonies to form a new Dominion. In the realm of politics, since there were now to be two levels of government (provincial and federal), it followed that twice the usual number of candidates would be required at the upcoming general elections. This in turn left a vacancy in North Victoria for the provincial legislature, and, since few men in the riding, which included the townships of Eldon, Morrison, Macaulay and Muskoka, were better known or more popular than A.P. Cockburn, representatives of both political parties soon approached him and asked him to stand as a candidate.

As events soon showed, Mr. Cockburn had no objections to running; in fact, he seems rather to have expected the invitation and been glad to assent. Having lived in the riding for several years and made its interests his own, he knew its needs intimately and realized that it would take government action to meet them. With a seat in the new Ontario legislature, it would be much easier to influence the government to carry out several projects vital to both the north country and his own steamboat enterprise. Besides, his chances were excellent. He was almost universally popular, and knew the area well. The main difficulty, as he explained in a letter to George Brown, the Reform leader, on March 7, 1867, was that many settlements in the riding were still unorganized or assessed too low to give them votes, but he hoped this situation would be changed at least regarding Morrison and Muskoka.

On July 1, 1867, Confederation was officially achieved. Shortly afterwards the nomination of Mr. Cockburn as the Reform party candidate was confirmed, and on August 23rd. the Orillia 'Expositor' carried the text of his election address. In it Mr. Cockburn reminded his readers that he had been a resident of North Victoria for eight years, and that he knew from his own upbringing what pioneer life was like. He assailed the defects of the government's Crown Lands policy, and called for a new law granting free lands to 'bona fide' settlers. He promised to support mineral exploitation, and reassured voters on the Trent waterway that he would give special attention to the improvement of navigation north of Fenelon Falls. (This was actually done when a lock was opened at Rosedale in 1872.) He praised Confederation as a great boon, and described himself as an independent in politics. His address concluded with the following words:

> I shall make it my business at an early date to see as many of you in your respective neighbourhoods as I can before the election takes place, when I shall be happy to give any information in my power and my views on any questions submitted to me.

The election took place the following September, and as was generally expected, Alexander P. Cockburn emerged the victor, defeating his opponent, Joseph Staples of Fenelon Falls, by 676 votes to 407. In Eldon and the Muskoka townships Mr. Cockburn won overwhelmingly, although he was slightly beaten in Fenelon. On October 4th, the 'Expositor' carried a report of a complimentary address accorded to him by several Bracebridge citizens after the election. They congratulated Mr. Cockburn on his victory, and regretted their own inability to take an active part in his election. They also applauded his steamboat venture, and expressed the hope that it would soon prove a profitable investment.

This latter point indicates that is was becoming common knowledge that the *Wenonah* had almost completed a second season without paying for herself. The little steamer had started on April 29th., only a few days after the ice left Lake Muskoka, with Mr. Cockburn himself usually at the wheel. As the 'Expositor' remarked,

> This handsome steamer has been newly painted, decorated and fitted out in splendid style for the convenience of the travelling community. The addition of a hurricane deck and other improvements adds greatly to the general appearance.
> The "Wenonah",.. having a large amount of towing to do, will make only tri-weekly trips between Gravenhurst and Bracebridge viz., Tuesdays, Thursdays and Saturdays, until further notice; she will also make bi-weekly trips to Baisong Rapids (Indian Village).

These towing duties probably related to Peter Cockburn's new sawmill down the Musquash River. The mill was moderately large, and capable of cutting about 75,000 feet of lumber daily. By June the firm of Cockburn and Son had already run about 28,000 sawlogs down the river, and was expecting to drive considerably more before the season ran out. Very likely the *Wenonah* was spending her alternate days herding some of those logs to the Musquash Falls. It is even conceivable that the season of 1867 was the first that the *Wenonah* ever ventured into Bala Bay, since there were still no roads to this side of the lake, and we do not hear of settlers in those parts until 1868. Of course, navigation into unfamiliar waters dotted with shoals, islets and narrow channels increased the likelihood of groundings, and with log booms in tow the steamer frequently had to manoeuvre close to shore to secure lines to the booms, making the risks even greater.

On one of her first trips into Bala Bay the *Wenonah* almost met with disaster. She had arrived, perhaps with a tow in hand, when suddenly the men on board realized that she was caught in the current, and being relentlessly dragged towards the Musquash Falls and certain destruction. Springing into action, they started ramming as much wood as they

A.P. Cockburn's Residence, Gravenhurst, Ontario.
Courtesy, Archives of Ontario S 3603

could into the firebox to generate more steam and set her paddlewheels churning in the opposite direction, just as fast as they could go. The steamer slowed down and sluggishly began to move the other way. But she hardly gained momentum before she lost it again. Then the engines prevailed a bit more, only to lose some to the current, then prevail a little further. For an agonizing half-hour or so it was a desperate struggle, but gradually the steamer managed to creep away from the cataract, until finally a line was secured from the capstan to a pine tree. Then with the help of her engines she was warped to safety. After that very close call a special log boom was laid across the channel above the falls as a precaution against incidents in future.

Despite her towing contracts the season of 1867 was not a good year for the *Wenonah*. Business was slow, the pace of immigration turned stagnant again, and periodic chartering of the vessel by adventurous tourists from the front could not offset the generally depressed conditions. Nor had the Ontario Government taken any action to improve navigation. No doubt it was for reasons like these that the steamer failed once again to produce a profit for her proprietor.[3]

Another perennial problem was that of the stage service. That, at least, was no longer A.P. Cockburn's direct concern. In the spring of 1867 he vacated this portion of the forwarding business — gladly, no doubt — to other operators. Starting in the winter of 1866-67 the tireless Alexander Bailey of Bracebridge began running teams over the road between his own community and Orillia, with stops at Washago, Gravenhurst and Muskokaville.

The other and more successful stage line of the period was founded by the Harvie family of Orillia. John Harvie, was the eldest of seven sons of a Scottish settler who had come out to southern Orillia Township in 1832. Before the advent of the railway Mr. Harvie ran a stage from Barrie to Orillia, and later, it would appear, to Washago. Now, in the spring of 1867, he formed a partnership with James Millard of Orillia and opened a line to Gravenhurst. Perhaps they bought out A.P. Cockburn's line. What is certain is that Cockburn never tried to compete with them, but immediately dropped his own stage service once Harvie and Millard were ready to start. In 1869 we find the following advertisement in the 'Northern Avocate', then being published in Parry Sound:

R. TATLE

S.S. "Wenonah" Final Version.

HARVIE'S LINE OF
ROYAL MAIL
STAGES

The subscriber begs leave to inform Tourists, and those in search of land in the Free Grant Districe of Muskoka, that he keeps a line of

STAGES RUNNING DAILY
BETWEEN
Washago and Gravenhurst.

Connecting with the steamers on Lake Couchiching, and the *Wenonah*, on Lake Muskoka.

John Harvie,
Proprietor

Before long Mr. Harvie would be assisted in the business by his son, John T. Harvie, and in time they would develop the most extensive stage line in the whole of Canada. For the moment, however, they confined themselves to the road between Washago and Gravenhurst, and Orillia and Gravenhurst during the winter months. A newspaper clipping dating from 1871 confirms that Harvie stages were then leaving Gravenhurst daily at 8:00 a.m. and returning from Washago upon the arrival of the local steamers from Orillia.

Unfortunately for all concerned, the stages were often overcrowded during the 1860s and '70s, while the Muskoka Road was not getting any better. Trips by stage were exceedingly slow and uncomfortable, and if a stage got bogged down in the mud the passengers were expected to get out and help pry it loose. A group of hardy Orillians who went for a cruise on the *Wenonah* in June of 1867 failed to make connections with either of the steamers on Lake Couchiching on their return trip, because the stage was unable to proceed any faster than a walk over the rocks, muck and potholes. (The party got out of an "ugly fix" only by putting in at the Washago Hotel for the night.) Similarly, a correspondent for the Orillia 'Expositor' wrote just a few weeks earlier that

> The most of our [Orillia] trade is derived from the northern settlements, and the least we should do would be to assist them in improving that break-neck road between Washago Mills and Gravenhurst. . . . The overland route between the Bay and the Severn Landing is in a dreadful state for want of repair, and if allowed to go neglected this summer it will be impossible to travel it next fall.

Thus it would appear that Muskoka's transport and settlement problems were by no means solved by 1867. But things were looking up. After the close of navigation, Mr. Cockburn could devote more time to political affairs, and immediately he began to put pressure on the Ontario government to survey more townships and reconsider its manner of disposing of lots in the Crown lands. The John Sandfield Macdonald administration was Conservative while A.P. Cockburn was a Liberal, but Cockburn was no doctrinaire fanatic, and was quite willing to support the government provided that its policies were progressive.[4]

Results were soon forthcoming. Obviously influenced by Mr. Cockburn's views, the government on February 28, 1868, passed "An Act to Secure Free Grants and Homesteads to Actual Settlers on Public Lands". This act made it lawful for the Lieutenant Governor in Council to "appropriate any Public Lands considered suitable for settlement and cultivation, and not being mineral lands or Pine Timber Lands, as Free Grants to actual settlers." Strict duties of settlement were set forth. The settlers must clear at least two acres 'per annum' during the first five years of occupancy, eventually clearing at least fifteen acres, and they must erect, and occupy, a substantial house at least sixteen feet by twenty. If all these conditions were met, a formal deed would be issued after five years had elapsed. Each settler over eighteen was entitled to 100 acres, but this figure was amended to 200 during the next session, evidently because so many of them were finding a disconcerting amount of rock on their lands. The Free Grant and Homesteads Act was a thorough and well considered enactment, but it did nothing to relieve the burdens of earlier settlers who had already purchased lands in the new townships and were still struggling to pay off the arrears. On December 9, 1870, Mr. Cockburn would present one of several petitions to the Legislature, pointing out the unfairness of giving free grants to new settlers while insisting that the early arrivals, who had suffered the greatest hardships, must pay for theirs.

Of course the new legislation was intended to apply to the entire Ottawa-Huron Tract, rather than just to Muskoka. Nevertheless, the main colonization campaigns were directed towards Muskoka and Haliburton. Starting on April 18, 1868, the Government of Ontario announced that the townships of Humphrey, Cardwell, Watt, Stephenson, Brunel, Macaulay, McLean, Muskoka and Draper were being opened up for location under the terms of the Free Grant and Homesteads Act, besides McDougall and Foley Townships in the Parry Sound District. Of these, Monck Township, northwest of Bracebridge, and neighbouring Watt, which surrounds Three Mile Lake, were to prove the most suitable for agriculture. In March of 1868, Muskoka was also made a territorial district for judicial purposes with Bracebridge as its centre. To this end, Morrison, Muskoka, Monck, Watt, Humphrey and Cardwell were detached from Simcoe County, while Ryde, Draper, Macaulay, Stephenson, Brunel, McLean and Oakley were soon transferred from Victoria. However, Muskoka was not to become a separate provisional county in its own right until 1888, and in the meantime the administration of justice was left to Simcoe, while municipal affairs remained divided between Simcoe and Victoria — quite an involved and costly arrangement. Still, it was sensible to gather all the new townships into one territorial district, since geographically they all lay within the same watershed, and commercially they all depended on Orillia.

How successful was the Free Grant and Homesteads Act? Though it largely failed to populate the Ottawa-Huron Tract, coupled with a renewed advertising campaign in Britain and Europe, it did give fresh impetus to settlement in the Crown lands. There was no rush of immigration at any time, but we do find a considerably expanded influx into Muskoka. In 1868 there were 407 free grants and 69 land purchases around the Muskoka Road, in 1869 there were 377 free grants and 39 purchases, while in 1870 the figures respectively were 652 and 61. The census of 1871 revealed a total population of 6,919 in the whole of Muskoka and Parry Sound, as compared with 670 in 1861. The records also show that in 1861, 8,622 acres had been located, and of these 211, or 2.45% were under cultivation, whereas ten years later 175,565 acres had been located, of which 7.3% were under cultivation. All in all, growth in Muskoka was steady but rather slow after 1867.

The Act also had the incidental effect of turning A.P. Cockburn's steamboat venture into a paying proposition for the first time, but the pessimistic proprietor was not feeling very hopeful as the spring thaw set in during 1868. For two seasons now he had been losing money with the *Wenonah*, and he knew he could not afford another year of failure. Perhaps he would soon have to give up. Perhaps he would have to sell the boat to someone else who might have better luck with her. As it happened, the ice broke up early that year, on April 15th., and within a week the *Wenonah* set off on her opening trip of the season, one full day before her neighbours the *Ida Burton* and *Carriella* resumed their runs on Lake Couchiching. This boded well, but after a busy opening week the *Wenonah* sustained another accident and remained out of service for over a month, while Thomas Robinson stepped into the breach as best he could with his sailboat, the *Wave*. For A.P. Cockburn, this must have been almost the last straw. But he persevered, and by June the steamer was going again. Meanwhile immigrants were arriving, in larger and larger numbers, and soon he could breathe a little more easily.

Str. "Carriella", on Lake Couchiching.

S.S. "Ida Burton", rival of the "Carriella".

Though the Ontario government was doing its best to promote and develop Muskoka, it was not doing so alone. Thomas McMurray of Bracebridge, owner and editor of the 'Northern Advocate', and J.C. McMullen of the Orillia press, himself a frequent visitor to the north, were staunch and vigorous defenders of the district, as was A.P. Cockburn himself. The genial steamboat owner spent parts of every winter, or whenever he had the time, writing immigration and tourist pamphlets, many of which he distributed on tours to the United States, and to this day he deserves to be honoured as the Father of the Muskoka tourist industry. Mr. Cockburn did more than this. He regularly attended the local fairs, and late in 1867 he took the initiative of calling a meeting of settlers at Bracebridge to discuss the idea of forming a Settlers' Association to disseminate reliable and useful information to incoming settlers. Admitting that many people had been attracted to Muskoka with exaggerated ideas as to its prospects, and then leaving once disillusionment set in, Cockburn proposed an organization to fight those influences and refute critics who were damning the entire district as a worthless block of rock. Since the settlers themselves needed to be optimistic, they warmly applauded A.P.'s proposal. The Association was established and Mr. Cockburn was elected president. By the summer of 1868 the first issue of the 'Muskoka District Settler's Guide' had been compiled, printed and paid for by the new group. More were to follow.

As more arrivals trooped in the older settlements grew larger and new ones came into being. One of them was Bala. In 1868 a Scot named Thomas Burgess paid his first visit to the Musquash Falls, almost certainly aboard the *Wenonah*. Impressed by the forests, the scenery and the water power, Burgess decided that this was a logical site for a community, and resolved to do his best to get it started. Accordingly he bought a large block of land, which he subdivided, and built a sawmill at one of the chutes, and also opened a small store to supply food for incoming settlers. The store, no doubt, was provisioned by the *Wenonah*, since it stood about seventeen miles from the nearest road. Soon a post office was opened, called "Bala", after the village in Wales. Thomas Burgess, the "laird of Bala", became reeve and postmaster, but the land adjacent to the falls is not much good for farming, and consequently the growth of Bala for many years was very slow.

The Old Stage Road over Moon River,
Muskoka Lakes.

Musquash Road Bridge, Moon River.
Courtesy, Archives of Ontario Acc. 9939

The Honourable John Carling, M.P.P.
Courtesy, Archives of Ontario S.413

Another settlement emerged at the opposite end of Bala Bay the following year when three men from Eramosa, Ontario — Joseph Coulter and George Jestin, both farmers, and William Torrance, a hardware merchant — arrived on board the *Wenonah*. What they found were lofty rocks near the landing place and vast, unspoiled forests broken only by the occasional Indian trapping trail, while the sole resident was a French Canadian axeman named Jenac, who was living on what is now Bala Park Island. Undaunted by the challenges, the three took up lots, and while Coulter and Torrance began erecting shanties, Jestin hired Jenac to build one for him and returned to Eramosa, where the others soon rejoined him. The following spring they were back with their families, as well as horses, wagons and a year's supplies. Disembarking from the steamer, Jestin discovered to his dismay that Jenac had left without building the shanty! They made do somehow, and by 1871, they were ready to bring in oxen and tilling equipment. Meanwhile about a dozen more settlers moved in, some with their families, and soon a small hamlet came into being. Another sawmill was built on East Bay, and in 1876 a post office was opened, called "Torrance" in honour of William Torrance, who became the first postmaster. For many years, however, Torrance was a farm settlement rather than a village. It did not coalesce until the coming of the railway in 1906.

Some other beginnings occurred during those years. Tondern Island in Lake Muskoka, site of the modern village of Beaumaris, had a squatter in residence around 1869. Further north, apparently around the mouth of the Indian River, a short-lived hamlet called Little Current flickered briefly as an early port of call for the *Wenonah*, but soon gave way to Baisong Rapids. At the rapids Chief Begahmegahbow's people, upset by the growing number of white men in their midst, moved away to Parry Island on Georgian Bay around 1867. However, J. Daniel Cockburn, who was a cousin of A.P., continued to run his trading post, and by 1867 a log hotel called the Polar Star was in business. As late as 1868 the rapids were still almost inaccessible by land, but the *Wenonah* was arriving about three times a week, turning the spot into a natural distribution point. There was also good water power available, and around 1868 a village plot was laid out. A post office was also opened at the home of Benjamin Hardcastle Johnston, who had earlier settled at Brackenrig on Lake Rosseau. Given the privilege of so doing, Johnston named the budding village "Port Carling", after his old friend the Hon. John Carling of London, Ontario, who in the summer of 1869 was taking a fishing trip in the neighbourhood.

By the end of the season of 1868, settlement was picking up in Muskoka, and the *Wenonah*, for the first time, had earned a tidy profit. Gratifying though all this was, there was still the problem of river navigation. No action had as yet been taken to build a lock at Baisong Rapids, and worse, the Indian River below the rapids was so bedeviled with boulders and sandbars that the *Wenonah* was usually forced to stop about half a mile south of Port Carling to unload her cargoes. Vexed by the government's inaction on the matter, A.P. Cockburn submitted a petition to the Legislature on December 17, 1868, signed by many of the residents of Muskoka, Macaulay and Monck, and calling for a lock on the river. Some of the arguments used are quite interesting:

> . . our Inland navigation . . is so constituted by nature that . . with a little government aid [it] will supply a high way for 7 months of the year, for the Transportation of freight and passengers, through the very heart of the district, at a very moderate cost compared with land conveyance, the distance being shorter by water, and journeys by steamer can be accomplished between Gravenhurst, Bracebridge and Rosseau, with greater expedition and ease and at less than half the cost now incurred by land travel which can scarcely be undertaken at all except in sleighing
> . . your petitioners also wish to explain that the removal of certain obstructions in the River between Lakes Muskoka and Rosseau are necessary before the benefit of the above system of navigation can be made properly available.

The petition closes with a reminder that there are vast tracts of land near the lakes which are certain to be settled rapidly 'provided that' the steamer route is extended.

Widespread opposition to the idea developed quickly. Some M.P.P.'s dismissed as absurd the notion of spending public money on a canal to link up a couple of frog-ponds. Roads Superintendent J.W. Bridgland, in a letter to Alexander Campbell, the Crown Lands Commissioner, dated June 24, 1867, gave as his opinion that a canal and lock on the Indian River would be "premature and extravagant", in that it would probably not be used by a steamer more than three times a week. Bridgland recommended a tram road instead, and Campbell agreed with him;. However, A.P. Cockburn continued to fight for a lock, and in this he was supported by the Public Works Commissioner, John Carling. It was Carling who laid down the policy that his Department was responsible for all provincial inland waterways except those assigned to federal jurisdiction, and in 1868 he visited the Free Grant lands and examined the site of the Baisong Rapids. In his report for that year, Carling agreed that navigational improvements to the Indian, Balsam and Otonabee Rivers were an urgent priority. In Muskoka, they would permit the steamer *Wenonah* to extend her runs into Lake Rosseau and Joseph, for a total distance of about 60 miles. The advantages for the future had not been overestimated, said the Commissioner, and the project deserved very serious consideration. Newspapers such as the Orillia 'Expositor' also favoured the idea of a lock.

As it happened, the viewpoint of Carling and Cockburn finally carried the day. A report of 1869 by Thomas Nepean Molesworth, the Assistant Engineer on Public Works, confirms that a contract was awarded on May 27, 1869 to a Mr. John Ginty, for the sum of $19,500, to build a lock at Baisong Rapids. In October of that year, Carling and Molesworth visited Port Carling to see how the work was progressing. They found the pace of construction rather slow, but reported the work done to date satisfactory. The contractor blamed the delay on the scarcity of suitable labour, but said that he was expecting to begin blasting operations over the coming winter.

As part of the overall project, dredging operations were to be carried out on the Muskoka and Indian Rivers. A channel, some 60 feet wide, was to be cut through the big sandbar near the estuary of the Muskoka River, which had been such a nuisance to the *Wenonah* on her runs to Bracebridge. Similarly, the shoals on the Indian River below Port Carling were also to be removed. The first dredging contract on the Muskoka waterways seems to have been awarded in 1869 to a settler named W. Whiteside, from whose family the small community and post office of Whiteside, north of Bala, derives its name. Molesworth's report of late 1869 notes that machinery for the purpose had been assembled at Bracebridge, but that nothing had yet been done. It was only in 1871 that the first steam dredge was built at Gravenhurst. One of its first operations was to clear a channel through the shoals on the Indian River. Other tasks followed.

On the whole, the needs of navigation in Muskoka received prompt and serious attention. This was in sharp contrast with other inland waterways such as the Trent-Kawartha Lakes, where steamboat men generally received little sympathy or assistance from the authorities. The difference in attitude originated perhaps from the fact that Muskoka was then a pioneer region being actively sponsored by the government, which accordingly favoured the navigating interests as an aid to settlement, wheras the Kawartha Lakes, being more southerly, were already past the pioneer period. Besides, the influence of mill owners and lumber companies was formidable in the Trent Valley, whereas little lumbering had been undertaken in Muskoka by the 1870s. For that matter, the Kawartha Lakes were then, as now, a responsibility of the federal government, whereas the Muskoka Lakes have always been under provincial jurisdiction.

Before the spring of 1869, A.P. Cockburn had decided that the time was ripe to place a second steamer on the Muskoka Lakes. Several factors probably contributed to that decision. The lock at Port Carling was at last under way, and the government was already offering inducements to some entrepreneur to put a steamboat on Lake Rosseau. If Cockburn failed to act, someone else might. Besides, having two boats offered several obvious advantages: one could take freight and passengers while the other was towing, and if one ran aground or was damaged, the other could lend a hand or act as a reserve boat. However, Mr. Cockburn was still somewhat short of funds. The *Wenonah* was still unpaid for, and, as an act of benevolence he had mortgaged the rest of his property to help his unfortunate friends in the lumber trade. What he needed, in short, was a small, relatively inexpensive vessel of shallow draught that could be crewed by just two or three men, to take on part of the work load of the *Wenonah*. The result was the arrival of the steamer *Waubamik*.

The *Waubamik* is something of a mystery today. She was never registered, at least, not under that name, and no pictures of her have ever been found. Nonetheless, an intensive search has disclosed a little information. The boat was small, with a keel-length of 41 feet (probably about 45 overall), a beam of eight feet, and a gross tonnage of 7.23. She was propeller driven, with two low-pressure engines and, no doubt, a vertical boiler. She also had one deck and a round stern. According to the Orillia newspapers she was a pretty little craft, capable of carrying 40 passengers at speeds of ten miles per hour, while much later an old timer from Beaumaris was to recall that she had a small cabin both fore and aft of the engine room, and an open bow and stern.

The *Waubamik* began as the steamer *Dean*, built at Buffalo in 1866. The following year she was imported to Lake Couchiching to compete with the *Carriella* and the *Ida Burton*. Then in 1869 A.P. Cockburn purchased the *Dean* and hired a local settler from Morrison Township to transport her up to Gravenhurst for the fee of $150. According to tradition, the feat was accomplished in March by fabricating a crude sleigh mounted on runners shod with steel from some discarded saws obtained at the Washago sawmill. Two teams of horses were used to drag the sleigh and its precious burden over the snow. At times the men had to cut trees and branches aside to make any headway, and there was always the possibility that the load might tip over! Luckily it arrived safely, and come spring the craft was repainted, refitted and launched with her new name, *Waubamik* (or *Wabamik*), meaning "white beaver".

The *Waubamik* completed her first trip to Bracebridge on May 1, 1869. She seems to have handled all the freighting and passengers that spring, while the *Wenonah*, by inference, was busy towing logs. During the seasons of 1869 and 1870 Mr. Cockburn resumed command of the *Wenonah*, while the *Waubamik* was entrusted to the amiable Aubrey White of Bracebridge,[5] a former employee at Alex Bailey's trading post who had received his first training at the helm under Captain McKay.

Str. "Waubamik".
A reconstruction, based on registry information plus a description by the late Mr. Horace Prowse of Beaumaris.

The *Waubamik* did not remain on Lake Muskoka very long in 1869. By the start of the summer, when the *Wenonah* finished her spring towing, the smaller steamer had been transferred to Lake Rosseau. Tradition says she was hauled on rollers past the Baisong Rapids. Thus the *Waubamik* became the first steam vessel to appear on the upper lake, as well as the first propeller to ply anywhere in Muskoka. Starting July 1, 1869, A.P. Cockburn advertised in the Orillia 'Northern Light' that the commodious *Wenonah* now "makes regular connections with the Lake Rosseau steamer, the "Waubamik" . . at Port Carling . . at 12 o'clock noon . ." Tickets for both vessels cost $1.75 each and were good for a week. "Meals and refreshments can be supplied on board". Some of the *Waubamik*'s duties probably included taking provisions to the head of Lake Rosseau for the Dodge Lumber Company, which was then opening a road into the interior of the Parry Sound District to its camps: A.G.P. Dodge seems to have provided some of the money for the boat.

Despite accidents and setbacks of the usual kind, steamboating continued to flourish as a steady inflow of settlers swelled the volume of the lakes trade. Unfortunately, work on the Port Carling locks was still proceeding at a snail's pace. On January 28, 1870, the 'Northern Light' remarked that

> The lock between Lakes Muskoka and Rosseau, we understand, will not be completed until next fall. We regret this delay, as it will retard the settlement of a large section of country..We trust that this important work will be prosecuted with vigor so as it may be accomplished by next August.

Unfortunately the 'Northern Light' was being overly optimistic about an early completion date. On December 30, 1870, Assistant Engineer Molesworth opened another report to his supervisors with the following words:

> This work was commenced in July, 1870, and from difficulties in connection with the blasting of rock, high water and other causes, has progressed very slowly, but I have reason to hope it will be ready for the navigation of Lake Rosseau early next season . .

The report continues with the announcement that all of the necessary materials for the project are now at hand, and that "The entire expenditure on the project comes to $16,200.90, while another $2,569.70 has been spent on dredging and blasting operations on the Indian and Muskoka Rivers."

Still another scheme to improve Muskoka's waterways was under way by 1870: a canal at Sandy Portage to link the two upper lakes, Joseph and Rosseau. The natural connection between them was the Joseph River, but the river was narrow in places and had a considerable current. The engineers reckoned that it would be much simpler and cheaper to dig a channel across the narrow portage near the south end of the two lakes, than to widen and clear the river, and Mr. John Carling agreed with them. Molesworth's report of 1870, alluded to earlier, confirms that this project was already far advanced.

> The work [continues Molesworth] was let to Mr. George Blain, on the 5th of February, 1870, for the sum of $7,865, for the excavation of the channel, dredging at both entrances, and crib-work piers at each end; and $1,500 for retaining walls of crib-work throughout on each side, to meet the piers at each entrance. The whole crib-work rests on a stratum of hard clay, which gives an excellent foundation . .
> The excavation of the channel connecting the lakes . . is nearly finished, and the waters are connected; but the dredging, especially in Lake Joseph, requires to be done, and this, as well as the crib-work, will be finished early in the summer of 1871.

The new canal had the effect of lowering the water levels of Lake Joseph somewhat and raising those of Lake Rosseau: originally the former body was about eighteen inches higher.

It was expected that the canal would be ready by the fall of 1871. A ceremony was planned for September, during which the *Wenonah* was to pass through for the first time. Unluckily, the channel wasn't deep enough, and the steamer ran aground in the middle of the celebrations! Not until July of 1872, after a lot more dredging, did the boats finally reach Lake Joseph.

During those years road construction, and reconstructions, were also making modest strides. From 1868 to 1871 an average of 30 miles of new road and two new bridges were built in Muskoka, while another 28 miles of older roads were improved. (During the next decade the annual average for the district was 75 miles built, 99 miles repaired and five bridges built at an average cost of $41,178.00.) The expenditures, borne by the Ontario Government, help explain why the authorities so greatly favoured the navigating interests. Canals and locks cost money, but once completed they required only occasional maintenance, whereas roads had to be repaired almost continually.

As landseekers pushed into the district along the colonization roads, branch roads were built to penetrate the backwoods. Many were opened to the waterways. In 1869 an arm of the Muskoka Road was extended east from Huntsville, then just appearing on the map for the first time, around the north side of the Lake of Bays. It met the Bobcaygeon Road near Dorset in 1874. In 1869, too, a side road was started eastward from Utterson, an infant backwoods community between Bracebridge and Huntsville, to the future site of Port Sydney on Mary Lake, while another road, the Maclean, was begun east from the Muskoka Road to the south end of the Lake of Bays, which it reached in 1876. Here, almost at once, the trim little village of Baysville came into being. Steamboats were soon to follow. Also in 1869 the Joseph Road was started westward from Falkenburg, about four miles north of Bracebridge, to Bardsville and on to Port Carling; from here it continued up the west side of Lake Joseph toward Parry Sound.

Perhaps the best illustration of the role steamboats were expected to play in supplementing the local road network can be found in the Rosseau-Nipissing Road. This 67 mile artery, the first to cross the entire Parry Sound District as far as Lake Nipissing, was begun at Cameron's Bay, at the head of Lake Rosseau, in 1869, the same year the *Waubamik* first went into service on that lake. Crossing the Parry Sound Road at the corners of Ashdown, the Nipissing Road was opened to the Magnetawan River in 1871 and to Lake Nipissing by 1873, while the Muskoka Road, by 1872, had only reached Perry Township, about ten miles north of Huntsville. In short, landseekers heading for the interior of Parry Sound or the Lake Nipissing country from the south were almost bound to travel 30 miles of their trip, from Gravenhurst to Rosseau, by boat: until the 1880s there was no other way. This was underlined by Mr. Molesworth in his *Report* to the Public Works Department in 1869, explaining the benefits to accrue from building the Port Carling locks: besides providing access to a local coastline of 150-odd miles, the new works "will also be the means of connecting . . the Muskoka, Nipissing and Parry Sound Colonization Roads, and thus of opening up communication through every part of the free grant lands . ."

While all these new roads were under way, the old Muskoka Road between Washago and Gravenhurst, now busier than ever, was disintegrating into quagmire. Around 1869 Kivas Tully, who was then chief engineer on the road, described it in the following terms:

> . . it is still a very bad state, and under the most favourable conditions, an ordinary passenger stage wagon, with a good team, takes three hours to perform the 14 miles; in fact, there are few places . . where the horses can go beyond a walk and the difficulties for loaded wagons are still greater.

Tully advised that it be planked. The Orillia newspapers had a lot to say about the road too. On September 17, 1869 the 'Northern Light' printed this commentary:

> There are holes in the centre of the road, filled with water, deep enough to bury horse, buggy and rider, and in order to escape such a catastrophe it is necessary to make a detour among the stumps and roots, to one side, which it is difficult to do with an empty buggy, much less a loaded wagon.

Conditions like these had other unfortunate effects. Passengers on the stages were so badly shaken and bruised that they frequently decided to get out and walk. Goods had to be transported in small quantities, which increased transport costs and resulted in many shipments being held up for weeks at Washago. Many items arrived at Gravenhurst broken and shattered. Pilferage was another problem. The government kept hoping that the locals would look after the Road — fond illusion! Finally the authorities caved in, and on February 25, 1870 it was announced that a grant of $25,000 was being made to plank the Muskoka Road from Washago to Gravenhurst.[6] The contract was assigned to the lumber firm of Peter Cockburn and Son, and in August we find them advertising for a hundred men to work on the road, at rates of $1.15 per day. The planks were sawn along the route, using a portable steam sawmill which was afterwards set up on Muskoka Bay to cut for local needs.

The planks lasted about three years. That they rendered the road temporarily passable is clear from an account of a trip taken to Muskoka by a party of Orillians in August of 1871, but despite the planking they did not enjoy the ride. As the 'Northern Light" reported,

> The drive between this place [Washago] and Gravenhurst is, at this season of the year, decidedly disagreeable. The roads are good, but the drivers have too much consideration for their horses, to exactly suit our ideas of locomotion. The fourteen miles so exhaust the steeds that three weary hours are spent in traversing this dusty road, and the scenery . . is somewhat monotonous, consisting . . first of pine and rock, and then of rock and pine, and then again of pine and rock . .

Furthermore, it did not take long before the planks began to rot. Worse still, forest fires destroyed some of the bridges and causeways in 1871 and 1875. As early as 1872, $25,186.69 had to be spent on additional repairs.

It was in the autumn of 1870 that, for the first time, a group of celebrities visited Muskoka. John Sandfield Macdonald, Premier of Ontario, and several members of his Cabinet resolved to take a tour of inspection to observe at first hand the roads and bridges they were paying for, as well as the suitability of the country for settlement and the condition and desires of the inhabitants. Included in the company were John Carling, Commissioner of Public Works, Stephen Richards, Commissioner of Crown Lands, Frederick Cumberland, Manager of the Northern Railway Company, and of course A.P. Cockburn, who put his steamers at the disposal of the group.

The party left Toronto on September 14, 1870 and reached Gravenhurst by sundown. The village had been making dramatic strides since 1866. It now boasted three stores, three hotels, a church, a sawmill and several homes, though its centre had shifted about half a mile north of Mickey McCabe's old tavern, closer to the steamboat wharf. A new sash and door factory plus a shingle mill were both in contemplation at the time. At the wharf the dignitaries boarded the *Wenonah* for Bracebridge. Here, much to their surprise, bonfires were lit upon their arrival, and the party given a tumultuous welcome. They were wined and dined, toasts were proposed, and "speeches, patriotic, and humerous, and explanatory, and promissory, were made up to two o'clock in the morning".[7] Bracebridge, they found, was also doing well: in 1871 Thomas McMurray would list amongst its establishments four large hotels, seven stores, two sawmills, a gristmill, two bakers' shops, two butchers' shops, a cabinet warehouse, a drug store, a book store, a courthouse, a Crown Lands Office, a registry office, a jail, printing office, churches, schools, an Orange Hall, savings bank, and more. Obviously, as McMurray predicted, Bracebridge was "destined to become a town of great importance".[8]

The government visitors took a short detour the following morning to visit Muskokaville and admire its majestic falls, before boarding the *Wenonah* for Alport and Port Carling. After viewing progress on the new lock, they took a cruise around Lake Rosseau aboard the *Waubamik*, and finally camped at the Sandy Portage, where about 30 men were busy working on the canal. That night, around their campfire where a true backwoods supper was enjoyed and patriotic songs sung, the dignitaries decided to give the canal site a new official name, and the next morning, just before leaving they nailed up a plank on a tree,

Port Sandfield, Ontario, Circa 1883.
Woodcut, Aikens' Historical Engraving Series

bearing the name they had chosen: "Port Sandfield", in honour of Premier Macdonald. The gentlemen then returned to the front, apparently convinced that the plan to people Muskoka was a good idea after all.

Very little seems to have happened at Port Sandfield until the early 1880s, when it suddenly started to blossom into a popular little tourist village. However, it was not here that the first tourist communities in Muskoka appeared, but rather, at the heads of the two lakes. Before 1870, scarcely anyone ever thought of Muskoka as tourist terrain, except a few groups of campers and sportsmen from the cities, who sometimes formed clubs such as the Muskoka Club on Lake Joseph and the Dwight-Wiman Club on the Lake of Bays. Such groups usually did not mix much with the settlers and tried to keep abreast of the spread of "civilization". Summer hotels in the Canadian bush, built avowedly for the tourist trade, simply did not exist at that time, and no doubt anyone who suggested the idea would have been considered perfectly mad.

As it happened, there 'was' someone mad enough to try it. That someone was not a Muskokan nor even a Canadian, but a very energetic and eccentric New Yorker named William H. Pratt. Perhaps the idea arose from discussions with A.P. Cockburn, who often took business trips to the United States. What is certain is that the venturesome Yankee visited the Lake Rosseau region in 1869, sizing up its prospects. He convinced himself that Muskoka, if better developed and publicized, could be turned into a tourist's and sportsmen's paradise; after all, was not the scenery spendid and the fishing excellent? The setting was rather remote from civilization, and the nearest railway station was about 80 miles away, but Pratt apparently figured that would be part of the novelty: a first-class hotel with all the comforts of home, set in the middle of nowhere!

Whatever his reasoning, W.H. Pratt selected the site he wanted, on a lofty hilltop at the head of Lake Rosseau, commanding a panoramic view of the lake, and went to work. By the summer of 1870 an impressive mansion was arising on the headland. It was formally called the Rosseau House, but usually it was simply called "Pratt's hotel". On August 26, 1870, the 'Northern Light' reported that

View of Lake Rosseau from "Pratt's" Balcony.
Charcoal Sketch by Edward Roper. 1883
Courtesy, Archives of Ontario

. . At the head of Lake Rosseau . . lives an enterprising American gentleman, named Pratt, who is erecting an hotel on a scale which has not (or rather will not have, when completed) its equal north of Toronto. Mr. P. has "calculated" the resources and promise of the neighbourhood; he has noticed the scenic advantages, the profusion of specled(sic) and salmon trout, bass and maskinonge; the haunts of the deer which abound there are not unknown to him, — and, let the tourist sportsman come along, he can "fix" them as far as an hotel keeper of the first order lies, and by the fall of 1871 will have his premises ready for accommodation of family parties . .

Incredibly enough, the mad scheme worked. Tourists were soon trooping to the Rosseau House in large numbers. Some eventually came from as far as England and the Carolinas, despite the fact that Pratt had the gall to charge very steep rates, up to $5.00 a day on the American plan, which was no mean sum in those days. He further made himself notorious by playing tricks on his guests. Nevertheless, the incorrigible American strove to justify his tariffs by making his hotel as splendid as possible, and adding new wings and improvements every year. His guests almost always came by steamer, as did most of the hotel's provisions and furnishings, which were regularly unloaded at the private wharf at the foot of the hill; from which point a carriage road wound its way up to the front verandah. W.H. Pratt thus founded an entirely new Canadian industry. Within a few more years a number of other wilderness resorts were established on the Kawartha Lakes, Lake Couchiching and Lake Joseph.

Pratt's hotel also had the incidental effect of helping to bring another village into being, though this would probably have happened in any case. Before Pratt arrived, scarcely anything existed at the head of Lake Rosseau except "one dingy-looking log house, almost buried in a swamp"[9]. This rustic habitation, located on the Parry Sound Road about midway between Bracebridge and Parry Sound, had itself been dignified by the name of the

"Rosseau House" hotel. Government surveyors had recommended the spot where the road met Lake Rosseau as a village site. An official plan had already been drawn up but for several years there was virtually no progress as the focal point for the area was the village of Ashdown, about two miles further up the Parry Sound Road at its junction with the Nipissing Road. Founded by James Ashdown of Weston and family as early as 1862, Ashdown Corners by 1869 possessed a store, a post office, a carriage and wagon shop, a Methodist church, an Orange Hall, a fair-sized hotel with bar, and several homes. Close by was the White Oak Creek, now called the Shadow River, which offered access to Lake Rosseau, and for a time the Ashdowns ran a sailing skiff to and from Port Carling to collect the mail.

Despite all its advantages, Ashdown Village was in trouble once a steamboat appeared on Lake Rosseau, and Mr. Pratt began building his hotel. When steamers assumed the job of transporting passengers and provisions through the district and unloading them at the new government wharf near Pratt's Point, the dormant site of Rosseau inevitably began to hum with activity. By 1871 Rosseau had sprouted a few stores, an immigrants' hostel, and several homes. For some years there was intense rivalry between the new village and Ashdown, but by 1879, judging from the 'Atlas of Muskoka', the lakeside community had definitely eclipsed the inland crossroads. Little by little, the people of Ashdown either shifted to Rosseau or moved away entirely. Today the corners is vacant, while Rosseau Village has over 200 inhabitants. Again, as with South Falls, the impact of the lake steamers proved decisive.

While Pratt was forging ahead with his hotel on Lake Rosseau, parallel developments were soon following on Lake Joseph. Here the "man of the hour" was Hamilton Fraser of Brampton, Ontario, a lawyer by training who had been bitten by the urge to try something new. In 1871 Mr. Fraser, in company with A.P. Cockburn, visited the head of Lake Joseph.

Summit House, Port Cockburn.
Charcoal Sketch by Edward Roper. 1883
Courtesy, Archives of Ontario

All they found there amid the trees was a single shanty, and a new short road built by the government the previous year to provide a link with the Parry Sound Road. However, the place had possibilities. They noted the safe anchorage, the abundance of land sloping gently down to the water's edge, and the overland distance of only eighteen miles to the rising port of Parry Sound. Here was the logical embarkation point for steamers on Lake Joseph. It could become the focal point for the entire lake and a centre of great importance. At the very least, it would be an excellent site for another hotel. Thus was conceived the vision of a new port on the Muskoka Lakes: Port Cockburn, another product of the steamboat era and the tourist industry.

Mr. Fraser began by purchasing a large block of land at the site and clearing part of it for a farm. By 1872, when steamers were in regular service on the lake, he was ready to begin construction of a large, three-storey hotel on a pine-studded promontory near the wharf. Though less elevated than "Pratt's", the new hotel still commanded a lovely view of Lake Joseph. It was called, aptly enough, the Summit House.

The results went according to plan. Port Cockburn became the Joseph terminus of the steamboat route, the government built a wharf at the end of the road, freight sheds and a post office followed, and the stage service from Rosseau to Parry Sound was extended to the new landing. The boats were soon calling three times a week, and by 1879 a small village had emerged, complete with boathouses, a store and several homes. Port Cockburn was, however, always noted primarily as a resort-community. Its hotel, like "Pratt's", catered more to sportsmen and vacationers than to land seekers, and after the untimely disappearance of the Rosseau House in 1883, the Summit House was for two more decades the largest and finest summer hotel in Muskoka.

Meanwhile, how were the steamers doing? If we can trust Thomas McMurray's testimony, both the *Wenonah* and the *Waubamik* were sailing crammed to capacity in 1870, at which rate they might not be equal to the demands of 1871. Lock and canal construction were proceeding, albeit slowly, and soon Mr. Cockburn was laying plans for his third steamer, this time not a small auxiliary like the *Waubamik*, but a large new side-wheeler that would eclipse almost every vessel then in service on any of Ontario's inland lakes. In design the new steamer was to be a scaled down copy of the majestic *Emily May*, then the queen of Lake Simcoe: the *Emily* was 144 feet in length, but Cockburn was planning his own vessel to be about one-sixth smaller. The cost of such a ship came to roughly $20,000, but A.P.'s credit was good and he found Captain Isaac May, who owned the *Emily*, disposed to lend him a large percentage of that sum.

Once arrangements were completed, work was started on the new steamer, at Gravenhurst, in the spring of 1871. Detailed information on this vessel is available.

> Her length of keel will be 115 feet; length of deck, 123 feet; breadth of beam, 19 feet; breadth over all, 31 feet; gross tonnage, 150 tons. She will be driven by a low-pressure beam engine . . The length of stroke will be six feet; the bore of cylinder 24 inches. Her boiler will be a return tubular . . weighing 8½ tons.
> The whole construction of this steamer is under the supervision of one of the most experienced mechanical engineers and draftsmen in the Dominion . . and, all things considered, I feel justified in stating that she will be a model of design, comfort and beauty . . Her average speed will be 14 miles an hour [an improvement on the *Wenonah*!], and she is expected to be launched on the 15th of April next.[10]

Whether on schedule or not, the new steamer was launched and christened the *Nipissing*, from the Indian word meaning "little body of water" (perhaps directly after the lake of that name). As events proved, she was a graceful craft and soon became very popular with the travelling community. Like the *Wenonah*, the *Nipissing* had two full-length decks, a pagoda-style wheelhouse, and a rounded, fantail stern. Also like the *Wenonah*, she originally lacked a hurricane deck, though this would be added at a later date.

S.S. "Nipissing".
Possible appearance of the Vessel, 1871-1876.

The Orillia newspapers confirm that the *Nipissing* was in service by late July of 1871. Mr. Cockburn himself took the wheel as captain, relinquishing the *Wenonah* to Captain George Pimlott of Gravenhurst, and the press is full of glowing tributes to the urbanity and courtesy of both of them. "Captain Cockburn", wrote one tourist in August of 1871,

> is one of the most attentive and obliging of men, and by his courteous attention to all his guests . . wins for himself hosts of fresh friends on every trip. He has secured as his caterer Mr. P.D. Davenport, formerly of New York . . who knows exactly how "to run that branch of the institution". Capital meals, cloths and napkins white as snow, glasses sparkling with brilliant clearness, and an assortment fo the best wines add a charm and luxuriance to the trip that does much to afford additional pleasure to the traveller.[11]

Service like that is almost unbelievable, in a pioneer region which only six years earlier had been almost an empty wilderness.

It was Mr. Cockburn's intention to have the *Nipissing* run on Lake Muskoka, where the traffic was heaviest, and to ply the *Wenonah* on Lake Rosseau. The *Waubamik* was to be a reserve vessel. Almost certainly the *Wenonah* was left on Lake Muskoka until the *Nipissing* was ready, but if the venturesome vessel-owner was expecting the Port Carling lock to be completed by then he was in for a bitter disappointment. It has been said that the original lock chamber had to be lengthened eight feet beyond the original plan to accommodate the *Nipissing*. Since two large steamers on Lake Muskoka and one very small one on Lake Rosseau did not make for a well-balanced service, Mr. Cockburn had no choice but to have the *Wenonah* "warped" (at heavy cost) over the Baisong Rapids to the upper lake. The feat was accomplished before mid-July, 1871, by building a succession of temporary coffer dams behind the steamer to raise the water levels high enough to float her through. Even then, transshipments remained very awkward, because the *Nipissing* was unable to reach the unfinished lock on account of all the shoals: her cargoes consequently had to be unloaded about half a mile below Port Carling.

From a newspaper clipping, dated 1871, we obtain some details of the boat schedule for that year. The *Nipissing*, we read, leaves Bracebridge daily at 6:30 a.m. for Gravenhurst, Port Carling and other points, calling at Little Current on Thursdays and Saturdays, and Point Kaye (near the north end of Lake Muskoka) on Wednesdays and Saturdays. The *Wenonah* in turn runs daily from Port Carling to Rosseau, calling at Windermere, on the east side of Lake Rosseau, on Tuesdays, Thursdays and Saturdays, and at Port Sandfield on Wednesdays and Fridays. Schedules must have been similar in 1872, except that the boats were making through trips on all three of the lakes. The return fare from Rosseau to Bracebridge and Gravenhurst in 1872 was $1.75, and from Windermere, $1.25. All in all, then, it sounds as if the service was fairly adequate, and cheap.

During her maiden season, the *Nipissing* sailed until November 17th., when an accident forced her into winter quarters. The *Wenonah* carried on a little longer. By that time the new lock at Port Carling was nearing completion at last, and on November 24th., just before the ice became too thick, the *Wenonah* became the first vessel to pass through the lock, on her way back to Gravenhurst.

The original Port Carling lock was a humble device compared to the elaborate concrete locks of today. But it was no mean achievement nonetheless, and its completion marked a great step forward, both for navigation and, as it turned out, the lumber trade in the district. The old lock remained in use for 31 years, until it was enlarged in 1902-03. Until that date it determined that the largest steamboats on the Muskoka Lakes should not exceed the 123 feet of the Nipissing, and until 1903, none did.

The season of 1872 proved about the best on record for the Muskoka steamers, which were now able to travel direct from Gravenhurst to Rosseau and Port Cockburn. Also heartening were the current dredging operations. The new steam dredge, which had already cleared the Indian River, was now engaged in removing silt around the Muskoka River delta. In 1873 it was hard at work further upstream, deepening some bends which, reported engineer Molesworth, ". . especially in low water, were found to cause great inconvenience to . . the steamer Nipissing . ."[12]

No sooner were operations completed on the Muskoka River than the dredge and its crew were transferred to Bala Bay to remove some snags in the narrow channels around Bala Park Island, which impeded access to the Bay. Hand in hand with this project went a more ambitious work, a dam at the Musquash Falls to regulate the water levels of Lake Muskoka. It was not only the navigating interests that were hampered by the drastic fluctuations every year. The local farmers also suffered, in that they found their marginal lands inundated every spring. It also made wharf construction difficult. Newspapers such as the Orillia 'Northern Light' had been advocating a dam as early as 1871, and no doubt Cockburn had been pressing for it as well. According to Molesworth, the necessary surveys were conducted in July of 1873, and the work actually started the following September. High water and other problems delayed the project, but in his report of November 16, 1874 Molesworth was able to announce that the dam was done, along with the dredging, at a total cost of $13,434.42; another clear indication of how highly navigation in Muskoka rated in the estimation of the Mowat administration. The new dam held the waters of Lake Muskoka at a fairly high level, and in so doing eliminated the need for many dredging operations. Unfortunately, it soon began to raise the lake levels 'too' high, resulting in floods during the seasons of 1875 and 1876, which in turn forced the government to spend more money, digging an extra channel at Bala to speed the outflow of water to Georgian Bay.

Mr. Cockburn could derive some further satisfactions during the 1870s. His career in politics was on the upswing. Early in 1871 his term in the Ontario legislature expired, but the Member for North Victoria declined to run again, explaining that business concerns were taking up too much of his time. Probably there was much truth in this, yet there may have been another reason for Cockburn's decision to leave provincial politics. The federal sphere was beckoning. Recently there had been a redistribution of seats in the House of Commons in Ottawa, and, since the census of 1871 had assigned a population of nearly 7,000 souls to the districts of Muskoka and Parry Sound, representation was given them as an electoral district for the return of one member. Who would enter the hustings to represent Muskoka in the elections of 1872? Since Mr. Cockburn was such an outstanding figure, and also so patently available, many prominent citizens of both political parties began urging him to stand as a candidate. Mr. Cockburn did, in fact, agree to run, and in June of 1872 was named standard bearer at the local Grit convention. His nomination filled some high ranking Conservatives with dismay, and with good reason. On June 20, 1872, a warning was sent to Sir John A. Macdonald that such were Cockburn's popularity and prestige in the Muskoka district that many reputed friends of the Government might rally to his support. Even "Governor" William Beatty, the steamboat and lumber king of Parry Sound, seemed likely to desert the cause and throw his very considerable weight behind the genial Grit. Another factor not very reassuring to the Conservatives was the fact that their own candidate, D'Arcy Boulton, was a resident of Toronto, and hence a relative stranger to Muskoka.

The fears proved well founded. Beatty did throw in his lot with A.P. Cockburn, explaining to his Conservative friends that he considered Cockburn a far more deserving man than his opponent. Such arguments were not likely to impress Sir John A. Macdonald, who was primarily concerned with getting as many Tories elected as possible, and on July 12, 1872 the Prime Minister observed in a letter to his friend Alexander Campbell, ". . It is quite clear that Beatty has sold us in Muskoka. Cockburn is the choice of the Reform Convention and has pledged himself to vote against us. Verily he shall have his reward."

Mr. Cockburn's reward took the form of a determined effort by the Conservatives to see his opponent win the election of 1872. The same applied to several subsequent elections as well. The result was a very spirited contest indeed. Mr. Cockburn based his campaign on a realistic appraisal of Muskoka's needs, stressing the importance of increased immigration and improved communications. He also voiced his disapproval of some of the sins of the reigning Conservative Government, especially its handling of the Manitoba question, its alleged mismanagement and extravagance in the building of the Intercolonial Railway, its failure to uphold the interests of Canada at the Washington Treaty negotiations, and finally, its refusal to pass legislation similar to that recently enacted in Ontario, to clamp down on election skulduggery. Finally, he reminded his readers that all his property was within the riding, that consequently his own interests were inseparably bound up with theirs, and concluded with the words, ". . should you honour me with your confidence, and charge me with the duties of your representative I shall to the utmost of my humble abilities, endeavour to deserve the one by a faithful discharge of the other."

Mr. Cockburn plunged himself into the fray with vigour, and when at last the hands were counted in mid-August he was deemed to have won with a comfortable majority of 126 votes. But then something unprecedented happened. The returning officer, a staunch Conservative who had already disallowed the Parry Sound vote on a technicality, because it was largely favourable to Cockburn, now refused to declare anyone elected for Muskoka! The matter was left in abeyance until the House met, but then Mr. Cockburn was at once awarded the seat. The returning officer was meanwhile called before Parliament to explain his conduct, and was never again employed in that capacity.[13]

Back in Muskoka, meanwhile, tourists and sightseers kept coming in ever-increasing numbers, thanks largely to the publicizing efforts of W.H. Pratt and A.P. Cockburn. On July 10-12, 1872, the Press Association of Canada was treated to a leisurely cruise through the lakes on the *Nipissing*, free of charge, of course: Mr. Cockburn was fully aware of the usefulness of entertaining such gentlemen! The first boating and sailing regatta on Lake Muskoka was held on October 12, 1870, and the second on September 29, 1871, off Browning Island. On the latter occasion the *Nipissing* was on hand with a shipload of spectators from Bracebridge. She also began calling at Yoho Island on Lake Joseph, the headquarters of the Muskoka Club (which now had several dozen members), Professor Campbell having struck up a friendship with A.P. Cockburn.

The *Nipissing* also had the honour of conducting a vice-regal tour in the summer of 1874, when the Governor General, the Earl of Dufferin and his Countess, paid a visit to Muskoka. The party took a train to Washago on July 28th., then proceeded north in special carriages which were packed aboard the *Nipissing* upon arrival at Gravenhurst. Then, as Lady Dufferin described it,

> . . When we left our carriages we got on to a steamer covered with flags, and steamed along a lovely place, called Muskoka Bay, into Muskoka Lake, and then through a most curious, narrow river, in which we twisted and turned . . and had only just room to move; sometimes we appeared to be going straight ashore, and then turned suddenly to one side and were saved. This river brought us to Bracebridge.

The carpenters were just putting the finishing touches on a set of arches spanning the village streets when the *Nipissing* blew her whistle and glided gracefully up to the Bracebridge wharf. On hand were a crowd and a band to greet the vice-regal party. The carriages were unloaded and a triumphal tour through the town followed, with some speeches and much fanfare. Lady Dufferin noted that the houses of Bracebridge looked very neat. The visitors spent the night aboard the *Nipissing*, a trifle awkwardly, since the steamer had no staterooms, and the next morning set off for Port Carling and Rosseau, where His Excellency mixed informally with the local settlers "in all stages of their existence". From here they proceeded to Port Sandfield and Lake Joseph. At Port Cockburn their carriages were unloaded again to take them to Parry Sound, where another steamer waited to take them to Collingwood. Apparently the Dufferins were delighted with the lake scenery, while Mr. Frederick Cumberland of the Northern Railway, who accompanied the party, afterwards remarked to Mr. Cockburn that the catering on the *Nipissing* was even better than that on the Great Lakes ship.

Indeed, by 1874 the only serious drawback to a visit to Muskoka was the perennial problem of the Muskoka Road as far as Gravenhurst. Even at the best of times a trip by stage was slow and bumpy; at worst it could be downright dangerous if bush-fires were burning. But even here, improvements were close at hand. In the distance men thought they could hear the puffing and chuffing of that marvellous machine called the iron horse, but we reserve that discussion to the next chapter.

Meanwhile, what can we say about the years 1866 to 1874? This much at least: that settlement, commerce and tourism were finally placed on a firm footing, that population was increasing, and that the earlier stagnation dogging the district largely lifted. In short, Muskoka, at least in the new urban centres, was starting to prosper. Many factors helped to make this possible: new and better roads, extended land surveys, a revamped immigration policy, various improvements to navigation, and vigorous entrepreneurial efforts, to say nothing of the scenic, lumbering and agricultural resources of the district itself. The central catalyst, however, was the lake steamers: without them, all other efforts would have been nearly useless.

Steamboating in Muskoka was just getting started during these years, and it was having its trials and tribulations. But it was no longer a mere experiment. It was now an economically viable and well established enterprise, squarely launched along the road to greater things.

FOOTNOTES

[1] The *Wenonah* was not entirely completed when she made that historic trip. Work on her cabins continued as late as August, probably using lumber cut at Alex Bailey's sawmill.

[2] Surplus cargoes may have been taken in scows.

[3] Whether the "Montreal Store" was doing any better is uncertain though we hear that it was well-stocked: it remained in business under the management of John Peter Cockburn, A.P.'s elder brother, until it fell a victim of the great fire of Gravenhurst in 1887.

[4] This drew an outraged scream of "traitor" from the Toronto 'Globe', until Mr. Cockburn, in a polite but firm exchange of letters, succeeded in vindicating his conduct, both for consistency and integrity, after which the 'Globe' ceased its attacks.

[5] White was later to become Deputy Minister of Lands, Forests and Mines for Ontario for 28 years.

[6] Plank roads were by no means uncommon in those days. Over 500 miles of such highways are said to have been built in Ontario between 1840 and 1860. There was no particular standard, but the planks were often sixteen feet long, twelve inches wide and three inches thick. About four or five such planks would be laid down and spiked to several rows of longitudinal "sleepers", with the next four or five offset to allow vehicles to get on and off easily. Finally, the road would be given a light coating of mud or gravel.

[7] Charles Marshall, 'The Canadian Dominion'.

[8] Thomas McMurray, 'Free Land Grants of Canada', 1871.

[9] Orillia 'Expositor', Sept. 17, 1874.

[10] Thomas McMurray, 'Free Land Grants of Canada', 1871.

[11] Orillia 'Northern Light', August 18, 1871.

[12] These operations cost $1,599.98. Unfortunately, a combination of deforestation along the river banks plus log drives and waves in the wake of the steamers were to accelerate erosion, which in turn were to make further dredging necessary.

[13] These questionable Tory tactics may have backfired on them, because Cockburn won his next contest, in 1874, by a resounding 309 votes over his opponent, John Teviotdale, a popular Bracebridge merchant, following the collapse of the Conservative administration in the wake of the "Pacific Scandal". Four years later the political pendulum swung back the other way, with the Conservatives recapturing two-thirds of the House of Commons; even so, A.P. Cockburn survived the rout of the Grits, narrowly beating W.E. O'Brien of Shanty Bay (Lake Simcoe) by 74 votes. So solidly entrenched was A.P. Cockburn that Sir John A. Macdonald himself tried tempting him with a seat in the Senate, as apparently the only means of getting him out of the Commons. Mr. Cockburn declined.

A train on the Northern Railway.
Courtesy, Public Archives of Canada C 35485

CHAPTER 3
Steamboating in the Railway and Lumbering Era
(1875-1885)

As the snow left the woods and the ice broke up on the lakes in the spring of 1875, Muskoka was stirred by some electrifying news: work on the Northern Extensions Railway was being renewed, north of the Severn River, and would perhaps be completed as far as Gravenhurst before the end of summer.

Nowhere else in Ontario was a railway so urgently needed. At that very time, Public Works Engineer Molesworth was reporting that traffic on the Muskoka Road was heavier than anywhere else in the back country, with the possible exception of the Upper Ottawa route to Pembroke. Already the freshly-laid planks on the Muskoka Road were splitting and rotting, and worse, summer bush fires burned out the bridges and causeways at Gibraltar and Beaver Creek. Settlers and storekeepers chafed at these disruptions. A Bracebridge merchant lamented that every single pane of glass in a shipment he had ordered from the front was shattered before it reached Gravenhurst. A.P. Cockburn gritted his teeth as the stages kept arriving late or not at all, forcing the *Nipissing* to waste time waiting for them. The tourist trade suffered too. Only a very hardy breed of traveller was willing to face a bumpy, dusty trip in one of Mr. Harvie's stages to enjoy the charms of the lake country beyond.

The cure for all these woes could be expressed in one word: railways. For any commercial navigation company plying ships on an inland waterway running through a sparsely populated pioneer district, a railway, or nowadays, an A-class highway, to an urban market centre is an absolute necessity if either the pioneer district or the boat service are to thrive. The Lake Simcoe steamboats provide a case in point. Until a railway was completed from the City of Toronto to Allandale in 1853, and to Belle Ewart in 1854, there were only two steamboats in service on Lake Simcoe, neither of which was prospering. After the railway arrived, the steamers entered their heyday, and soon, instead of two on the lake, there were more like ten.

By the 1870s the Muskoka steamboats were in a similar position to that of the Lake Simcoe steamers before 1853, and A.P. Cockburn was determined that his steamers, and the district as a whole, should enjoy the benefits of a railway. As early as the winter of 1868-69 he procured, at his own expense, a charter to build a railroad, either of wood or iron, between Lakes Simcoe and Muskoka.[1] Not having the capital necessary to develop his charter, Mr. Cockburn could do little more than talk to railwaymen and government officials, and to audiences everywhere, stressing the need for the railway and all the benefits it would bring: markets for the settlers, rapid shipments for merchants, a whole new watershed full of untapped timber for the lumber companies, and general prosperity for everyone. Soon railway talk was rampant throughout Muskoka. So anxious were people to have a railway that they declared themselves ready to donate time, land and labour to the project, and to tax themselves to meet the costs. Newspapers such as the Orillia 'Expositor' carried one editorial after another in support of the idea.

Finally, on December 24, 1869, a charter was obtained for the Toronto, Simcoe and Muskoka Junction Railway, which was authorized to build from Barrie to Orillia and beyond to an unnamed terminus on Lake Muskoka. The names of many influential people in Toronto and Muskoka appear on the list of 47 provisional directors, including A.G.P. Dodge of the Dodge Lumber Company of Parry Sound, A.J. Alport, now a Muskoka reeve, and, the owner of the Muskoka steamer fleet, who worked indefatigably to see the new line become a reality.

All these moves were momentous to the Northern Railway of Canada, which then had tracks running from Toronto to Barrie and Collingwood. It thus formed part of the route of entry to Muskoka, and came closer to the district than any other line. Obviously the Northern was the most logical candidate to build the new road, and evidently the most preferred. But the Northern was in no mood to rush into reckless expansionary schemes. Under the firm and cautious direction of General Manager Frederick Cumberland, the railway was just nicely recovering solvency after the chaotic blundering of its initial years of operations. When approached about a possible branch to Muskoka, Mr. Cumberland was ready to offer interest and sympathy, but he would not commit his Company to anything without substantial guarantees from the municipalities to be served.

Yet the formation of the T.S.&M.J.R. was not a development to be ignored. Cumberland obviously could not afford to let the new line fall under the control of any rival company, such as the Midland Railway, which was then extending its tracks from Lindsay to Beaverton and on towards Orillia. Both the Midland and the Northern derived most of their revenues from the timber trade, and as lumbering kept migrating farther and farther north it was clear that both railways would soon have to follow, or run the risk of losing the pineries to the other. Promises of cash subsidies from Barrie and Orillia helped to make the lure a little more tempting. Consequently the Northern Railway speedily bought a controlling interest in the T.S.&M.J.R., which was renamed the Northern Extensions Railway in 1871. A.P. Cockburn in the meantime had willingly surrendered his own charter at Cumberland's request.

Building the new branch was another matter. But money was being promised from sundry sources. In 1869 the Toronto city council passed a bylaw granting $100,000 to the project. Obviously Toronto, too, saw advantages in a direct line to the Free Grant territories. On February 15, 1871, the Ontario Government passed the Railway Fund Act to capitalize lines "leading to, or through sections of the country, remote from existing thoroughfares, or passing through thinly settled tracts or leading to the Free Grant territory, or to the inland waters", all of which the Northern Extension was proposing to do. Interestingly enough, there was nothing in the wording of this Act about possible benefits the lumber companies might derive from it: the railways were supposed to promote settlement, not lumbering. The same applied to a railway petition, signed by over a thousand Muskokans and presented to the Ontario legislature by A.P. Cockburn in 1870.

Frederick Cumberland, Manager of the Northern Railway, 1859-1881. Courtesy, Archives of Ontario S.124

Again, the emphasis was entirely on colonization, not forestry. All this was rather ironic, considering that the lumber companies proved to be the prime beneficiaries immediately after the new lines were built.

The Railway Fund Act assured the proposed Muskoka line of an additional $4,000 per mile. Around the same time a deputation from Muskoka, including Thomas McMurray and John Teviotdale of Bracebridge and accompanied by A.P. Cockburn, met with Cumberland and Frank Smith, president of the T.S.&M.J.R. in Toronto. Smith assured the Muskoka delegates that the Company was prepared to contribute $10,000 per mile to the new line, but warned that the Muskoka municipalities themselves must raise $2,000 per mile to have the branch extended north of Rama Township (Washago). On March 1, 1871, the reeves of Muskoka, at a meeting held at Bracebridge, approved the proposed expenditure, to be paid by instalments as each mile was completed.

Work was started on the Northern Extensions in 1871. The line was opened to Orillia on April 1, 1872, just in time to forestall the Midland Railway, but beyond that, progress was slow. Bridging the Atherley Narrows proved very expensive, and railway building in the Shield was not easy. The winters were cold and cash was short. Barrie and Orillia each realized 82% of their subscriptions, but Muskoka never raised more than 70% of hers. As a result, the railway was not opened to Washago until August 8, 1873, and it took another entire year to advance the rails the next two miles to Severn Bridge. Here, work ground to a halt.

To many, it looked as if the railway would never cross the Severn. Worse still, the country as a whole was now caught up in a depression. But A.P. Cockburn continued to push for the railway, exhorting his constituents to help, reassuring them that the work stoppage was only temporary, and insisting that more capital would indeed be found. More deputations to the government and the Company finally bore fruit, and in 1875 work was resumed with fresh vigour. The construction crews had nothing to work with except picks and shovels, plus ox-teams to haul gravel and black powder to blast through ridges of granite. Notwithstanding, the rails kept creeping northward; furthermore, the line was built to very high standards. Finally, in August 1875 the tracks reached Gravenhurst, and on September 28th. the first work train rolled in from Severn Bridge. What a day that was! Settlers who had been promised the line for so many years flocked to Gravenhurst from miles around to see the train for themselves. Barrels of beer were rolled out into the streets by the hotel keepers as townsmen joined the railway navvies in whooping it up. To the north, Bracebridge and Huntsville rejoiced as well, as if the iron horse were already at their own doorsteps.

A.P. Cockburn and the railway officials were not quite as jubilant, since there was still a gap of a mile or more between the end of steel and the shores of Muskoka Bay. Unless that gap could be closed, much of the value of the new line would be nullified. It took over two more months to extend the tracks down a convenient ravine to the lakeside, where the shoreline was artificially extended with cribwork and fill to form a wharf within a sheltered inlet. Here a shed was immediately erected, and given the name "Muskoka Wharf Station", which henceforth became the usual embarkation point for the lake steamers. By that time, however, the season of navigation was almost over, and the boats derived little benefit from the railway that year.

But the occasion called for celebrations nonetheless. A special train carrying over 200 picked passengers from Toronto and all points along the way came chugging into Gravenhurst on Saturday, November 13, 1875 for the formal opening of the Northern extension. Frank Smith, Frederick Cumberland and President Thompson of the Northern Railway were along for the trip. They found Gravenhurst decorated everywhere with flags and a large crowd gathered at Muskoka Wharf. As the train rolled in, the whistle of the locomotive blended with continuous blasts from the *Wenonah*, the *Waubamik* and the *Nipissing*, which were all assembled by way of welcome. The passengers all crowded aboard the three steamers and were taken on a short cruise around the Bay. A dinner at the Township Hall followed, with speeches and loyal toasts, and finally, in the late afternoon the assemblage broke up, well pleased by the day's events.

Muskoka Wharf Station, N.R. Co. System, 1882.
Terminus of the Northern Railway, 1875-1885. The above illustration symbolizes the close
alliance between the railway and the Navigation Company.
Lithograph from a M. & N. N. Co. Brochure, 1882.

They had reason to be. Gone were the days of doubt and uncertainty about freight deliveries to and from Lake Couchiching. Gone, too, were the days of bumpy, dusty trips by stage over the south Muskoka Road. Almost instantly the stage service to Gravenhurst vanished, as the Harvie brothers shifted their runs northwards to Bracebridge and beyond. It was now possible for the tourist, the entrepreneur or the prospective settler to travel from Toronto to Rosseau, a distance of 143 miles, or 155 miles to Port Cockburn in complete comfort for eight months of the year. Sixty miles into the pioneer Shield country at moderate rates, when just sixteen years previously the whole region had been a silent, empty wilderness.[2]

As the Northern Railway neared Gravenhurst, hopes ran high that the line would immediately be extended to Bracebridge, but such hopes were vain. The Company had its access to the Muskoka pineries and connections with the steamers which already served Bracebridge; that was enough for the moment. Besides, around 1875 railwaymen were becoming more interested in east-west transcontinental lines. Any extension further north into Muskoka would have to wait. At that time there were no communities of any size to the north of Muskoka. Settlement was just starting to invade the Magnetawan country, and North Bay and Sudbury were still to be. The Canadian Pacific Railway did not exist. Hence it is not surprising that Muskoka should be regarded as a 'cul-de-sac' or dead-end route. In 1871 we find the Northern Railway's board of directors alluding to the Muskoka line as a "new feeder of very considerable value to its mainline"; in other words it was reckoned only as a feeder.

In one sense, the railway reached Muskoka at an inauspicious moment. The year 1875 was right in the middle of a severe economic slump that had been dogging Canada and most of the Western world since 1873. It is hard to gauge the precise effects of the depression on Muskoka, but it seems to have had a discouraging impact on tourism and lumbering. People do not, as a rule, travel for pleasure when money is scarce. It is noteworthy that not a single new resort hotel was built in Muskoka while the depression persisted. New ones began to appear only in 1880 and afterwards, by which time the economic skies were brighter, but until then Pratt's hotel at Rosseau, and Fraser's at Port Cockburn, had the lakes all to themselves. It was rather cruelly ironic that A.P. Cockburn's first tourist and sportsmen's guidebook for Muskoka appeared in 1874, just when times were turning very bad.

If the depression was unfortunate for the resort industry, it may have been indirectly beneficial to settlement. As the verdant green of American pastures turned rust brown under the glaring sun of hard times, the steady flow of land hungry Canadians across the

Gravenhurst, Ontario, Circa 1880.

border seems to have slackened a bit. Statistics show that the population of Canada increased about two percent faster from 1871 to 1881 than during the previous decade. Some people, more or less denied the American alternative, and not caring to go as far away as distant Manitoba, were now prepared to reconsider the Ontario Government's still-standing offers of free land in northern Ontario. Census reports prove that by 1881, some 66% of the settlers in Muskoka and Parry Sound were native Ontarians, as compared with only 52.3% in 1871. The records also reveal that the total population of the two districts rose from 6,919 in 1871 to 27,204 in 1881, an increase of 29.3%. All in all, such an increase was considerable, but not very rapid. Even so, it was faster than the corresponding rate for Manitoba, where the population grew by only 28.8% during the same period. By 1881, too, we find 11.92% of the occupied lands in Muskoka-Parry Sound cleared and under cultivation, as opposed to 7.3% in 1871 and 2.45% in 1861. Thus in some areas at least, Muskoka was starting to resemble the more settled lands to the south.

Unhappily most of the new settlements were not very prosperous. Visitors continually commented on the wretchedness of the roads, the long cold winters, the haggard look of the settlers, and, most of all, the superabundance of rock. The government tried to help matters along in 1871 by partially clearing land and building shanties in Ryerson Township in southern Parry Sound, to ease the burdens of the settlers, but this paternalistic experiment proved a complete failure. Some of the settlers, too, tried to rebuff the critics by holding fairs featuring large displays of grain crops and livestock. They took especial pleasure, for example, in a record sized turnip weighing 88½ pounds which was grown on a Muskoka farm. The first fall fair at Bracebridge was held in 1868 and thereafter repeated annually; others were held at such places at Gravenhurst, Rosseau, McKellar Village and Dunchurch in Parry Sound. A.P. Cockburn usually made a point of attending the local fairs, and besides granting special rates for visitors on his steamers, he often arranged to have various

Members of Provincial Parliament and other celebrities in attendance. He would also see that there were well planned receptions for these dignitaries, complete with banquets and flowery toasts praising the prospects of Muskoka agriculture.

Despite all the fanfare and optimism, however, nothing could nullify the unrelenting truth that most parts of the Canadian Shield are totally unfit for farming. By the 1870s several of the older townships abounded with abandoned lots reverting to bush. It was another bad sign when A.J. Alport, whose farm near the mouth of the Muskoka River was the envy of the district, decided to sell his holdings and leave in 1873. British emigration societies remained active during the period, the Mowat administration continued to encourage settlement in Northern Ontario, and we also hear of colonies of Swiss and Scandinavian settlers being organized in several parts of the Muskokas. Yet by the end of the decade so many people were foresaking their lots for the West that W.E. Hamilton complained in the Atlas of 1879 that "Manitoba fever" was reaching epidemic proportions. Indeed, for a time the port of Rosseau actually became known as the "gateway to the West", as people kept arriving on the lake steamers to catch a stage for Parry Sound.

Despite everything, population grew during the 1870s and '80s. This no doubt was beneficial to the steamers, especially after the railway arrived. So much freight was arriving on the boats that three freight sheds had to be erected at both Bracebridge and Rosseau to cope with it. According to W.E. Hamilton, no less than 2,811 tons 1,210 pounds of freight left the railway sheds at Muskoka Wharf for various points in Muskoka in 1878. Another source for the same period remarks that, while Cockburn had used only a single cart to load up the *Wenonah* for her maiden voyage in 1866, it was now common to find one hundred tons of cargo awaiting transshipment to the boats at Gravenhurst. Additional freight sheds were built at other unloading centres such as Tondern Island on Lake Muskoka, Windermere on Lake Rosseau, and Port Cockburn.

Meanwhile, new refinements were being built into the boats themselves to make them more comfortable and efficient. In 1874 the engines and hull of the *Wenonah* were overhauled to give the stubby old ship greater speed. A condensing heater, utilizing steam from the boiler, was installed at the same time; a welcome addition on cold dark nights out on the lakes! In 1877, Muskoka's first marine railway was built at Gravenhurst, near the old government wharf at the foot of the Bay. It was immediately used to haul the flagship *Nipissing* out of the water to be refitted and repainted. At the same time the *Nipissing* was given a new cabin on the promenade deck, plus a badly needed hurricane deck to provide shelter for passengers and crew. In 1878 the *Wenonah* was also put in drydock and extensively remodelled. Probably her cabin space was enlarged, since the vessel's tonnage figures show an increase from 62 to 113 about this time. Possibly she was lengthened as well, though there is no proof of this.

From a schedule published in June 1877 we get another glimpse of the operations of the Muskoka steamboats, this time after the railway arrived. The *Nipissing* leaves Rosseau at 7:30 a.m., calling at Windermere, Port Carling and Bracebridge by 11:00 a.m. After dinner she leaves for Gravenhurst to connect with the 1:00 p.m. train, calling at both Muskoka Wharf and the old town wharf. She then begins the return trip, arriving at Rosseau again at 7:00 p.m. Mondays and Fridays were especially arduous, since the steamer then had to take in Lake Joseph as far as Port Cockburn on the afternoon trip, and consequently did not reach Rosseau until 10:00 p.m. The *Wenonah*, meanwhile, is confined strictly to Lake Muskoka, leaving Bracebridge bright and early at 5:00 a.m., arriving at Gravenhurst at 7:00 a.m., returning to Bracebridge around noon, and making two more trips in the afternoon and evening, except on Tuesdays and Saturdays, when she returns by way of Walker's Point, Point Kaye, Torrance and Bala. (Obviously the most heavily travelled route was between Gravenhurst and Bracebridge: not for nothing did A.P. Cockburn complain about the difficulties of trying to work out a satisfactory service on such an awkward configuration of lakes as those of Muskoka!) The *Waubamik* is not mentioned in the above timetable: she is said to have been sold to a Toronto skipper in the spring of 1876 and used briefly to take special parties to Bracebridge.

S.S. "Nipissing".
This recently discovered photograph shows the vessel at Muskoka Wharf, probably around 1879
Courtesy, Mr. Bill Gray, Port Credit

S.S. "Nipissing".
From the Collection of the late Mr. Claude Snider, Gravenhurst.

S.S. "Wenonah".
This is the only known photograph of the vessel, taken probably during the 1880s.

The steamers connected with an assortment of stage lines: a daily stage from Bracebridge to Falkenburg, Utterson and Huntsville, a triweekly stage to Port Sydney (where a new steamer service was just being inaugurated), another triweekly stage to Muskoka Falls and Uffington in Draper Township, and a biweekly stage to Baysville. From Windermere on Lake Rosseau a triweekly stage carried the mail to Dee Bank Village, Ufford, Beatrice, Raymond, Ullswater and the other settlements around Three Mile Lake, while from Rosseau a daily stage ran to Parry Sound and a triweekly stage up the Nipissing Road to Magnetawan, with a semi-weekly run as far as Lake Nipissing.

As a rule, merchants and forwarders seemed fairly pleased with the boat service, barring the occasional accident or delay. However, according to a credible tradition storekeepers had one bone of contention to pick with Mr. Cockburn: they complained that a barrel of whiskey never reached Port Carling without some of its contents being drawn in transit. Determined finally that at least one barrel should arrive intact, Mr. Cockburn had it set upright on the main deck of the steamer, where he proceeded to guard it by sitting on it for the entire trip. However, one crew member was just as determined not to be deprived of his "wee drappie". Accordingly, he measured the distance from the stoke hold to the barrel with his eye, went below to throw some more wood into the fire box, bored a hole up through the deck with an auger, then through the barrel head with a gimlet, drew off a pail of whiskey, and plugged up the hole.

At times, the boat crews or their passengers were known to indulge in other forms of mischief. One Saturday evening around 1877, a couple of Gravenhurst storekeepers decided to close up shop and take a moonlight cruise on the *Wenonah*. The steamer, now commanded by Captain Charles Percival[3] of Bracebridge, set off on her rounds up the lake, but at Point Kaye the skipper announced that he was going ashore for the night, and left the vessel in charge of the mate, Alexander Link. The men decided to take an overnight cruise up to Lake Rosseau. This meant, of course, locking through at Port Carling. On their way up the Indian River, Link solemnly warned his passengers that they must be very quiet when passing through the lock, since the lockmaster, Patrick Obeirne, was a dour old Irishman who disliked having anyone use the locks on Sunday, as a matter of religious principle, and if aroused would refuse to let them return. They locked the *Wenonah* through in dead of night without disturbing anyone; no one in the village seemed to know they were there. From here they took in a sail to Windermere, and returned just as the dawn was breaking on Sunday morning.

Stealthily the party eased the *Wenonah* through the locks once again and started down the river. However, just at that moment one of the passengers could not refrain from blowing a shrill blast with the whistle, arousing the entire village. Windows flew up as people peered out to see what was going on. "What in the world did you do that for?" cried Link in consternation. "Obeirne will raise Cain! He will report to A.P."!

Sure enough, a letter was dispatched to Gravenhurst in which the lockmaster indignantly complained about the "unseemly" conduct of the *Wenonah*'s crew on the Sabbath. Sandy Link made a point of intercepting that letter at the navigation office. It did not reach A.P. Cockburn until some weeks later, when Link showed it to him, along with a copy of another letter which Link had written to Obeirne in A.P.'s name, expressing regret and promising that such an event would not occur again. A.P. Cockburn got quite a laugh out of the whole affair.

Of course, there were times when pranks threatened to get out of hand. One day, probably in 1876, the *Nipissing*, commanded by Captain James Kirkland[4] of Woodville, Ontario, was picking up a crowd at Rosseau for a regatta. Perhaps some of the passengers had had a little too much to drink, because some of them began to get very boisterous and run up and down between decks, and also from side to side, making the steamer roll as she churned along. Such foolishness was potentially dangerous, and the crew tried in vain to get them to stop. Finally the captain locked the door on the companionway, so that "them that was on the upper deck had to stay on the upper deck and them that was on the lower deck..had to stay on the lower deck and in the cabin".

In the meantime, a new influence was at work on the local scene, an influence strong enough to revolutionize the economy of the entire district. The lumbermen had arrived in force on the Muskoka Lakes.

From the local viewpoint, they came at an opportune time. As we have noted, fur trading could never provide a livelihood for very many people, while agriculture in the district was gradually proving illusory. As for mining, that scarcely went any farther than a brief flurry of excitement following the discovery of a few gold nuggets in a ("salted"?) Gravenhurst well in 1877. But Muskoka still had one major resource to exploit, and that was wood. The lumbermen had left the Muskoka basin largely untapped until this point because they had been busy laying waste the areas further south, and because they hadn't been able to surmount the hurdle of the overland trek from Lake Muskoka to Lake Couchiching. The railway, of course, changed all that. The double line of steel now made the transport of sawn lumber an easy matter, all year around, direct from Gravenhurst to Toronto; whence it could easily be shipped to such American cities as Buffalo and Oswego. Trains could also take equipment and supplies and, if necessary, steam tugs to the Muskoka Lakes. The coming of the railway also placed the entire Muskoka watershed, including the Huntsville lakes, the Lake of Bays, and tributary lakes and streams as far north as the modern Algonquin Park, within striking distance of Gravenhurst, as well as Toronto. Lumbering in Muskoka suffered a distinct geographic disadvantage compared with the Ottawa Valley, in that transport costs were higher. Nevertheless, when the industry moved in, it created new towns, (not all of them permanent), new transport routes, a new commerce, and for many, a whole new way of life. Thousands of poverty-striken settlers, after trying for years to clear a few acres in the bush, and to coax a few potato tubers or wheat shoots to grow among the stumps in sterile Shield soil, now turned with relief to the nearby lumber camps to work, which did not make life any easier for their wives and children back in the shanties. The longer the farmers left their lots, the more agriculture was neglected. More and more settlers concentrated on raising hay to feed the lumbermens' oxen without practising crop rotation. By the 1880s farming in Muskoka was declining in productivity and becoming quite dependent on the lumber trade. Under these conditions, family life deteriorated and "boozing" flourished: many are the stories of young lumberjacks flocking into Gravenhurst shortly after payday to spend their wages on beer and whiskey, afterwards to return, penniless anew, to the camps.[5]

Shier Company Lumber Camp at Crooked Lake, near Baysville (1909). Courtesy, Mr. Brad Robinson, Dorset

The only hindrance to an immense boom in Muskoka lumbering after 1875 was the depression, which nearly paralysed the industry. According to the Crown Lands report for the above year, both the square and sawn lumber trades were in a state of stagnation, with cash sales virtually unknown. Similarly, an eminent Canadian historian[6] has observed that lumber exports from Canada dropped from a total of $29,000,000 in 1873 to a mere $13,000,000 in 1878. All this resulted from shock waves following a price collapse in the United States in 1873. The experiences of one small lumberman of the day, Captain Robert Dollar,[7] may perhaps be taken as typical. As Captain Dollar relates in his 'Memoirs', in 1872 he went to Muskoka, formed a partnership, and

> . . bought timber on land owned by farmers and started lumbering for our own account, making our headquarters at Bracebridge...It was a new country just opened by the Government, and there was a good opportunity. Business was booming at this time, and we did not sell our logs, expecting to get a higher price when we would deliver them at the market the following summer; but . . . at that time along came Black Friday in New York, which paralyzed business throughout not only the United States but Canada as well. When we came to sell our logs we found we had made a loss of what little money we had put in as well as about $5,000.00 more . . .
> In order to pay up the debts, my partner and myself had to go to work on wages . . it took three years' hard work to get even with the world again.

Captain Dollar was not alone. Even so large an outfit as the Dodge Lumber Company got into trouble and passed into other hands about this time. Alexander P. Cockburn, too, was caught up in the crisis in a very direct way. In 1874, having been induced to join a friend in purchasing a third interest in a square timber exporting concern, he suddenly found himself in debt to the commercial house of James Gibb Ross and Company of Quebec for $17,000 on the transaction. Fortunately, the firm proved reasonable and did not press for immediate payment, though it required security on Mr. Cockburn's property. Gradually, over the next six years, Mr. Cockburn's boats earned enough for him to liquidate most of the debt.

It is evident, then, that the Canadian lumber industry was in very bad shape at the time the railway was extended to Gravenhurst. Despite all their troubles, many firms reacted positively to the opportunity. Instead of waiting passively for an upturn, they laboured to create it. To return to Captain Dollar, whom we left with his debts just barely cleared away, we learn from his 'Memoirs' that, about 1875, he made a new partnership with Herman Henry Cook, the former agent for Dodge and Company, and

> He furnished the money and I the brains and hard work. Having the experience of previous years I was extremely cautious and careful, and made a success of the new venture from the start.
> . . . In 1876 I had started eight camps in Muskoka district, and besides these I started a camp to get out saw logs on one of the islands of Georgian Bay . . .

The Orillia 'Expositor', in May of 1876, notes that the Cook firm had about 35,000 logs ready to be sawn. Also during this period, we find new mills of all sizes and descriptions going up all around the shores of the Muskoka Lakes: at East Bay, near Torrance, in 1876, at Rosseau Falls in 1877, at Rosseau proper by 1879, at Brackenrig and Windermere on Lake Rosseau about the same time, and at Port Sandfield and Walker's Point early in the 1880s. The Burgess mill at Bala was still cutting, and Bracebridge still had three. There were others besides, cutting mostly for local needs.

But the main beneficiary of the industry was Gravenhurst. This town seemed to have been designed by Nature to be a lumber centre. Unlike Bracebridge, where the harbour is small and ringed by lofty, precipitous cliffs and hills, the harbour of Gravenhurst on Muskoka Bay is surrounded, on the south and west sides, by acres of almost level land, upon which thousands of board feet of lumber could be stockpiled. By 1875 Gravenhurst was also

Logs on Muskoka Bay, near Gravenhurst.

a railhead, and furthermore, railway officials were assuring the lumbermen that the line would definitely not be extended for at least the next ten years. This in turn made Muskoka Bay all the more desirable for mill sites, since it was obviously to the advantage of the lumbermen to build their mills as close to the railway sidings as possible. From the mariner's point of view, Muskoka Bay made a very safe and spacious harbour, which could accommodate a great many logs: Captain Levi Fraser estimated that it sometimes sheltered about 50,000,000 feet of timber. Since Gravenhurst was geographically at the southern-most tip of the entire Muskoka Lakes basin, it was able to control lumbering operations not only throughout Muskoka proper, but also in large parts of Haliburton and the districts of Parry Sound and Nipissing as well. The only possible alternate exit for this vast region was at Bala, by way of the Moon and Musquash Rivers, neither of which has a suitable harbour at its estuary. As a result, Bala never became an important lumber town (it never had more than two sawmills), while Gravenhurst got the lion's share of the mills; a predominance it never lost.

Once the railway arrived, sawmills sprang up at Gravenhurst like mushrooms. Some of these were built by local entrepreneurs like Peter Cockburn, who erected a steam powered mill in 1876. Others were built or acquired by powerful companies such as the Rathbuns of Deseronto, who bought Cockburn's mill in 1888 and proceeded to acquire another. By the autumn of 1876 there were at least four saw or shingle mills at Gravenhurst, two of which were on Gull Lake, immediately east of town. Two more were erected in 1877, and more afterwards; among them were the Thompson and Baker mill, the Fraser mill, the Brydon mill, the Hotchkiss and Hughson Company mill, the Woodstock Company mill, the King mill . . until by 1879 there were seventeen sawmills at Gravenhurst, and in 1883, fourteen. So numerous were they by 1880 that one firm, Crone and Patton, had to build 'outside' of Muskoka Bay, on the south shore of the main lake, and this case was not exceptional. About 30,000,000 feet of lumber plus 35,000,000 shingles left Gravenhurst on Northern Railway trains in 1883 alone, besides another 50,000,000 feet of logs and square timber valued at $500,000. Professor Arthur Lower has calculated that the period of maximum production was from 1883 to 1890. At times, only Ottawa and perhaps Midland were doing any better. Truly Gravenhurst had become the "Sawdust City".

The most successful of the Gravenhurst firms was the Mickle and Dyment Company Ltd. This outfit began inconspicuously in 1877 when Charles Mickle of Cargill, Ontario, came to Gravenhurst, formed a partnership with William Tait of Orillia, and built a sawmill near Muskoka Wharf. Within a year and a half Mr. Mickle bought out Tait's interest and soon afterwards bought an adjacent mill. In 1884 he made a partnership with Nathaniel Dyment of Barrie, thus laying the foundations of the mighty "M.D." empire. Besides Gravenhurst, the firm operated mills at Bradford and Barrie, and later at Severn Bridge and Fenelon Falls as well. Theirs was the last sawmill to shut down in 1933 when the days of the Gravenhurst timber trade finally came to an end.

As might be expected, the population of Gravenhurst grew rapidly over those years; from about 1,200 in 1878 to 2,454 in 1887, the year it was incorporated as a town. (Bracebridge had only about 1,200 residents at that time.) At least half the population of Gravenhurst worked for the lumber companies. The town had no other industries, except a foundry and a gingerale bottling works. Nothing else took root in the "Sawdust City", where lumberjacks "six feet three inches in stocking-feet, all bone and muscle" were the pride of the town. (Sometimes they were also the terror of the town, as when the jacks came trooping in from the camps looking for booze and excitement — and usually finding both!) "Those were the days," said an old-timer of the 1880s, "that made Gravenhurst the envy of the north. Those were the days when men were men. Girls were peaches and not painted dolls and snobs were an unknown animal."[8]

How did steamboats fit into this new world of humming sawmills, six-foot lumberjacks and unpainted girls? In answer, we can state that without steam tugs, it would have been totally impossible to conduct lumbering on a big scale, or to concentrate the industry at Gravenhurst. In most localities, logs could simply be cut in the bush over the wintertime and rolled into the rivers in the spring, when river drivers could guide them downstream to the mills. Not so in Muskoka, where the size and scope of the lakes were a great potential hindrance. Steam tugs were needed to bag the logs with booms and tow them to the mills at the railheads. Some tugs could tow timber rafts a half-mile in diameter, without losing any logs on rock filled rapids. In short, the boats converted the lakes from handicaps into highways in the movement of millions of feet of timber. The only alternatives at the time would have been building hundreds of miles of railway spurs all through the district, or hauling the logs overland, neither of which would have made sense in this area. The boats also towed rafts and scows loaded with cut lumber from sawmills "up the lakes", thereby enabling some operators to locate their mills miles away if they chose. Almost all the provisions taken to remote lumber camps, were also transported by boat. The tugs had a beneficial effect on men's morale, too, in that they were used occasionally for picnics and moonlight cruises which added a little colour to the rather drab lives of the millhands. This form of recreation was at least a little more wholesome than boozing.

As lumbering moved in to become the mainstay of the Muskoka economy — a situation that persisted until around the turn of the century — it is not surprising to find that almost all the new steamers to appear on the Muskoka Lakes right after 1875 were tugs. Predictably, the first one to arrive belonged to A.P. Cockburn.

Obviously Mr. Cockburn was reading the trends of the times when he resolved to acquire a tug. Perhaps he was also influenced by the fact that both his father and his brother John Peter were planning to run sawmills on Muskoka Bay. In any case, immediately after the railway was officially declared open Cockburn bought the steamer *Simcoe* on Lake

Mickle-Dyment Sawmill, West Gravenhurst.

Lumber Yards, West Gravenhurst.
(View facing North-East. The Mickle Sawmill is in the background.)

Steam Tug "Simcoe".
A reconstruction, based on registry information and pictures of contemporary tugs from the Niagara region.

Couchiching and arranged to have her taken to Gravenhurst on a railway flatcar. Little is known about the *Simcoe* today, but thanks to an official shipping register, the most elementary facts are available. It seems she was built at Buffalo, N.Y., in 1866, under the name *M.C. Simons*, and registered 15.25 tons. Tradition says the vessel was used as a gunboat on the Niagara frontier during the Fenian scare. In June of 1867 she was imported to Lake Simcoe and put to work towing lumber barges and timber rafts to the sawmill at Belle Ewart. She was small and plain, only 49 feet in keel by 12 in beam, and had a single deck and a round, fantail stern. Her only remarkable features were her engine, a high-pressure model generating an exceptional 45 hp. (very good for the times), and her long remembered chime whistle, which, commented the Orillia 'Expositor' in 1867, "can be heard at a distance of twelve miles in calm weather."

The *Simcoe* spent a total of nine years towing on Lakes Simcoe and Couchiching before A.P. Cockburn purchased her from the Longford Lumber Company in 1875. She spent the last five years of her existence on the Muskoka Lakes, mostly towing log rafts; first under the command of Captain George Pirie, a popular Scot who was tragically drowned from her deck on the night of June 27th., and afterwards by Captain Charles Sweet[9] of Gravenhurst. Little is known of her activities in detail, except that she once attended a regatta on Lake Rosseau in 1876, along with the *Nipissing*. Sailing races had been scheduled, but the lake was calm as a millpond that day, and it was decided to race the steamers instead. The sight of the big sidewheeler, laden with excited passengers, pitted against the little screw tug on a course to the Indian River, was a thrilling spectacle, but after a close race the *Simcoe* won by a few lengths.

Apparently the *Simcoe* had little competition in the towing business, as only a few other tugs are known to have sailed on the Muskoka Lakes during the seventies. (The depression did not really lift until 1878.) One exception was the little steamer *Pinafore*, which was built as a screw yacht at Port Carling in 1876. With a length of 28.6 feet and a tonnage of 1.61, the *Pinafore* was owned by Captain John Rogers of Port Sandfield, who is remembered today chiefly as a hydrographer and compiler of some of the earliest known maps of the lakes. Captain Rogers used his vessel for all sorts of chores, including scowing, fishing trips and excursion cruises, until 1886. He may have been the first free-lance steamboat man in Muskoka.

A story is told about the *Pinafore*, near the end of her career. She was venturing into Bala Bay one night when a heavy fog set in, and rather than tempt fate Captain Rogers snubbed the vessel to a tree, then went ashore and lit his pipe, while the engineer, Charles Vanderburgh of Port Carling, banked the fire and filled the boiler. No one knew just where they were, but the deckhand made a good supper, after which they all retired to get some sleep. After midnight, however, a rooster began to crow. The fog was still as thick as pea-soup, but Vanderburgh at once roused the captain, announcing that he knew where they were.

"Where?" asked the captain.

"We are near Packer's, because I heard Packer's rooster crow," called back Charlie.

"How do you know it was Packer's? It may have been anybody's".

"Oh, I know that bird," replied Vanderburgh confidently. He was right. The three left their bunks, got up steam, steered in the direction of the sound, and arrived at the Packer farm on the south side of East Bay, safe and sound.

In the meantime, other enterprises, likewise dependent on towing operations, were starting to appear in Muskoka. A very persistent effort was made during the late 1870s to attract manufacturing industries to the district, a campaign that continues to this day. The initiative was taken primarily by Bracebridge. That bustling little community, whose population had swollen from a few dozen in 1866 to 750 a decade later, had just been incorporated as a village in 1875. North Falls had already pioneered by having the region's first sawmill (1862), the first gristmill (1864) and the first woollen mill (1872). In short, Bracebridge had practically monopolized Muskoka's fledgeling industries, except for sawmilling and shingle manufacturing. Starting in 1875, the village resolved to advertise in the Toronto newspapers, inviting correspondence from tanning companies, iron foundries,

Str. "Rosseau" scowing tanbark, Indian River.
From the Collection of the late Mr. Lester Turnbull, Dundas

Steam Tug "Queen of the Isles." Scowing tanbark on the Muskoka River during the 1890s.

woodenware makers and the like, and offering a bonus of $2,000 to any that would locate in Bracebridge. In 1876 the Beardmore Company of Toronto won this bonus, with the added benefit of a ten-year exemption from municipal taxation, on the promise that a tannery would be established within a year. In 1877 the new tannery was opened on schedule, beside the Muskoka River shortly below the falls. It proved quite successful, although it did not remain in the hands of the Beardmores beyond 1882. The tannery imported its hides from Central and South America, but obtained the tanbark from local hemlock, a tree which had hitherto been regarded by lumbermen as mere trash.

The Beardmore tannery opened an important new phase in the lakes trade of Muskoka, in that it consumed roughly 4,000 cords of tanbark 'per annum'. This tanbark would be purchased from local farmers and, for the most part, towed to the tannery in scows. A newspaper advertisement, dated June 1879, announces that Beardmore will pay $3.00 a cord for well-saved hemlock delivered to the tannery, or $2.25 a cord delivered to the shores of the Muskoka Lakes in lots of not less than a scowload. That presumably meant that roughly $10,000 to $12,000 was being distributed annually throughout the region of the three lakes. The farmers would usually do their cutting over the winters.

How was all this tanbark to be collected? For the first few seasons the tannery relied on A.P. Cockburn's fleet to tow in most of the bark. The Toronto shipping registers list a scow called the *Beaver*, which was built for Cockburn at Gravenhurst in 1877, the same year as the tannery. The *Beaver* was evidently used in tow of the *Simcoe*, since both were officially entrusted to Captain Sweet. The new scow was 70.5 feet by 18, with a draught of five feet, which suggests that she could handle perhaps 50 cords at a time. At that rate, she could theoretically have supplied the tannery with a year's consumption of tanbark in roughly 80 trips, not an impossible performance over a season of seven months, especially if a portion of the bark arrived (as it undoubtedly did) by other means. The *Beaver* was sold in 1879 and

Str. "Jennie Willson", with excursionists.

90

replaced by the *Otter*, a slightly larger scow, which in turn was joined by the *Mink* (1880), which was 52 feet by 16, and the much larger *Bruin* (1881), which was 97 feet by 25. The *Mink* and the *Bruin* both lasted until 1910, and they were probably not the only ones owned by A.P. Cockburn. There must have been a fair amount of bulk freight crossing the lakes in those years to justify the construction of such craft.

The Beardmore tannery did not choose to remain dependent on the Cockburn boats for long. In 1879 its owner, George S. Beardmore of Toronto, had a small screw tug built for him and transported by rail to Muskoka. The vessel, the *Jennie Willson*, was just 36.3 feet in length and registered five tons. Named after the manager's daughter, the *Jennie Wilson* towed for the tannery for six years and ran pleasure trips, until she proved too small for the workloads demanded of her and had to be sold. Nonetheless, she lasted a total of 30 years, a long life for a small Muskoka tug.

The *Jennie Willson* seems to have been replaced by the steamer *Chateau*, a tug which first appeared sometime in the 1880s, but of which nothing further is known, except that she had disappeared by 1893. The tannery was later to use additional tugs, and meanwhile it also developed its own fleet of scows.

Despite the coming of the Beardmore Company, the attempt to attract industry to Muskoka during the 1870s and '80s largely failed. Those that did move in almost invariably located in Bracebridge. In short, manufacturing, unlike lumbering, failed to revolutionize the economy of Muskoka.

A few more tugs can be chronicled from this period, though little is known about them. One was the *Hockrock*, a small 30-foot screw steamer of 2.83 tons, built in 1880 for the Crone and Patton Lumber Company, which had a sawmill at the mouth of the Hoc-Roc River, at the south end of Lake Muskoka. Another was the *Flora Barnes*, a 64-foot tug of 11.83 tons which was built at Port Carling in 1881. Captain Levi Fraser, himself a tug captain, has preserved a tradition that the *Flora Barnes* once grounded on a shoal near Mortimer's Point, on the west arm of Lake Muskoka. Her crew tried rocking her loose by tying a line to a tree and heaving back and forth, but just when she seemed all set to roll off the rocks, the line snapped and all hands spilled into the drink. There were no casualties. Later, during the winter of 1882-83 the *Flora Barnes* was seized by the Village of Bracebridge for unpaid taxes. While still under seizure she was destroyed by fire on February 2, 1883. If the townspeople thought that was the end of the affair they were soon undeceived, because the owner, Captain Thomas Barnes of Wentworth County, launched a suit the following March for what he claimed was unlawful seizure. This led to a colossal court case, held at Barrie in 1884, in which the verdict went in favour of the plaintiff, and the Village of Bracebridge was ordered to pay a total of $3,671.00. plus costs. As a result, Bracebridge was saddled with what were called the Flora Barnes debentures for the next twenty years.

Not all the new steamers of the 1870s were tugs. Two small steam yachts are known from this interval. One was the *Helena*, a 44-foot half-decked screw vessel of 9.06 tons, built at Gravenhurst in 1877 for A.P. Cockburn and undoubtedly named in honour of his wife. Her skipper was Captain Joseph C. Huckins of Toronto, who was later to buy her and move her to the Lake of Bays. The second yacht, the *Kate Murray*, was a trim little craft of 2.35 tons, built at Hamilton for Charles Vanderburgh of Port Carling, whom we have already encountered on the *Pinafore*. Vanderburgh apparently used the *Kate Murray* for pleasure trips, and also to tow logs to his sawmill. Later he built a small resort on the Indian River, and used the yacht to help entertain his guests. The *Kate Murray* lasted until 1902, but her last years were spent mostly towing.

In the meantime, how were the Cockburn steamers faring? Very well, apparently. By 1878 the depression was lifting, immigration was steady, and there were plenty of logs to tow. The boats were now confirmed more strongly than ever as an integral part of all transport services north of Gravenhurst. All mail, freight and passengers bound for Bracebridge, Huntsville, Rosseau and Lake Nipissing, except in winter, were transported on the Cockburn line.

In 1878 the fleet still consisted of only three vessels. Mr. Cockburn had sold his smallest steamer, the *Waubamik*, in 1876. She went to the aforementioned Captain Huckins, who removed her to Baysville, where we shall soon find her again. The steamer that eventually followed her was the *Rosseau*, which was purchased while still under construction at Gravenhurst in the fall of 1879. The *Rosseau* was 70 feet in length, 11.6 feet in beam, had a half-round stern and a register tonnage of 35.71. Her engine power was considerable, delivering up to 20 hp. In appearance she looked a trifle odd, with her rather boxy cabins and tall, ungainly stack contrasting with the fine lines of her hull. Perhaps she was originally designed as a yacht, only to be remodelled as a workboat. In any case, the *Rosseau* was usually used as a tug and scowboat, though like most tugs she was occasionally engaged for picnics and pleasure cruises.

The *Rosseau* entered service in 1880, under the command of Captain George Bailey of Bracebridge, who at 33 had just gained his master's ticket. A son of Alexander Bailey, the pioneer fur trader and mill owner at North Falls, the young man was a born boatman, having rowed or paddled over every portion of the Muskoka Lakes. As a youth of nineteen he had been aboard the *Wenonah* for her maiden voyage in 1866, and resolved at that moment to devote his life to steamboating. He would have joined the *Wenonah*'s crew straightaway, but his father had other plans, and it was only in 1867 that Alexander Bailey gave his son permission to enroll as a deckhand on the *Wenonah*. Since then he had worked his way up from the bottom, serving as part-time wheelsman under Captain McKay and Captain Pimlott, then as mate on the *Nipissing* under Captain McKay and Captain Pimlott, then as mate on the *Nipissing* under Captain Kirkland and his successor, Captain John Scott.[10] Now Bailey had his own vessel to command. This was only the start of a distinguished career that would span a total of 55 years, ending finally with George Bailey as Commodore and senior captain of the Line.

Bailey's earliest assignments were usually to tow timber rafts to the Gravenhurst sawmills and provisions up the lakes to the lumber camps, along with Captain Sweet on the *Simcoe*. So heavy were the workloads that double crews had to be engaged. As it happened, though, the *Simcoe* and the *Rosseau* sailed together for only one year. Then in 1880 A.P. Cockburn decided to do away with the *Simcoe*. His reasons are not entirely clear. Perhaps he had become convinced that larger tugs were necessary to cope with the immense drives of logs. (Sometimes a single tow might contain 20,000 logs.) Perhaps the *Simcoe* was growing leaky and unseaworthy by her fifteenth year, leaving him no choice. What is certain is that Cockburn wrote to the Toronto registry office on December 10, 1880 to advise that the tug *Simcoe* had just been broken up at Gravenhurst, although it is said that her wheelhouse was

Str. "Kate Murray".
Sketch from *Muskoka Illustrated*, by G.M. Adam, 1888
Courtesy, Metropolitan Toronto Library.

Str. "Rosseau", towing on Muskoka Bay.

used to ornament a point on Gibraltar Island, west of Beaumaris, for many years. The *Rosseau* in turn was sold in January of 1881 to John Speirs Playfair, a Toronto dry goods merchant. This move was probably a mere formality, since Playfair was already joining Mr. Cockburn as a partner in the steamboat business. The local newspapers continued to speak of the *Rosseau* as part of the Cockburn fleet until 1884, when she was sold to the Bracebridge tannery.

Before we follow the fortunes of the boats into the 1880s, let us pause for a look at developments on the North Muskoka Lakes.

FOOTNOTES

[1] No doubt this move was merely a gesture, meant to prod some of the existing railway lines to act, since transport firms as a rule do not like the prospect of independent operators acting within their own spheres of influence.

[2] The south Muskoka Road, having been set in "good order," was meanwhile abandoned by the Works Department to the care of the local townships.

[3] Captain Percival later left the boats to run a hotel at Port Sydney, only to be killed as a result of a freak accident there in 1884.

[4] Captain Kirkland was a veteran Great Lakes sailor who had recently been master of the Kawartha steamer *Vanderbilt* on Sturgeon Lake.

[5] It is not surprising to find a notable increase in the number of temperance societies and police constables in the district around this time.

[6] Arthur R.M. Lower, 'The North American Assault on the Canadian Forest', 1938

[7] Captain Dollar afterwards founded the Dollar Line of ocean steamships.

[8] Gravenhurst 'Banner', December 19, 1929

[9] Captain Sweet died in 1887, perhaps of alcoholism, to the great regret of his shipmates.

[10] Captain Scott served on the Muskoka steamers for a decade until 1881, when he left for California.

Utterson, Ontario (facing North)
Courtesy, Mr. George Johnson, Port Sydney

CHAPTER 4
Steamboats Appear on the North Muskoka Lakes
(1877-1885)

While the Muskoka Lakes steamer fleet was entering its second decade, other parts of the district were just starting to enjoy the benefits of regular boat services. In 1875, for example, an English engineer named Thomas Stanton put a small steam-launch called the *Pioneer* in service on a route from Severn Bridge to Sparrow Lake, around which there were a number of farms and good timber, but no passable roads, except in winter. This proved the beginning of a service that would continue until the First World War, but the Sparrow Lake region belongs to the Trent-Severn waterway rather than Muskoka.

Meanwhile, settlement was spreading north of Bracebridge. As an example, by 1877 the village of Utterson, located at the junction of the Muskoka Road and the Brunel Road, about nine miles south of Huntsville, was a lively, ambitious hamlet with two churches, two hotels, a school, a post office, and a daily stage service. Huntsville was doing even better. Its first settler, William Cann, had erected a shanty on the Vernon River between Lake Vernon and Fairy Lake as early as 1862, well before any surveys had been conducted. Cann engaged in a little trapping and fishing for a year, before selling most of his land to Captain George Hunt, a retired British Army officer from Montreal, who became the first businessman in the area. A man of some means and strong views on liquor, Captain Hunt opened a small store which carried a small stock of tea, tobacco, flour and pork, all of which had to be hauled overland from Orillia, a distance of 60 miles. He also lobbied vigorously to have the Muskoka Road extended to the Vernon River, and when a post office was opened — named "Huntsville" in his honour — the captain became the first postmaster, which entailed regular walks to Utterson to collect mail. His home served as a temporary church and schoolhouse until proper buildings could be built. Despite the herculean labours of Captain Hunt, the community grew slowly. By 1875 there were only eleven resident families, with a sawmill, gristmill, two log stores, one hotel, a physician, and a telegraph line to serve them. It was a sad day for the little village when Captain Hunt was stricken with typhoid and died in 1882, at the age of 57.

During the early years, Huntsville and the other northern settlements suffered all the usual hardships of isolation resulting from bad roads. As late as 1879 the stages on the Muskoka Road required an average of eight hours to complete the 20-mile trip from Bracebridge to Huntsville. Many settlers preferred the alternative of travelling part of the way by boat, which in this case meant unloading wagons at the east end of the Brunel Road where it comes out on Mary Lake, a few miles from Utterson, and from here using dugout canoes to proceed up Mary Lake and up the serpentine North Muskoka River to Fairy Lake, at the west end of which stood Huntsville. The only serious drawback to this thirteen-mile trip was a ten-foot waterfall and rapids near the foot of Fairy Lake.

At the Mary Lake landing, a very small hamlet was already emerging. A squatter named John McAlpine had taken up land near the outlet of Mary Lake in 1868 and did his best to assist those coming after, by ferrying them across the river in his dugout (popularly known as the "Man-Killer"), and putting them up at his home if necesary. As additional families moved in, McAlpine and his neighbours raised a crude sawmill and built a dam at the foot of the lake. In 1870 he successfully petitioned A.P. Cockburn, then the Memeber of Parliament for a bridge to carry the road across the river. However, the following year Mr. McAlpine left the district, and his mill and most of his lands were acquired by Albert Sydney Smith, a gentleman of some means from Stratford, Ontario, who had paid a visit to Muskoka in 1871. He was captivated by the picturesque rolling hills and dome-shaped islands of Mary Lake, and saw a vision of a prosperous mill town developing along the shore, encompassing both the falls and the landing. In good English tradition, Sydney-Smith saw his own role as that of village squire. Accordingly, he laid out a village plot, rebuilt and enlarged the sawmill, and added a grist and oatmeal mill. His neighbours were not idle either. Some of

Mary Lake, from Port Sydney (facing North-East).
The village Anglican Church appears at left.
Courtesy, Mr. Victor Clarke, Port Sydney

them opened a store, then a school and a church. In 1873 the fledgling community decided to call itself "Port Sydney" in honour of its most prominent citizen, and on January 1, 1874 this name became official when the post office adopted it.

The very name of Port Sydney shows that its residents were already contemplating a regular boat service and hoping for great things from it. The village was, like Gravenhurst, at the foot of a whole network of lakes and rivers that, with a few modifications, could be adapted into a waterway extending about 28 miles through a number of promising new settlements. Huntsville felt the same way. In 1875 Dr. F.P. Howland, who was already a leader on the local scene, commented that "Our [Huntsville] merchants and all interested in the carrying trade are very anxious that a steamer should run on these waters."

The Government of Ontario agreed. Obviously impressed by great success of the Cockburn fleet on the lower lakes, and dismayed by the never-ending outlays needed to keep the local roads open, the Public Works Department ordered a survey made of the Muskoka River north of Mary Lake in 1873. By January of 1874, according to engineer Molesworth, an appropriation of $20,000 was made for navigational improvements. Of this, some $16,900 was granted to a Mr. John Carroll to build a lock past the falls, while the balance was to pay for a 600-foot channel needed to connect the lock with the river upstream. The actual lock chamber was to be 88 feet six inches in length, considerably less than the one at Port Carling.

A later report submitted by Molesworth on November 24, 1875, confirms that the lock above Mary Lake had been completed by that date. Unfortunately, the report goes on, there were shoals above the new lock, and another one below it, and still another under the road bridge at Huntsville, which would all have to be removed by hand dredging before boats could use the waterway. Also, it was noted that the bridge at Huntsville was too low to allow a steamer to pass under it, and therefore would have to be raised. Nor was this all. Mary Lake required a new stop log dam at its exit to maintain the water-levels, the old dam having been washed away by a flood the previous spring. The government, however, paid all these additional bills promptly, though the total costs ran considerably higher then the original $20,000. By 1875, extensive repairs were made to that section of the Muskoka Road between Bracebridge and Utterson, with more outlays following on the road to Port Sydney, to make certain that stages would be able to reach the new terminus. All that, before anyone had even built a steamer! The contrast with the lower lakes is striking. A decade earlier, A.P. Cockburn had been running steamboats for three years amid incredible difficulties before the government provided any help, whereas on the upper lakes every possible assistance to steam navigation was being provided in advance. The people of Port Sydney did their part by building a wharf over the winter of 1876-77. Now everything was ready, but where was the boat?

Actually, the new steamer was not long in coming. By the winter of 1876-77, three gentlemen from Port Dalhousie were hard at work building it, next to Sydney-Smith's sawmill. Their names were Alfred Denton, master mariner; John Smiley, engineer; and John James Denton, clerk; the three had incorporated themselves as Denton, Smiley and Company, following invitations to establish a boat service. The steamboat, called the *Northern*, was in many ways similar to A.P. Cockburn's *Wenonah*, being a double-decked sidewheeler with a horizontal 25-hp. high-pressure engine geared to the paddle-shaft, thus dispensing with a walking beam. Her hull was 74.5 feet in length by 15.6 in beam, while her overall proportions, encompassing the paddle wheels, were about 80 feet by 24. She drew a modest 4.9 feet of water, registered 62.14 tons, and was capable of carrying over 200 passengers and a lot of freight.

By June of 1877 the *Northern* was ready. Years later, an old settler would recall being at Port Sydney during his youth, on June 18, 1877, and seeing the steamer "slide down the ways into the waters of Mary Lake to the music of a fife and drum band aboard the ship to give [her] . . a welcome to the water and a "bon voyage" salute. That was surely a gala day for Port Sydney."[1]

The *Northern* was not a particularly elegant boat. Her hull was flat-bottomed and a trifle scow-like, with a square stern; her bow between decks was unenclosed and she never had a hurricane deck. Her tall, slender stack was hinged to allow her to pass under the bridge at Huntsville. Still, she proved a great success, plying daily from Port Sydney to Huntsville and Lake Vernon on a round trip of 56 miles with seven ports of call. Except for winter travel she practically cancelled out wheeled traffic on the Muskoka Road from Utterson to Huntsville, and for eight years, 1877 to 1885, the standard pattern of transport was as follows: Toronto to Gravenhurst (115 miles) by train, Gravenhurst to Bracebridge (16 miles) by steamboat, Bracebridge to Port Sydney (13 miles) by stage, and Port Sydney to Huntsville (15 miles) on the *Northern*. No doubt the quaint little woodburner was busy towing logs between her regular passenger runs, and sometimes she was used for picnic cruises, occasionally ascending a few miles up the Big East River from Lake Vernon.

Her coming was highly beneficial to the communities on her route. For the next eight years Port Sydney blossomed, while her inland neighbour and chief rival, Utterson, began to wither. Huntsville prospered even more, and by 1879 it could boast three churches, a public school, an Orange Hall, a temperance hall, two hotels, five general stores, a hardware store, harness shop, wagon shop, two sawmills, and a weekly newspaper.

Huntsville also had its competitors. A rival village called Port Vernon was emerging about eight miles away, at the northwest corner of Vernon Lake. Here the presiding genius was Captain Charles Hood, a former St. Lawrence River mariner who first visited the region about 1875. Greatly impressed by the scenery and the water power of the Fox River where it empties into the lake, Captain Hood felt that this would make a splendid site for a town. He bought the property, built a dam and a sawmill, opened roads and bridges, and laid out a complete town plot on both sides of the river. An eccentric individual of grim

S.S. "Northern".
Sketch from *Muskoka Illustrated*, by G.M. Adam. 1888,
Courtesy, Metropolitan Toronto Library

determination and driving energy, Captain Hood soon attracted a fair number of people to his "town", and soon Port Vernon possessed two or three stores, three churches, a school, two hotels, and about fifteen homes. There were even sidewalks along its main street. Once the *Northern* began to call, Port Vernon also became the chief distribution centre for Stisted Township and a string of new settlements to the north. In 1877, by popular demand, the name Port Vernon was officially changed to "Hoodstown", in honour of Captain Hood.

Though the *Northern* proved very profitable, she was not spared the usual trials and tribulations common to steamboats in the backwoods. In the spring of 1879, for example, the lumbermen drove about 35,000 sawlogs over the government dam at the Fairy Lake lock, where they formed a jam some distance below. The backed-up pressure from the current overflowed the breakwater, filling the canal with sand and gravel. It was quite some time before the *Northern* could get through the canal again. In 1877, the suggestion was made that a canal should be dug through the marshy creek linking Fairy Lake with Peninsula Lake, thus permitting the *Northern* to extend her runs another five miles eastward towards the Lake of Bays, but owing to costs this improvement had to wait until 1888.

While the *Northern* was opening a whole new chapter in the history of Muskoka steam navigation, parallel developments were under way on the Lake of Bays. As noted earlier, a sideroad called the Maclean, branching off from the Muskoka Road at High Falls, was slowly extended eastwards until in 1876 it reached the southwest corner of the Lake of Bays, at the mouth of the south branch of the Muskoka River. The site is less hilly, hence less scenic, than Port Sydney or Huntsville, but it was very suitable for a mill town, with excellent water power and plenty of level land. The first settler, William H. Brown, arrived in 1877 and soon erected a dam and a sawmill, which became the nucleus of the little village of Baysville. The new community grew steadily, but for decades it was frustratingly remote, despite a biweekly stage service. Meanwhile, another settlement already existed on the Lake of Bays about eighteen miles away, at the east end, where the Bobcaygeon Road crossed the narrows near Johnny-Cake Bay. Originally called Cedar Narrows, this spot was renamed Colebridge about 1865, in honour of Zachariah Cole and his wife, who built the first store. Much later, when a post office came to be opened there in 1883, it was discovered that another place in the province already bore the name of Colebridge; consequently Cedar Narrows was renamed "Dorset". Zack Cole had meanwhile added a hotel, as a considerable influx of settlers, lured by the promise of free land grants, moved into the area from Minden in 1868. For quite some time Dorset had much closer links with Haliburton than Muskoka: as late as 1879 there was still no road of any kind running between Dorset and Baysville.

This situation began to change in 1878 when the steamer *Dean* entered service on the Lake of Bays. The *Dean* was A.P. Cockburn's former steamer *Waubamik*, now sold to Captain Joseph Huckins. According to local sources Captain Huckins had the little vessel loaded onto a wagon at Bracebridge and laboriously dragged up Hunt's Hill with the help of the local citizens. The heavy load proved too much for the soft roads, and it took two days to cover the first five miles. A lumberman named Steve Fortin then took over the job of moving the boat. He did so by building a long sled, loading the craft onto it, and dragging it the rest of the way to Baysville using several horse teams. The whole effort took two weeks. Captain Huckins then took over, refitted the boat, and restored her original name. Thus the much-travelled *Waubamik* added another "first" to her record: the first steamer on Lake Rosseau, the first on the Lake of Bays, and the first propeller steamer anywhere in Muskoka.

The early steamboat period on the Lake of Bays is poorly documented, and therefore we cannot say much about the *Dean*'s activities there. Population was then very sparse, and passengers aboard the little craft must have noted only the occasional clearing as she puffed her way along to such calling places as Bigwin Island, Dwight Bay and Dorset. Probably she ran only three regular trips a week, on the arrival of Harvie's stage, and alternated by towing logs. Yet she was apparently profitable, since Captain Huckins is said to have used her for four seasons.

Presumably the little *Dean* was growing leaky and unseaworthy by the season of 1881, by which time she was fifteen years old. At any rate, we soon find a new steamer on the Lake of Bays. In 1883 an advertisement mentions that James Harvie's northbound stages are connecting daily with the steamer *Northern* at Port Sydney, and triweekly at Baysville with the steamer *Helena*, a vessel of nine tons. Since A.P. Cockburn's yacht, the *Helena* was about that size, and since Captain Huckins had once been running it for him, it seems reasonable

Dorset House, Dorset, Ontario
Courtesy, Mr. Brad Robinson, Dorset

to suppose that Cockburn's yacht was in fact identical to the Lake of Bays boat, and that Captain Huckins bought her about 1882 to replace the *Dean*. The *Helena* was running again in 1884 and probably as late as 1886, when Captain Huckins is said to have had two steamers in service. What finally happened to her is unrecorded, although in 1976 an old-timer from Birkendale, on the Lake of Bays, remarked to this writer that he had heard of both the *Dean* and the *Helena*, and that in his boyhood he had seen the submerged wreck of a very early steamer, lying in about nine feet of water about a mile north of Baysville. Undoubtedly the remains of both vessels lie somewhere in that area.

Captain Huckins' new steamer, built in partnership with William H. Brown, was the *Excelsior*, a fine double decked ship listed at 23.55 tons. The *Excelsior* was 70 feet in length by 15 in beam, and could carry at least 150 passengers. Her engine, a vertical 9.63 hp. model, was installed by George Robertson, a Scot from Norway Point, and the official launching drew people from miles around to watch. Clearly, with a vessel her size, steamboating on the Lake of Bays was entering a whole new phase.

Just how dramatic it was, no one could have foreseen. Plying from Baysville, which was then the gateway to the Lake of Bays, the *Excelsior* began regular trips, calling at all the wharves and post offices on the lake, bringing in commodities from the outside world, and frequently running picnics and charter trips. She was not permitted to monopolize this market for long. Almost immediately came disquieting reports of a rival steamer being built near the mouth of the Oxtongue River by a settler named George Francis Marsh, who already had a sawmill at Marsh's Falls. The new steamer was even larger than the *Excelsior*, though not quite as long. Captain Huckins ran his own ship until the fall of 1886, but there wasn't room for two competing services on the Lake of Bays, and in the end the 'palm of victory' was to go to Captain Marsh.

We shall have more to say about the Lake of Bays in succeeding chapters, but for the present let us turn our attention briefly to some new developments in the Nipissing country, which were soon to have major consequences both on Lake Nipissing and the lakes of Muskoka.

S.S. "Excelsior".
A reconstruction, based largely on registry information. Most of the superstructure detail is conjectural.

Baysville, Ontario (view facing West)
Courtesy, Archives of Ontario Acc 9939

FOOTNOTES

[1] Captain Levi R. Fraser, 'History of Muskoka', P.68

Steamers at Sturgeon Falls Circa 1910.
S.S. "Northern Belle" (left), S.S. "Highland Belle" and S.S. "Elgin L. Lewis".
Courtesy, Mrs. Rita Moon, Sturgeon Falls

CHAPTER 5
Steamboating on Lake Nipissing
(1881-1962)

At the start of the 1880s Canada as a whole was prospering. The depression had lifted, times were generally good, the Conservatives were back in power in Ottawa, and once again the nation was becoming excited about the renewed prospect of a transcontinental railway all the way to the Pacific. In Muskoka, Mr. Cockburn's steamboat line was sharing in this prosperity. Though the records of the firm have disappeared, we have Cockburn's own testimony that, by 1881, he had almost paid for the steamers *Nipissing*, *Simcoe* and *Wenonah*, which together were valued at more than $31,000, excepting $4,000 still owed on the latter boat to his inlaws, the Proctors. Moreover, he had succeeded in reducing his debt to James Gibb Ross and Company from $17,000 to $5,000, the balance of which was extinguished when the firm agreed to accept stock in the new Navigation Company. Put together, all this suggests that his net profits between 1868 and 1881 came to something like $39,000. Furthermore, Mr. Cockburn found it possible to build an additional three steamers in 1881, at a cost of $23,000.

Some very ambitious schemes were afoot during the winter of 1880-81. The Canada Central Railway, later to be merged into the Canadian Pacific Railway network, was gradually being pushed up the Ottawa Valley towards the eastern end of Lake Nipissing. To Mr. Cockburn, watching all this from his vantage point in Parliament, these developments came as a reminder of the Northern Railway's extension to Muskoka Wharf and the mutually profitable arrangements ensuing both for the railway and his steamers. Once again, a railway from the cities was preparing to tap a major lake. The general consensus was that the new line would pass through the newly emerging hamlet of Nipissingan, or Nipissing Village, at the terminus of the Rosseau-Nipissing Road from Muskoka, then, the only land-route to the big lake. With regular stages already bumping their way overland from Rosseau, Nipissingan was easily the busiest spot in the entire region. With settlement also increasing, there would soon be plenty of scope for steamboats, which would be needed to supplement the railway and service the shores and harbours of Lake Nipissing, especially Sturgeon Falls. Opportunity was beckoning.

Gradually, in conversations with some of his deskmates in the Commons, notably Mr. Donald A. Smith, the future Lord Strathcona, the idea arose of forming a joint-stock company, to encompass and expand Cockburn's existing fleet, and to place a steamer on Lake Nipissing. Smith offered to invest $5,000 to $10,000 in the proposed scheme, and when others also showed interest, Mr. Cockburn drew up a private prospectus, stating the aims of the new venture. These included improvements to the existing plant, the inauguration of steam navigation on Lake Nipissing, and perhaps new operations on the Magnetawan River system as well. He predicted that the new company would earn a net profit of $12,000 during its first year alone: in fact, the actual returns for 1881 came to $12,430.37. What followed was the organization of the Muskoka and Nipissing Navigation Company.

The charter of the new company, dated January 10, 1881, spelled out its aims exactly and authorized it to issue stock to a total value of $100,000, to be divided into 2,000 shares worth $50.00 each. The *Wenonah*, *Nipissing* and *Rosseau* were taken over at the rather low valuation of $34,075, which is to say that Mr. Cockburn received 681½ shares for them. Actually, Mr. Cockburn always held the lion's share of the Company's stock: out of 1,280 shares subscribed, he owned 800. Donald Smith subscribed for 100 shares or $5,000, while John S. Playfair of Toronto purchased 10. The Honourable Alexander Mackenzie, M.P. and former Prime Minister of Canada, also purchased $1,000 of company stock and became its first president, with Mr. Playfair as vice-president. Both of these men were among the first six directors of the Company, the others being Robert Hay, a merchant from Toronto; Larratt William Smith, a Toronto barrister-at-law; Herman Henry Cook, the lumber firm owner; and Mr. Cockburn. John Alexander Link of Gravenhurst, Mr. Cockburn's bookeeper and former mate on the *Wenonah*, was made secretary-treasurer, while Mr. Cockburn himself was appointed general manager. For about 20 years there were few changes in the composition of the board, except that Alexander Mackenzie retired as president late in 1882, to be succeeded by J.S. Playfair, with a Barrie lumberman, Richard Power, now in the vice-president's chair.

The new Company was to prove both a triumph and a curse to its prime founder, A.P. Cockburn, in that it both aided and frustrated his plans. While he could now contemplate far more ambitious operations, he was no longer free to make his own business decisions. Henceforth he would be obliged to share power with other men, many of whom had not half the interest, or a quarter the expertise, that he had. Worries and regrets he had always known, but these had hitherto been of his own making. It becomes quite a different matter to be caught up in the errors and follies of others, without being able to prevent them.

Immediately after the Company was organized, before any of the 44 shareholders were asked to contribute anything, Mr. Cockburn began construction of his three new steamers. Two of these were built at Gravenhurst; the third, perhaps, was built there in sections, but assembled near Lake Nipissing.

There were comparatively few settlers living around the big lake in 1881. A handful of brave souls were starting a few clearings and building shanties at Callander Bay and Sturgeon Falls, a few miles upstream from the lake. North Bay did not exist. The real focal point for the area was Nipissingan, now Nipissing Village. The first settlers arrived there about 1863, from Eganville and vicinity in the Ottawa Valley, and for years their only contacts with the outside world were along the old canoe route to Pembroke. After the Nipissing Road was rendered passable in 1874 Nipissing Village grew steadily, until by 1881 it could boast two stores, two hotels, a blacksmith shop and a municipal hall. By 1880 a sailboat called the *Louise* was being used to carry freight and passengers around the lake, but soon proved unequal to the task.

Improvements were already under way, at Chapman's Landing on the South River, barely a mile from Nipissingan, where a group of men were busy building a new propeller steamship, which was, rather grandly, christened the *Inter-Ocean*. Comparatively little is known of this, the first of many steamboats on Lake Nipissing. No photos of the vessel have yet been discovered, and, aside from a terse description in a Toronto shipping register, the only real information about her comes from an elderly resident of Nipissing Township who actually remembered seeing her slide stern first from the ways into the South River in the spring of 1881.

The *Inter-Ocean* was apparently a conventional, all-purpose passenger and freight steamer, with a length of 103.4 feet, a beam of 22.5 feet (probably a precaution in the event of storms on a large and shallow lake), and a register tonnage of 98.12. She was of oak construction, with two full-length decks, a hurricane deck and a round stern. Powered with a 15-hp. high-pressure engine, she was of course a wood-burner, and is said to have had a twelve-foot boiler which was fuelled from the stern end.

Using Nipissing Village as her home port, the *Inter-Ocean* began making regular trips to all points on the lake, usually departing at 8:00 a.m. and arriving at Sturgeon Falls about 11:00 a.m. It generally took her about an hour and forty-five minutes to reach the beaches of North Bay, but this was then a minor port of call. The main calling places were Callander and Sturgeon Falls.

As expected, the little steamship proved a tremendous boon to the local settlers, and played no small part in the growth and expansion of Nipissing Village. Sturgeon Falls received a post office just weeks after the *Inter-Ocean* first blew her whistle in the basin below the cataract. The steamer, commanded by Captain Alfred Burritt, a veteran Great Lakes sailor from Thornbury, carried passengers and freight of all sorts, including livestock, and also conducted the first sightseeing cruises on Lake Nipissing. Undoubtedly she was a welcome sight to many a weary landseeker after bouncing and jolting over the Nipissing Road in a stage for 67 miles, and to merchants and settlers dependent on her for the delivery of provisions. Business was so good that within two years the Navigation Company decided to add another steamer to the Nipissing division, and accordingly purchased a new 50-foot screw tug called the *Sparrow*, then under construction across the lake at Duchesay Creek,

Captain Alfred Burritt, Master of the "Inter-Ocean".
Courtesy, Ms. Ruth Burritt, Weston

S.S. "Inter-Ocean".
A reconstruction, based largely on registry information and the detailed recollections of the late Mr. William Armstrong of North Himsworth. Mr. Armstrong declared the above sketch a fairly accurate likeness.

Steam Tug "Sparrow"

near North Bay. A staunch little vessel of 25.23 tons (later increased to 36.17 when the boat was lengthened), the *Sparrow* assumed most of the towing of logs on the lake, while the *Inter-Ocean* carried most of the freight and passengers.

All looked bright for the Muskoka and Nipissing Navigation Company. Business was brisk and its boats were busy. Its faith in the prospects of the Nipissing region seemed fully justified. The Ontario Government lent a hand by building a dredge in 1883 to help deepen portions of the Sturgeon River and other shallow spots.

Then the first blow fell. As the C.P.R. drew close to the lake in 1882, its promoters suddenly announced a change of plan. Originally it was expected that the railway would run south of Lake Nipissing and pass through Nipissing Village. Instead, a new route was selected, skirting the north side of the lake and running due west past a shallow and exposed spot which by a stretch of imagination was called a bay: North Bay, which then consisted of a few shacks fringed by the forest. The new route also went straight through the port of Sturgeon Falls. Overnight the village of Nipissing saw its hopes of becoming a major port and distribution centre dashed forever. In an age that worshipped the iron horse, all spoils and honours went to the place that possessed a railway. North Bay was a poor port, but a good site for sidings.

It need hardly be added that the change of route did not improve the earnings of the *Inter-Ocean*, which now found herself largely supplanted: apparently it also prompted Alexander Mackenzie to withdraw from the Company. Ironically, the steamboat made a modest contribution to her own obsolescence, in that she is said to have hauled stones from the Manitou Islands to help build a railway bridge at North Bay for the C.P.R!

The railway's arrival left little work for steamboats on Lake Nipissing, beyond the towing of logs. Here again though, times were changing. Mr. John Rudolphus Booth, the Ottawa lumber king, was eying the pineries of the Lake Nipissing region, and wondering how to add another territory to his vast timber empire. He decided to build a short railway from the east side of the lake, near Callander, to Lake Nosbonsing, from which point logs could be conveyed into the Ottawa. Late in 1883 Booth made overtures to the M. & N.

Navigation Company. He offered to give it large towing contracts at good rates, but he insisted that the Company in turn should build a paddlewheel steamer for that purpose. Booth even offered to supply the machinery for such a vessel, but he would not look at the *Inter-Ocean*: in his judgement she drew too much water for the shallow bays of Lake Nipissing. All this seemed like a golden opportunity to A.P. Cockburn, who went to Ottawa and worked out an agreement with Booth, subject to ratification by the Company board of directors. Upon his return, the board, for some reason, vetoed the entire transaction. In vain the Manager protested, sensing that a fatal mistake was being made.

The decision did prove fatal, as far as the Company's operations on Lake Nipissing were concerned. Shrugging his shoulders, Booth simply proceeded to build his own steamer, a powerful light-draught paddlewheel tug which he named after himself, and used her do do his own and any other towing he could get on Lake Nipissing. By 1885 the *John R. Booth* was in regular service.

For the Navigation Company, this was the second great shock. During 1884 and 1885 the *Inter-Ocean* continued to sail from the stranded port of Nipissing Village, and meeting the trains at North Bay and Sturgeon Falls, but all the east-west traffic was now running overland and she earned little money. The final blow came in January 1886, when the Northern Railway, which was then being extended north from Gravenhurst to connect with the C.P.R., reached Callander and re-routed the main north-south traffic away from the Nipissing Road and the waterways forever. There was no point in continuing the struggle any further. Nipissing Village was now a complete backwater, and the steamer a redundancy.

In the spring of 1886, the *Inter-Ocean* and the *Sparrow* were offered for sale. The larger vessel was soon sold, at a heavy loss, to a pair of businessmen from the Collingwood area who hoped to use her on Georgian Bay. Three local men agreed to sail her to the French River outlet, but one look at the Chaudiere Falls revealed the hopelessness of trying to warp

Steam Tug "J.R. Booth"
Courtesy, Mr. Alex Dufresne, Callander

G.T.R. train at Callander.
Courtesy, North Himsworth Museum, Callander

the ship downstream. Orders were given, and the little steamer was ignominiously broken up. Every piece of metal in her construction, down to the last iron spike, was extracted and salvaged, but all the timbers were piled up and burned. The *Sparrow* was on hand to bring back the fragments, and later they were incorporated into a new steamer on Georgian Bay, also called the *Inter-Ocean*. Years later Captain Burritt, who had moved away with his family to Thornbury, was to write to friends in Nipissing that, every so often, he could hear the whistle of the old *Inter-Ocean* echoing across the waters of Georgian Bay like a ghost from the past.

The *Sparrow* was luckier. On May 3, 1886, she too was sold, to John B. Smith of Callander, who kept her profitably employed towing logs and scows until 1927.

The steamboat era on Lake Nipissing did not die with the *Inter-Ocean*, nor even with the *Sparrow*. On the contrary, it would continue as late as 1960, and during the 80-year span nearly 50 steam-vessels (mostly tugs) would ply on the big lake; not counting a few more on nearby Trout Lake, Lake Nosbonsing and the French River.

Following the demise of the *Inter-Ocean*, the passenger boat service fell into abeyance for a time. However, there were soon at least half a dozen lumber companies active in the area, and several used tugs. For seventeen years the *John R. Booth* (which registered 194.23 tons) plied slowly back and forth, endlessly feeding logs in to the landing at Wisa-Wasa, just south of Callander; whence the Booth Company tram-railway ran them across to Lake Nosbonsing. Here a little tug called the *Nosbonsing* (18.67 tons) took over, hauling them across the lake to continue their journey to the Ottawa. In 1902 the *John R. Booth* was hauled ashore and burned at Wisa-Wasa. The Company also ran a few small tugs used for "sweeping" up stray logs, and in later years acquired an "alligator" or warping tug, the *Monarch* (renamed the *Wisawassa*), to bring in the booms until the firm ceased operations on

108

Steam Tug "Screamer" at North Bay.

Steam Alligator "Woodchuck"
Courtesy, Mr. Alex Dufresne, Callander

Steam Tug "Callander"
Courtesy, North Himsworth Museum, Callander

Lake Nipissing. From Callander, meanwhile, the John B. Smith Company relied on the powerful little *Sparrow* to deliver its logs, mostly from the Sturgeon River, until 1922 when it acquired a top-heavy little tug called the *Screamer* to replace her. The *Sparrow* spent her last few years as a coal tender, servicing the *Screamer*. In 1906 the firm also built the screw-tug *Sea Gull*, which it later sold, and in 1926 built an alligator tug called the *Woodchuck*, which lasted until 1955. Finally, in 1930 it built its last tug, a fine big coal burner also called the *Sea Gull*, which remained in service until the Company closed its mill at Callander in 1960.

Another firm, the Davidson and Hay Lumber Company of Toronto, which opened a mill at Cache Bay around 1887, also used a few steam tugs, mostly to tow and to transport men and supplies to its camps near Frank's Bay, on the south side of the lake. The most celebrated of these was the *John B. Fraser*, a large, 99-ton double decked sidewheeler which on November 7, 1893 fell victim to the worst disaster in the history of Lake Nipissing. While on her way from Callander to Frank's Bay with several men on board and a scow in tow, the old ship somehow caught fire near the Goose Islands and was soon out of control. The engineer apparently perished in a vain attempt to stop the engines. Everyone panicked except the captain, and though a boat was lowered, it was immediately upset by the paddlewheels. As a result, 21 men were drowned or frozen to death in the water when the flames forced them overboard. Seven managed to reach the scow, which was later washed ashore. After the initial shock, the incident was almost forgotten, until a team of divers from North Bay managed to locate the wreck of the *John B. Fraser* in 1972. The Davidson and Hay Company meanwhile went bankrupt, and was bought out by the George Gordon Company of Pembroke in 1900. This firm used alligators to warp logs into Cache Bay.

A number of tugs, some of which doubled as passenger boats, were also owned by free-lance captains. Among them were the *Hazel B.*, built in 1892 and later renamed the *Callander*, and the *Dalton K.*, built in 1915. At least two fishing tugs are known: the *Dauntless*, imported from Gravenhurst in 1892, and the *Osprey*, which arrived from the Niagara region around 1902. Two more tugs, the *Catharine C.* (1903) and her successor, the *Maggie K.* (1912), were used by the Department of Public Works, apparently as dredge tenders.

Meanwhile, the passenger business was slowly reviving. In 1894 the lovely steam-yacht *Camilla* (36.50 tons) was imported from Lake Simcoe by John Ferguson, one of the leading men of North Bay, who for a time hired Captain Burritt to run her for him. A small passenger steamer called the *Olive* was also in service before 1893, and in 1899 the steamer *Queen* (12.49 tons) was built at North Bay, and soon became a towboat on nearby Trout Lake. Also during the 1890s Captain William Windsor of Callander, formerly owner of the *Dauntless*, acquired the steamer *Albino*, and later (1900) the *Van Woodland*, another big yacht from Lake Simcoe, to carry freight and passengers until 1906.

The most systematic boat service, however, was established by Captain John Ashley Clark and family of Sturgeon Falls. In 1891 the Clarks built the steamer *Empress* (27.61 tons), both to tow for the family sawmill, and to run freight to the French River or the west arm of the lake. She was also used extensively for excursion cruises. As business grew, the *Empress* was replaced in 1905 by the *Northern Belle* (169 tons), which was licensed for 300 passengers and ran picnics and charter cruises to all parts of the lake, even to the forsaken port of Nipissing Village. In 1907 the Clarks purchased the *Van Woodland* and enlarged her into the *Highland Belle* (24.07 tons), as a smaller running mate for the *Northern Belle*. Concurrently another firm, known as the French River and Nipissing Navigation Company, imported the small steamer *Elgin L. Lewis* (30.40 tons) from Orillia in 1905 to ply from Sturgeon Falls to the French River, but this operation lapsed around 1917. Both the *Elgin L. Lewis* and the *Highland Belle* were dismantled about that time, and soon afterwards the *Northern Belle* went to the North Bay and French River Navigation Company, to operate from North Bay.

At that time Sturgeon Falls was the distribution centre for various small communities around the west arm of the lake, such as Lavigne, Noelville and Monetville, and in 1918 the firm of Michaud and Levesque, which still runs a department store at "the Falls", imported the handsome steamer *Queen of Temagami* (24.70 tons) from the lake of that name, to continue the work of running provisions and passengers to the west arm settlements. However, here as elsewhere, road improvements to that region soon allowed trucks to take over the business, and in 1923 the *Queen of Temagami* went to the Ottawa River.

Steam Tug "Dalton K."
Courtesy, Mr. Herb Knapp, Callander

Steam Tug "Dalton K."
Courtesy, Mr. Alex Dufresne, Callander

S.S. "Northern Belle" and Str. "Osprey" (Fishing Tug)

S.S. "Modello"

Only two large passenger steamers remained on Lake Nipissing after that. The *Northern Belle*, now under Captain Angus McKenny of Callander, continued to run excursions from North Bay until June 28, 1928, when she was destroyed by fire at her wharf. The last passenger steamer on the lake was the *Modello* (29.47 tons), which arrived from Lake Simcoe around 1922, and was used by the Temiskaming and Northern Ontario Railways boat-divison (later the Ontario Northland Boat Line) to service the lodges and cottages on the upper French River, which were, and still are, inaccessible by road. The *Modello* plied faithfully until 1945, when she went to Lake Temagami and was dieselized. Her successor was the *Chief Commanda*, a steel-hulled twin-engine diesel which served until 1975, and was then replaced by a twin-hulled aluminum-built craft known as the *Chief Commanda II*, which continues to run to this day. The last steamboat on Lake Nipissing, the aforementioned tug *Sea Gull*,(the second) was offered as a memorial gift to the City of North Bay in 1960, but the city council, indifferent to its heritage, refused to take her. Consequently the veteran vessel, still in excellent condition, was handed over to the wreckers and cut up with chain saws. On that note ends the long saga of the steamers on Lake Nipissing.

Steam Tug "Sea Gull".
Courtesy, North Himsworth Museum, Callander

Muskoka Wharf Station, Circa 1884.
S.S. "Nipissing" appears at right.
Courtesy, Archives of Ontario ST 1173

CHAPTER 6
The Muskoka Steamers and the Tourist Trade
(1880-1885)

The fleet on the Muskoka Lakes was doing very well, catering to immigrants, merchants, lumbermen, and tourists, in spite of the relentless spoliation of Muskoka's scenic beauty by lumberjacks and forest fires during the 1870s and '80s. Parties of campers and sportsmen never ceased coming to hunt deer or fish in the local lakes and streams but as long as the depression persisted the numbers of newcomers did not warrant the construction of new hotels.

Muskoka would never have become the renowned recreation area it is today, had it not been for the efforts of vigorous promoters who tried valiantly to make its attractions known to the outside world. The Northern Railway, realizing the revenues it could derive from so doing, spent considerable sums encouraging people to visit Muskoka. About 1882 it was advertising itself as

> . . the Great and Only Line running to the far-famed Muskoka District, the Sportsman's Paradise and Free Grant Lands of Ontario. Fast trains Daily from Toronto and Hamilton, connecting with Steamers of the Muskoka Navigation Company for all Points on the Lakes. Fishing, Hunting, Camping, Delightful Summer Resort for Families . .

Besides the railway, various friends of the district, such as Thomas McMurray and W.E. Hamilton, were mindful of Muskoka's possibilities as a land of recreation. However, McMurray was obliged to leave the area in 1874 amid financial difficulties, and within ten more years Hamilton also left. Muskoka missed them considerably. It fell to A.P. Cockburn to carry on their work, and for the next three decades he assiduously did so, pouring out a stream of periodicals and guidebooks to lure tourists into the district. In 1877 he also promoted and edited the 'Canadian Lumberman'[1], Gravenhurst's first newspaper. He doubtless found space to mention such factors as Muskoka's 700-foot elevation above the sea: its pleasant, bracing air: its freedom from pollens causing hayfever: and its congenial summer climate. (He probably gave less stress to mosquitoes, blackflies and poison ivy.) So extensively did he advertise, in fact, that both his contemporaries and modern researchers have given him most of the credit for rescuing Muskoka from the fate of other Shield settled territories in Ontario, such as the North Kawartha Lakes, where the inhabitants languished in destitution after the lumber trade passed. In Muskoka, the tourist and cottage industries have become central to the local economy, not mere appendages to it. Today no other part of Ontario relies so heavily on a transient summer population.

Around 1880 the persistent propaganda of Cockburn and the railway suddenly began to pay off, enough that new resorts could be established. In most cases it happened almost accidentally. Parties of hunters and anglers, mostly Americans, would call upon farmers lucky enough to have located near the lakes, asking for directions to the best areas for fishing and shooting. Sometimes they also requested food and overnight accommodation. As they offered cash for what they consumed, the farmers were willing to oblige, and as they kept coming back, year after year in larger and larger numbers, the farmers gradually started building extensions to their homes. In time, the farm evolved into a summer boarding house, and sometimes the boarding house evolved into a resort hotel, as amusements such as tennis courts, croquet grounds, rowboats and the like were added. The tourist might look down condescendingly on the grimy bearded settler, and the settler might glare back resentfully at the haughty tourist, but each soon realized how useful the other could be. No doubt these early "resorts" would be judged simple and unpretentious, but most visitors during the 1880s do not seem to have expected all the comforts and amenities of city life out in the bush.

The Rosseau House ("Pratt's Hotel").
Picture taken shortly before the fire of 1883.

The Monteith House, Rosseau

Every single one of the new resorts was located on one of the three major Muskoka Lakes, usually close to one of the steamboat wharves. The tourists always arrived by steamer, and so did the mail and any hardware or supplies needed from the towns; consequently any aspiring resort that did not have a wharf lost little time in building one. Many resorts grew their own foodstuffs, but they depended on the steamers for almost everything else. The boats soon became attractions in themselves, as visitors started requesting charter cruises and picnics on them. In short, an extensive summer resort industry in Muskoka would have been almost impossible without the lake steamers.

Until 1880, the only tourist hotels in all the Muskokas were still the two giants of the previous decade, Pratt's Rosseau House and the Summit House at Port Cockburn. Both of them were doing very well. The palatial profile of "Pratt's" seemed to catch all the limelight, and competing with it seemed a waste of time. Despite the odds, however, a few other places modestly began opening their doors. In 1880 the artist R.G. Penson, who had taken up land on a beautiful sandy bay at the south end of Lake Rosseau, near Port Carling in 1869, now opened his home as a small tourist haven, called Ferndale. He gradually added a boathouse, bathhouses and other buildings, until Ferndale House began to ressemble a village in itself.[2] Shortly afterwards John Monteith built another hotel called the Monteith House (at first simply called "Monteith's") in the heart of the village of Rosseau, actually daring to compete with "Pratt's". The Monteith House also catered to tourists and built its own steamboat wharf, but it was more like an inn than a resort. Once Pratt's hotel disappeared, Monteith's began to flourish, and by 1884 it had added a billiard room, bathhouses, two new wings and a large maple-floored roller skating rink.

As for Pratt's, which had been growing larger and more splendid every year, its time unhappily ran out on the evening of October 6, 1883, when fire suddenly broke out and speedily reduced the great multi-winged mansion to a heap of glowing cinders. Everything was destroyed, including the outbuildings and stables, along with most of the furnishings. The twenty guests and staff all escaped safely, and mercifully Mr. Pratt and his wife were away at the time. The Rosseau House was never rebuilt, but, heavy though the loss was, in a sense the great hotel had served its purpose. It had made summer vacations and sporting trips to Muskoka fashionable, and its tragic disappearance left the way clear for other entrepreneurs to try their hand.

One of these was Enoch Cox, a free grant settler from Stratford-on-Avon in England, who had taken up land near Port Sandfield in the 1870s. Soon despairing of farming, Cox tried building a cedar hotel around 1882, on high ground overlooking the steamboat canal from the north side. He called it the Prospect House. That its prospects were indeed good may be judged from the fact that, whereas it was taking about 60 guests in 1883, by 1886 it was handling twice that number. Surrounded by shady groves and endowed with spacious verandahs and a good beach, Prospect House was long noted as a sportsmens' haven. Mr. Cox was fortunate to secure the services of his neighbour and son-in-law, Captain Rogers, owner of the little *Pinafore*, which was frequently chartered for fishing trips or special cruises. Meanwhile, the *Nipissing* was soon calling every day, which was fortunate, since the farm soon ceased to contribute much to the hotel.

Almost overnight the Prospect House turned Port Sandfield from a mere name into a thriving, thought small, community. Whereas in 1880 the site had consisted of literally nothing but a lofty wooden bridge spanning the canal, plus a few scattered homes, by 1886 Port Sandfield had a church, a store, a second small inn and several homes, plus a school and sawmill in close proximity. It was taking its place as one of Muskoka's best-loved tourist centres.

Across the lake, similar developments were taking place at Windermere. This little village was first settled as early as 1864 by Thomas Aitken, a hearty Shetlander who moved in from Peterborough County to farm. Along with a few neighbours, Aitken spent several winters clearing land near the east shore of Lake Rosseau, before taking up permanent residence around 1869. By that time the steamer *Waubamik* was running, and soon a post office called "Windermere" (named after scenic Lake Windermere in Westmoreland) was opened in Mr. Aitken's home. As the chief boat landing between Port Carling and Rosseau, Windermere became the central distribution point for the whole of Watt Township, and the

The Prospect House, Port Sandfield

Windermere House, Windermere Circa 1890

Craigie Lea House, Craigie Lea, Lake Joseph

Stratton House, Port Carling

Hamill's Point Hotel, Lake Joseph
Courtesy, Public Archives of Canada PA 67285

Port Carling House,
Port Carling

Clevelands House,
Minett Circa 1890

Regatta Scene at Beaumaris, Circa 1895.
The stern of the S.S. "Nipissing" appears at the left. The smaller boats have not been identified.

starting point for the local stages. Notwithstanding, the place grew slowly. Some of its inland neighbours, such as Dee Bank Village, seemed much better favoured. By 1878 Dee Bank was an appreciable little manufacturing centre, with a store, inn, saw-and-grist mill, school and several homes.

Then Windermere came to life. Finding more and more excursionists disembarking from the lake steamers in front of his home, Thomas Aitken soon supplemented his meagre income by feeding and housing them. By 1883 he was advertising that he could take 35 guests. Four years later he was catering to one hundred. By then his little home had turned into the Windermere House, a three-storey hotel some 65 feet by 33. It was also a post office and express office: hotel keepers were expected to handle those departments too. The new hotel proved a great success, and it is still in business today. The village of Windermere grew around the hotel, and soon sprouted several steam sawmills and stores. A second hotel, the Fife House, was opened in 1888. Eventually Windermere became an incorporated village, while the Dee Bank Village has ceased to exist.

Again and again during the 1880s we find the same pattern recurring. New hotels at the steamboat landings became the nuclei of emerging villages. What happened at Windermere and Port Sandfield also applied to Minett, on western Lake Rosseau, which started off in 1869 as C.J. Minett's farm. By the 1880s, having been assured of a boat service, Mr. Minett was also taking guests, and not later than 1887 his home had expanded to become the Clevelands House, now one of the finest summer resorts in Muskoka. As at Windermere, the old family farm is now a golf course. A few miles south of Minett arose the Woodington House on a lofty hilltop commanding a splendid view of the lake. Other hotels were likewise appearing around the older centres, such as the Rossmoyne Hotel and the palatial Maplehurst near Rosseau, and the Stratton House and Vanderburgh House at Port Carling.

Not all the new hotels centred on Lake Rosseau. The Hamill Hotel on Hamill's Point, Lake Joseph, and Craigie Lea House near the entrance to Little Lake Joseph, were both built during the 1880s. On Lake Muskoka, about 1882, one H.C.Guy, and after him Thomas Currie, founded the resort-business at Bala by building the River View Temperance House.

A much more famous hotel was also under way on Tondern Island at the same time. First settled around 1867 by Paul Dane, who named it after a place near Waterloo, Belgium, Tondern Island became one of the first calling places for the *Wenonah*. In 1873 the island was purchased and divided by two Englishmen, Edward Prowse and John Willmott, who expanded Dane's clearings and built homesteads. Later, as the inflow of tourists kept increasing, Mr. Prowse erected a large hotel with a large square tower and a mansard roof, directly facing the steamboat wharf, on the very spot where Paul Dane had built his hearth and shanty about sixteen years before. He named it the Beaumaris, after a village on the Island of Anglesey. Very quickly the new resort became predominantly an American summer colony, and even today Beaumaris is often dubbed "Little Pittsburg". Many families have been summering there for three or four generations. By 1886 Mr. Prowse had refined his hotel by the addition of bowling alleys, billiard rooms, and a profusion of small boats. For many years, however, the Beaumaris Hotel stood almost alone on Lake Muskoka, probably because of the intensity of the lumber trade. It was long said that the Muskoka tourist country began at Beaumaris. Gravenhurst was definitely not yet a tourist town.

Other examples of new summer hotels and boarding houses could be cited, but from the above it should be evident that Muskoka was well on the way to becoming Ontario's favourite playground. The first summer cottages were also appearing at this time, especially around Beaumaris and Windermere. Impressive though all this was, it was only the prelude to a much greater rush that started during the late 1890s, in what might be considered the "golden age" of the summer resort industry. As the lumber trade busily wrought its own extinction, and agriculture slowly proved itself illusory in all but a few favoured places, the tourist industry was gradually perceived for what it was, a lifesaver.

All this was exceedingly gratifying for A.P. Cockburn's steamboat enterprise, which was soon assured of business beyond anyone's wildest dreams. Certainly it was fundamental to the establishment of the Muskoka and Nipissing Navigation Company in 1881. That spring Mr. Cockburn was already having two new steamers built at Gravenhurst.

Both of the new vessels were tugs, intended as replacements for the *Simcoe*, which had just been scrapped. The larger of the two was the steamer *Muskoka*, a round-sterned screw vessel listed at 67.31 tons. With a length of 94 feet and a beam of 15, the *Muskoka* was a rather blunt nosed tug, over twice the size of the *Simcoe*, and powered with two high-pressure engines giving a combined horsepower of 60. No pictures of her in her original guise have been found, but she had a single deck with a bank of cabins surmounted by a pilot-house. For over a quarter of a century she was to be a familiar sight on the lakes, though repeatedly remodelled: at least five different versions of the vessel are known. She was very slow, and could not exceed eight miles per hour. Nonetheless she was unbelievably tough, and for years she was usually the first steamer in service in the spring, often before the ice broke up. A government inspector commented at the time that the *Muskoka* was one of the best tugs he had ever examined, and that it was a needless waste of lumber making her so strong.

On May 6, 1881, the following announcements from Gravenhurst appeared in the Orillia 'Packet':

> The new tug *Muskoka* is still on the ways. The builders expect to launch her this week. She is 90 feet long, has two cylinders, and five feet screw, and is expected to be an A1 tug. She will be commanded by Captain Sweet.
> The new harbour tug will be a first-class vessel of her size. She will be 50 feet long, cylinder 10 × 14, and will be launched in a few days. She will . . be commanded by Captain Foote.

The harbour tug in question was the steamer *Lake Joseph*, likewise built for A.P. Cockburn. She was a rather odd little craft, with a 10 hp. engine, a length of 52 feet, a beam of 10.3 and a draught of about four feet. She had an experimental "V"-shaped bottom, which was hoped would make her faster (it didn't). She even lacked a wheelhouse! Still, the *Lake Joseph* proved a very serviceable tug, and was used by the Navigation Company for fifteen years. Her skipper, Hamilton A. Foot of Foot's Bay on Lake Joseph, had just obtained his certificate in 1881; later he would leave to command ships on the Great Lakes and the Pacific Ocean.

By the summer of 1881 the Navigation Company had three tugs in commission, whereas in 1876 there had been only one. Until the mid-1880s these three, the *Lake Joseph*, the *Muskoka* and the *Rosseau*, seem to have had very few competitors in the log towing business. One exception at this time was the *Ontario*, a small 43.5-foot tug of 7.67 net tons, built at Walker's Point, Lake Muskoka, by Captain Harper Walker, a settler who engaged in lumbering and log towing as well as farming. According to local tradition, Captain Walker originally intended to call his own boat the *Muskoka*, and actually had the name registered, when the Navigation Company, in applying to register their own tug with the same name, found out what had happened. The Company then made overtures to Captain Walker, asking him if he would agree to change the name of his boat in return for a consideration. Being a kindly, easy-going man the captain agreed, and renamed his vessel after the province instead of the district.

In the meantime, a problem was surfacing between the Navigation Company and the lumbermen. Many of the lumber companies were dependent on the Navigation Company tugs to get their logs moved to the mills. However, the lumbermen and the boatmen did not always get along well. Difficulties arose in confined waters, such as the Gravenhurst Narrows and Muskoka Bay, which might be entirely clogged up with timber rafts, or the Muskoka and Indian Rivers, where the river-drivers usually let their logs loose to drift downstream, to be bagged together with booms on the open lakes. The loose logs were a

S.S. "Muskoka".
A reconstruction of the vessel's probable appearance when first built in 1881.

menace to navigation, and as early as 1876 we find Public Works Engineer Molesworth alluding to the situation in the following words:

> At the entrance to the Muskoka River, at the period of the runs of timber, much inconvenience and delay, as well as cost, is occasioned by the difficulties besetting the way of the steamboats in getting up or down, or to and from Bracebridge. These difficulties arise from the obstacles formed by the large number of logs in transit down this river, and the collecting of them in booms at the lake. It is desired to correct this by the enlargement of a cut already made, but not wide enough, so that steamers can have a separate entrance to the river, from that occupied by a boom of logs at the proper outlet.

In May of the same year the Orillia 'Expositor', was suggesting an enlargement of the lateral cut through the peninsula at the river delta, or some booms or piers near the estuary to contain the logs and leave a channel for the *Nipissing*, or both. The lumbermen themselves, claimed the paper, were willing to admit that the existing mode of securing booms was confused and improper. Twice that spring the booms had given way, spilling logs all around the entrance to the river. Molesworth's report of 1877 again had to repeat that sorting booms at the delta were still causing "very great inconvenience" to public travel, especially in May and June: again a wider and deeper channel was recommended. Bracebridge merchants, complained as freight was being held up and tourists prevented from reaching town. Yet the alternate channel was not dredged until after 1880.

Even with this done, the steamers sometimes got into trouble on the river, if not from the logs themselves, then from trying to avoid them. One time about 1882 the *Nipissing* was entering the estuary, when she discovered the *Muskoka*, solidly grounded at the "Cut". The *Nipissing* completed her trip to Bracebridge, then went back to help. First a line was run out through a mooring chock near one of the gangways of the *Nipissing* to the *Muskoka*. Both ships then reversed engines, only to rip the mooring chock and a few stanchions out of the *Nipissing*. Next, the two steamers came alongside to unload some of the cordwood from the *Muskoka* and lighten her. Then a new line was passed through the *Nipissing*'s hawsehole to the *Muskoka*, and again the two vessels began backing up. After a considerable strain the *Muskoka* finally jerked loose.

This was not the end of mishaps. The two passenger-steamers, the *Nipissing* and *Wenonah*, were particularly vulnerable to log damage, in that both were paddle wheelers. Sometimes they might find their way to port blocked by a sea of logs, though the lumber companies tried to co-operate by leaving a path open when the passenger ships were expected, (or said they did). Despite their best efforts the captains were often unable to prevent logs getting caught in the paddle wheels, which as a rule hurt the paddle wheels more than the logs. It soon became evident that a screw driven ship, with its propeller set along the keel well below the waterline, would be better suited for coping with those churning logs. Speed would also be a desirable trait in the new steamer. Besides, the passenger business was increasing anyway. So it was that the steamer *Kenozha* was designed and built at Gravenhurst, and launched in the spring of 1883.

The *Kenozha*, whose name is an Ojibwa word meaning "pickerel", began her life as a medium-sized vessel, similar to the *Inter-Ocean* but narrower, with a length of 100.8 feet and a beam of 18.2, which made her slightly larger than the *Wenonah* and the *Muskoka*, but smaller than the *Nipissing*. She registered 123.87 tons and was originally equipped with a sixteen horsepower high-pressure engine which could drive the vessel at twelve miles per hour. On July 14, 1887 the Toronto 'World' carried an article that speaks of the *Kenozha* as the fastest ship on the lakes and capable of carrying 250 passengers.

The new steamer, resplendent with her gleaming white paint, with a red bottom, black trim and a red and black stack, was launched with great fanfare. On her deck was the newly-formed Gravenhurst Town Band, playing 'See the Conquering Hero Comes'. After the usual speeches and applause, a bottle of champagne was broken over her bow, and the vessel slid down the ways. Instead of landing smoothly in the lake, she started to keel over. The music dissolved into cacophony as the bandsmen lost their balance. The cornet player threw his cornet into the lake while grabbing for something to hold onto. The drummer, trying to make the best of both worlds, rolled his drum up the sloping deck with one hand while clawing his way up to the rail. Things could have been worse, though: the ship could have capsized, but she didn't. She was, however, left stuck on the ways, and it was not until the following day that she was safely floating. An investigation revealed that some of the supporting blocks left on the ways had jammed under the vessel's keel, causing the mishap.

S.S. "Lake Joseph" (Tug).
The only known photograph of the vessel, taken around 1895. The S.S. "Oriole" can be glimpsed at left.

S.S. "Kenozha", Original Version

S.S. "Kenozha", Second Version. A small cabin has been added to the aft promenade deck.

A.P. Cockburn and the Marquis of Lansdowne aboard the S.S. "Kenozha" at Beaumaris, 1884.

The *Kenozha*, was a handsomely proportioned little ship with fine lines. In some ways she looked like the later propeller steamers, but she also retained a few old-fashioned features, such as extra wide dining room windows and an outside catwalk or passageway around the curve of the stern on the main deck. She was also a little low on headroom between decks. She soon proved a favourite with the public, making three round trips daily between Gravenhurst and Bracebridge during the spring. Her usual commander was Captain John Henry of Gravenhurst, who was destined to serve the Navigation Company for fully half a century. Captain Henry grew very fond of the *Kenozha*. She handled so well on the Bracebridge run that he vowed she knew the way by herself.

The *Kenozha* did not always stay on the Muskoka River route. According to a timetable published later in 1883, the new steamer had been transferred to the Lake Joseph route, leaving Muskoka Wharf on the arrival of the noon trains from Toronto and Hamilton and sailing direct to Port Carling, Port Sandfield and Port Cockburn, returning the next morning by way of Bracebridge. The *Nipissing*, now under Captain George Rose, a veteran boatman from Lindsay, left Gravenhurst at the same time and plied daily to Bracebridge, Beaumaris, Port Carling, Windermere and Rosseau, returning the following day. The old *Wenonah*, now under Captain James Reide of Orillia,[3] provided a morning service, leaving Gravenhurst at 7:00 a.m. for Walker's Point, Torrance and Bala, returning daily.

In late August of 1884, the *Kenozha* was given a special assignment, that of conducting the Governor General, the Marquis of Lansdowne and his aides on a tour of the Muskoka Lakes with A.P. Cockburn. The tour generally went well, with the people of Beaumaris assembling in their best bib and tucker to receive their distinguished guest. Unluckily, the new steamer was still having teething troubles with her engines, and consequently had to make a second, unscheduled stop at Beaumaris, much to the surprise of the local people. But the trouble was not serious, and Lord Lansdowne and his party were entertained for an hour at the Beaumaris Hotel until the *Kenozha* was again ready to depart.

Soon after the *Kenozha* made her début, the staunch little *Wenonah* made her last trip. By the end of the season of 1885 the tired old sidewheeler had completed twenty seasons on the lakes, always starting in the early spring, always finishing in the late fall. For twenty years she had towed thousands of sawlogs, carried tons of freight and hosted thousands of visitors. For twenty years, she had bucked ice and logs, and had grounded on countless rocks and shoals: but for such rough treatment, she might have had a longer life. As it happened, by the fall of 1885 the *Wenonah* was worn out. She was then decommissioned, and her engines transferred to another vessel. For a few years she was turned into a houseboat, which the Cockburn family and others used occasionally for fishing trips, but Mrs. Cockburn did not care for such outings because the old boat had mice aboard. Then the old *Wenonah* was towed up to a small island in northern Lake Muskoka, now known as Cinderwood, and abandoned in a small cove. Local residents began tearing her apart for firewood. Finally, about 1890, the owners of the island asked the Navigation Company to get rid of the wreck. The hulk was towed away into deep water by the steamer *Muskoka*, filled with rocks, and scuttled. To this day, however, a few of her timbers are still preserved at nearby Barlochan.

In a sense, the Muskoka lake steamers enjoyed their period of maximum utility during the decade from 1876 to 1885. As feeders to the one and only railway line linking Toronto to the southernmost corner of the entire lakes system, and as providers of the only speedy, comfortable and reliable transportation north of the railway terminus in a time of steady immigration, expanding tourist travel, and a booming lumber trade, it is not surprising that the Cockburn company boats thrived, and that operations were extended to new waterways as well. Though the Lake Nipissing division of the new Navigation Company soon proved abortive, the Muskoka Lakes fleet was consolidated with six vessels instead of three. It was a prosperous interval.

But intervals come to an end, and conditions are subject to change. In 1886 a new crisis was on the horizon for the Muskoka and Nipissing Navigation Company.

Beaumaris Hotel, Beaumaris, Circa 1900.
Steam-Launch "Siesta" at Dock

S.S. "Wenonah" derelict at Cinderwood Island.
Sketch by one of A.P. Cockburn's daughters. Courtesy, Ms. Mary Fowler, Beaverton

FOOTNOTES

[1] The *Lumberman*, alas, died the same year, perhaps because Cockburn found it was taking up too much of his time.
[2] Ferndale is still in business today, though the original hotel has long since disappeared.
[3] Captain Reide was a former master of the *Carriella*.

Alexander Peter Cockburn, M.P., photographed in 1879.
Courtesy, Public Archives of Canada PA 33609

CHAPTER 7
Steamboating in the Post-Railway Period
(1886 et seq.)

Twenty years had passed since the sturdy little *Wenonah* had first blown her whistle at Gravenhurst in 1866. Much had happened in Muskoka. The district had been so extensively opened up that in some areas the pioneer period could be considered almost over. A railway had been opened as far as Lake Muskoka. The lumber trade was operating at full tilt. Tourist hotels were numerous and growing, even though the overall economic scene in Canada was not prosperous during the years following the completion of the C.P.R. in 1885. As for A.P. Cockburn's steamer fleet, it had grown from one vessel in 1866 to six in 1885, and though the *Wenonah* was retired that year, a new steamer was soon under construction to replace her. With its virtual monopoly of transport facilities north of Gravenhurst, the Navigation Company was thriving. The future seemed assured.

Then the roof fell in. Railway construction was resumed.

Ever since the tracks of the Northern Railway reached Gravenhurst in 1875 there had been agitation throughout Muskoka, spearheaded by Bracebridge, to have the line extended further north. The northern communities still suffered from the old drawbacks of roads that were wretched except in winter. They considered their problem ameliorated, but not solved, by the lake steamers, and wanted the benefits of a regular year-round railway service. Of course, this applied to both the east and west sides of the lakes, but in spite of all sorts of resolutions and petitions, nothing was accomplished for years. By the end of the decade, people were becoming discouraged. Railways were not discussed during the elections of 1878 and 1882, and Mr. Cockburn, M.P. for Muskoka, had nothing to say on the matter. This gave rise to rumours, encouraged and spread by the Conservatives, that Gravenhurst was to be the permanent terminus of the line, and that Cockburn himself was secretly using his influence to make certain of this, on the grounds that an extension of the railway would be ruinous to his steamboat venture. There is no evidence that these rumours were true, but they were certainly credible, and became so widespread that Mr. Cockburn found it necessary to write a public letter to the Bracebridge newspapers, denying the allegations. In part his letter read as follows:

> Certain parties, having chosen for political purposes to wilfully misrepresent me with reference to railway extension beyond Gravenhurst, I deem it necessary to state that I have neither by word or action given the least ground for the circulation of these gross fabrications. It is also argued by designing persons that railway extension beyond Gravenhurst would be fatal to my steamboat interest; nothing could be further from the fact as with railway facilities established throughout the District the general business of the country would be increased to that degree that the loss of the through business to Bracebridge would not be felt. A good trade would still exist between Bracebridge and the western and northern portions of the District adjacent to the lakes. Having a coasting distance of upwards of 140 miles and assuming that the trade between Bracebridge and Gravenhurst is lost there would remain a distance of 120 miles not interfered with. Therefore it does not require much calculation to show that the arguments of my calumniators are untenable ... At the same time I now take the opportunity of pledging myself, both in my private and public capacity, to heartily assist in getting the railway extended at the earliest possible date.

If Mr. Cockburn was being entirely honest in this letter, and not merely polishing his rhetoric for political reasons, it would appear that he had overlooked a very important factor in his calculations. He had failed to realize that there was far more at stake than just the trade between Gravenhurst and Bracebridge. There was also the question of the entire

G.T.R. Train Entering Bracebridge, around 1895.
(Note the timber-slide past the falls in the foreground.)

Utterson Station. G.T.R. (C.N.R.)
Courtesy, Mr. George Johnson, Port Sydney

Utterson, Ontario (facing West)
Courtesy, Mr. George Johnson, Port Sydney

Grand Trunk Railway Station, Huntsville.
Courtesy; Archives of Ontario, 13889-3.

forwarding business beyond the railway terminus. Most of the cargoes bound for Rosseau, for example, were destined for places farther north, up the Nipissing Road. The commerce leaving Gravenhurst utilized the lake steamers because they were infinitely preferable to anything else available, but it would be quite content, as commerce always will be, to take advantage of any faster means of conveyance. The existing routes involved tiresome transshipments from trains to steamboats, and from steamers to stages, which remained crude, slow and uncomfortable. A through railway could change all that by offering speedy, safe and reliable transportation all year around without transshipments, wherever the rails were laid. Steamers could offer competitive rates, but not comparable speed or convenience, as they were obviously confined strictly to such waterways as Nature happened to provide. If the Lake Simcoe steamboat proprietors had not known all that before the railways were extended up to Orillia and Washago, they had found out afterwards, to their cost. Once the railways went beyond Lake Simcoe, the local steamers lost almost all their freight revenues and most of their towing contracts, leaving little for the survivors to do except run pleasure cruises. Mr. Cockburn was failing to realize in his letter that, once a railway was opened into the Parry Sound district, the Muskoka steamers would be reduced almost entirely to servicing the regions close to the three Muskoka Lakes.

It might be remarked in passing that the rumours about Mr. Cockburn's attitude towards the railway expansion failed to stem his career in politics. A gerrymander, engineered by the Macdonald government in 1882, tried to produce the same effect. Before the election of that year the Conservative administration, in one of the most brazen maneouvres ever taken by any government to keep itself in power, redrew the boundaries of several constituencies to its own advantage. Mr. Cockburn's riding of Muskoka, including Parry Sound, was an obvious target, and was therefore cut up into three chunks, with portions going to three new constituencies. Cockburn decided to stand for the new seat of North Ontario, which he described as a "mutilated and unshapely riding . . which comprises a length of 125 miles by a breadth of less than five miles at one point, with the detached township of Scugog thrown in as a make weight." But Northern Ontario also included Bracebridge, Gravenhurst and several Muskoka townships, plus Beaverton, which had been Cockburn's place of residence since 1873, out of deference to his wife. Again Mr. Cockburn entered the lists, and won. It proved, however, his last victory. To sum up in his own words,

> . . before another election the Franchise Act of 1885 became law, which not only introduced a new class of votes, but also improperly enfranchised the Indians of Rama and Scugog, who were wards of the Government and voted accordingly. I was therefore defeated [by Frank Madill of Cannington], which..to some extent was a relief, as I never gave regular attendance at Ottawa, having invariably made all other interests subservient to my navigation duties in Muskoka . .[1]

To return to the railway: by 1881 speculations were taking a very serious turn. The Northern — now the Northern and North Western, having formed a joint executive partnership with its rival, the Hamilton and North-Western Railway in June of 1879 — was prospering at this time, hauling lumber south and freight north. Furthermore, in 1881 the Government cancelled its expansion debts. On March 21st. of the same year it secured a charter to build north from Gravenhurst to Callander, and thence to Sault Ste. Marie, but there was widespread opposition to the plan, and the Sault portion was too long and costly to be realistic. However, as the C.P.R. built through North Bay and beyond, the desirability of opening a connecting link became obvious, and there were numerous politicians pushing for it. In May of 1882 the Dominion Government voted a subsidy of $6,000 per mile for the proposed extension to Lake Nipissing. This was raised to $12,000 a mile the following year, but still there were delays, since the Northern and North Western executives could not agree on how to split the profits. There was, moreover, a widespread sentiment that no single company should have exclusive rights on the new line. Once, in reply to a question from Mr. Cockburn, Sir Charles Tupper explained to the House of Commons that "The

Government have given a promise that this line should be kept independant [sic] and it was because of the difficulties of making arrangements on this basis that the delay had taken place."

Finally, in July of 1884 the rival interests of the Northern and its partner were resolved, and the following autumn work was started on the Northern and Pacific Junction Railway. Using only men, horses, graders, picks and shovels to do most of the work, the contractors managed to grade a roadbed of 111 miles and extend the rails about half this distance within a year. The new line went past the old village of South Falls and directly through Bracebridge, but for a time it was debatable which route it would take beyond this point. Naturally, there was intensive lobbying by rival communities in its path, notably between Port Sydney and Utterson, and between Huntsville and Hoodstown, but in the end the railway opted to pass through Utterson, bypassing Mary Lake, and then swing northeast through Huntsville, more or less following the old Muskoka Road. From there it wound its way up to the Magnetawan River, crossing at the village of Burks Falls, and continuing north past the west side of Stoney Lake (now called Lake Bernard) where Sundridge now stands, across the South River, and finally to Callander. Expensive bridges were required at Bracebridge, Burks Falls and South River, but on January 27th., 1886, the first train pulled into Callander. From here it was only a few more miles to North Bay.

In the spring of 1886, before the effects of the railway extension became obvious, the Navigation Company added another steamer to its fleet to replace the *Wenonah*. The newcomer was the *Oriole*, an ornate little screw vessel which registered just 48.45 tons. With a keel-length of 75 feet and a beam of 14.5, the *Oriole* had two decks, a round stern, a tiny hurricane deck, and a small octagonal pilot-house crowned with a pagoda style dome. Soon she was further embellished with a beautifully carved little wooden oriole set on top of the dome; a gift from Captain George Bailey, who was later to carve a splendid wooden pickerel to ornament the pilot-house of the *Kenozha*.

Apparently the *Oriole* was purchased by the Navigation Company while still under construction, which may explain her rather unusual appearance. Powered by a steeple compound engine, she could go about ten miles per hour, and was commonly used on the Muskoka River run to Bracebridge: probably A.P. Cockburn figured that a small steamer would be sufficient on this route, now that the railway was completed. Her first master was Captain Peter Lindsay, who was followed within a year by Captain Edward F. McAlpine of Southwood, Ontario, who first joined the crews of the lake steamers in 1880. A genial, humourous Ulsterman, Captain McAlpine looked the very picture of an "old salt". He served the Navigation Company for a total of 47 years, and built up an enviable record for caution and dependability.

Unfortunately, the *Oriole* did not prove a very popular vessel. Her small size, plus her comparative narrowness, gave her a tendency to roll, hence she was regarded with some mistrust. Nor was this feeling entirely unfounded. Once, after she had been in service a few years, she nearly capsized while rounding the Devil's Elbow, a very tricky bend in the Muskoka River. Later she would do much worse than this.

As the season of 1886 unfolded, and the railway was formally opened to Nipissing Junction, near North Bay, in April of that year, the Navigation Company must have had moments of wondering whether it should even have bothered to replace the *Wenonah*. We have already noted what the railway extension did to the Lake Nipissing division of the Company's operations. On the Muskoka Lakes, the effects were only a little less disastrous. According to A.P. Cockburn's later reminiscences, business was "nearly paralysed" on the lakes, as freight receipts dropped by about 75% after the railway was opened. This, surely, is a graphic illustration of how heavily both the Muskokas and Parry Sound Districts had previously depended on the services of the lake steamers. So completely were the arteries of trade and commerce shifted that stage traffic over the Rosseau-Nipissing Road declined to a mere trickle. Every community along the road, except perhaps Magnetawan Village and Rosseau itself, fell into decline or disappeared altogether, while the corresponding villages along the Muskoka Road, which were now served by the railway, expanded and flourished. In time some sections of the Nipissing Road were abandoned and became impassable,

Captain Edward F. McAlpine

S.S. "Oriole" (Original Version)

including a portion north of Rosseau, and even today only parts of this old pioneeer road are still in use. On the Muskoka Lakes, meanwhile, the Navigation Company was in for some lean years, and not until 1892 was it again able to issue a small dividend.

Yet the Muskoka steamboats survived the crisis. How was this possible? Two obvious answers suggest themselves immediately: log towing and the tourist traffic. While both these factors remained important, it is also true that the boats continued to carry a lot of freight and passengers. The extended railway tapped the lakes system at only two points (Gravenhurst and Bracebridge) on a somewhat north-easterly course on its way to Huntsville, whereas the Muskoka Lakes, conforming to the rolling Precambrian topography of the region, lie on essentially a northwest to southeast plane. Furthermore, the extreme irregularity of the shorelines made it a foregone conclusion that most of the coastal communities would never be serviced by railways, though paved highways would be a different matter: to this extent, A.P. Cockburn was right in his letter to the Bracebridge press. In this respect the Muskoka Lakes form a sharp contrast to Lake Simcoe, which has a fairly regular outline, along which railways could, and did, build quite easily to almost every hamlet along its shores. Thus the usurpation of the lakes trade by railways was bound to be far more complete on Lake Simcoe than it ever could be in Muskoka.

On the North Muskoka Lakes, meanwhile, steamboat men also found it possible to adapt to the new situation. Huntsville was the only port actually served by the railway, and since the local lakes extend mostly east and west of Huntsville, they were well suited to become feeder routes to the railway. The same applied to the Magnetawan River system.

The stage service from Bracebridge to Port Sydney died almost instantaneously once the railway reached Utterson. The same applied to the teams bumping their way over the Rosseau-Nipissing Road. For the lumbermen, however, the extended railway was an immense boon. The Northern's new tracks cut directly across most of the large rivers flowing westward through the Parry Sound District to Georgian Bay, thus "short-circuiting" the natural water routes ordinarily used for floating out timber, and offering a quick convenient new route directly south to Toronto. Wherever the railway crossed an important waterway, a lumber town usually sprang up, each controlling the timber limits in the watersheds upstream. Thus Huntsville burgeoned and took on new life where the railway crossed the Vernon River, and Burks Falls did the same once the line crossed the Magnetawan River. Another town sprang up at the South River in much the same way, while Callander, seemingly ruined when the C.P.R. bypassed it, staged a rapid recovery after the Northern arrived. To some extent Bracebridge also shared this new prosperity, but despite everything Gravenhurst still retained its predominance as a sawmill centre. Very few firms moved their mills from Muskoka Bay to places up the line after 1886.

The Muskoka Navigation Company, still reeling from the loss of its revenues and forced to withdraw from Lake Nipissing in 1886, was now anxiously casting about for some new theatres of operation that might restore its prosperity. One likely prospect seemed to beckon from the valley of Magnetawan.

FOOTNOTES
[1] Mr. Cockburn did try campaigning again, but in the contest of 1891 he was again defeated by Frank Madill in North Ontario. Twice more during the decade, in 1890 and 1894, the Grits, facing an increasing trend towards Toryism in Muskoka, called on him to redeem the district in the provincial legislature, but again, on both of these occasions he was unsuccessful. The campaign of 1894 was his last attempt, although he continued to take an active interest in the fortunes of the federal Liberal Party.

S.S. "Wenonah" and S.S. "Wanita".
Courtesy, Magnetawan Museum

CHAPTER 8
Steamboating on the Magnetawan
(1879-1906)

Of all the rivers flowing through the Parry Sound District, none is larger than the Magnetawan. It finds its source in the highlands of what is now Algonquin Park, and drops about 800 feet in its westward flow to Georgian Bay. Many a nameless log driver found an unmarked grave along its banks beside the various chutes and waterfalls that punctuate its progress. The name, variously spelled "Maganetawan", "Maganattawan", "Magnatawan" or "Magenattawan", is said to be derived from the Ojibwa word "Mawgawnettewang", meaning "a long channel": an alternate name "Neyetawa" apparently means "swift flowing channel".

The Magnetawan valley was an Indian hunting and trapping ground for centuries before the first curious white men were attracted to it. Many Europeans had visited sections of the valley, among them were Captain Baddeley in 1835, Alexander Murray in 1854, and A.P. Cockburn in 1865. All noted the diversified forests suggesting extensive tracts of fertile soil amid the rolling hills, the numerous maple groves which the Indians tapped for sugar, the excellent fishing and the numerous waterfalls affording fine millsites. The region had its attractions, but it was not until the late 1860s that the first settlers began to move in.

The earliest arrivals migrated inland from Parry Sound. One of them was an Irishman named Samuel Armstrong, who was a relative of "Governor" William Beatty of Parry Sound. By 1865 Armstrong had a number of lumber camps operating in the valley, with his headquarters at Ahmic Lake. In 1867, he and his men blazed the Great North Road through the bush from Parry Sound to Lake Manitouwaba, where the village of McKellar now stands. By 1870 this road had been extended to Ahmic Lake, and soon a branch was extended to Magnetawan itself, which by Armstrong's reckoning had about ten inhabitants in 1871. About that time the Dodge Lumber Company opened the Nipissing Road from Rosseau to Magnetawan, and began hauling supplies over it. It is said that Mr. Armstrong practically founded the village of McKellar, by opening a store, a boarding house, and a water-powered sawmill. He paid his workmen with provisions from the store. A post office was opened at McKellar in 1874, by which time the little community had two hotels and several homes. In 1881 Mr. Armstrong's sons, Samuel and James, imported a small 27-foot steam-launch from Toronto to tow logs to their sawmill. Built in 1878, the *Ada* registered 1.68 tons. She remained on Lake Manitouwaba until 1885, when she was transferred to Ahmic Lake.

Farther east, Magnetawan was making even faster progress. Located amid some partly arable lands sloping gently down to a narrow point in the river, where there was a ten-foot waterfall, Magnetawan could hardly fail to become a good-sized village, especially considering that it was the only practical place within miles for crossing the river. The first "bridge" was hastily built on floating logs, which had the disconcerting tendency to sink down every time a team passed over it. After 1875, when the Nipissing Road was rendered passable for wheeled vehicles, Magnetawan Village grew rapidly. By 1878 it could boast two taverns, four general stores, a tin shop, baker's shop, watchmaker's shop, a flour and feed store, a grist and sawmill, a post office, Crown Lands office, a schoolhouse and three churches, plus several private homes. So bright were its prospects that it was once favoured to become the district seat, but Governor Beatty of Parry Sound managed to secure that honour for his own town.

Another of Magnetawan's advantages was the fact that the river was navigable upstream for a distance of 23 miles, as far as Burks Falls; in part utilizing Lake Cecebe. Burks Falls itself was named in honour of David Francis Burk of Oshawa, who built the first shanty at the falls in 1876 and remained to become one of the community's leading citizens. Though its waterpower is superb, the site is exceedingly hilly and awkward for a village. Furthermore, it remained inaccessible by road until 1880, when the Muskoka Road finally went through from Huntsville. Growth at Burks Falls was therefore slow for several years. Not until 1884 did it get a sawmill.

The first steamboat to run between Magnetawan and Burks Falls was the *Pioneer*, a small yacht built at Magnetawan in 1879. A 34-foot craft with a round stern and a four horsepower high-pressure engine, the *Pioneer* drew less than three feet of water, which was fortunate, since no dredging or other navigational improvements had yet been made to the river. Built by Henry Walton, a local handyman, she was listed at 7.54 tons, and is said to have had a little bowsprit in the form of a spear. Her owner and master was Edward A. Morris of Magnetawan, a merchant and gentleman farmer who served for a time as a justice of the peace. His sons sometimes acted as crew.

Plying the river every other day, the *Pioneer* was used largely for delivering groceries and provisions to the settlers at their numerous clearings along its banks. Sometimes those provisions included hay. We hear of cattle starving to death around Dunchurch and vicinity, near Ahmic Lake in the spring of 1885, because the ice broke up late that year, preventing the steamer from resuming her rounds. Occasionally the *Pioneer* also ran passenger cruises, as in September of 1884, when she hosted a number of hunters heading for Burks Falls.

No sooner was the *Pioneer* in service than people began talking about the need for a second steamer, to run downstream from Magnetawan to the far end of Ahmic Lake, a distance of ten miles. This in turn led to demands for a lock at Magnetawan, so that steamers could travel direct from Burks Falls to Ahmic Harbour, from which point the Great North Road continued to Parry Sound. True to its policy of assisting settlement in the north country wherever possible, the Ontario Government approved the lock scheme in 1883, and by December work had started. The lock chamber was originally slated to be 100 feet by 24, but in response to a local petition in 1884 this was increased to 112 feet by 28. (Obviously someone was contemplating quite a fair-sized steamboat for the waterway!) By 1885 the project was well advanced. Much of the timber for it was towed in from nearby Port Anson, where the Nipissing Road passes a corner of Ahmic Lake. A spring freshet in April of 1886 caused some further delays, but by the beginning of the summer the lock at last was ready. Built of cribwork filled with stone, it had a lift of about 10½ feet. In addition, a swing bridge and some wooden wing dams were also built, while the boulders in the channel below the lock were blasted out and a dam built at Knoepfli Rapids to control the water levels of Ahmic Lake. Some additional dredging (by horse-power) and blasting was carried out in the river to get rid of the shoals and boulders below Burks Falls. Once this was done, operations were transferred to the exit from Lake Cecebe, near Magnetawan.

In the meantime, a steamboat was ready to use the new lock. But not the little *Pioneer*. This aptly-named craft is not mentioned after 1885, and according to local tradition her hull now lies scuttled at Magnetawan, where the local marina now has a boathouse. Nor was it the *Ada*, which had apparently been moved from McKellar to Ahmic Lake by the Armstrong brothers in 1885 to connect with the *Pioneer*. The first steamer actually to use the new lock was the *Wenonah*, built at Burks Falls by the Muskoka and Nipissing Navigation Company in 1886.

The steamer *Wenonah* was not the old sidewheeler built by A.P. Cockburn on Lake Muskoka twenty years before, although she looked very similar and in fact inherited the engine as well as the name of the earlier ship. Several factors underlay her arrival. The Navigation Company's charter gave it the right to run steamers on the Magnetawan, and in 1886 the Company was badly in need of additional revenues. Furthermore, the same railway which had ruined the Company's business on Lake Nipissing and dealt such a crippling blow to the Muskoka Lakes trade had also been built to within half a mile of Burks Falls, where a station was erected. This put the valley within easy access by rail. No doubt it was A.P. Cockburn who pushed the idea of putting a steamer on the river, running in conjunction with the railway. He had never forgotten his favourable impressions of 1865, and had never lost interest in the valley. Probably his influence was at work behind the scenes when the lock was built. In any event, Cockburn was planning a steamer as early as 1885, and the following year she was ready. Some members of the Company board of directors, however, were not enthusiastic about the new division, and only gradually did their opposition diminish.

The second *Wenonah* was somewhat larger than her Muskoka namesake, being 94.6 feet in length by 18 in beam and registering 89.90 tons: this made her the longest, and, with one later exception, the largest steamboat ever to ply on the Magnetawan. She was also the only paddlewheeler on the waterway (unless we count one or two "alligators" or warping tugs which arrived later) and she was screw driven as well. Her two engines gave her a combined horsepower of 14.2. On her runs she proved commodious and efficient, and very popular with the travelling public. It is said that she was capable of alternating her paddlewheels, so as to be able to pivot her way around tight corners in the river. Under the command of Captain John Templeman of Burks Falls, the *Wenonah* first passed through the Magnetawan lock on July 8, 1886, on her way to Ahmic Harbour.

Except for the *Ada*, the *Wenonah* was the only steamer on the waterway. The Navigation Company lost little time in buying the smaller craft, which is said to have been lengthened and rebuilt as the screw launch *Cecebe*, though it is more likely that the *Cecebe* (31.7 feet, 7.72 tons) was an entirely new vessel that merely inherited the engine from the *Ada*: the 'Muskoka Herald' comments that the hull of the old *Ada* was swept downriver from Burks Falls during the spring floods of 1888, while the *Cecebe* was still in service. As a rule, the *Cecebe*, under Captain Angus Kennedy of Burks Falls, would take small parties daily from the Falls to Magnetawan upon the arrival of the northbound train, returning in time to connect with the southbound train the following morning, while the *Wenonah* plied daily all the way to Ahmic Harbour.

The new boat service was an immense convenience to the Magnetawan communities, especially those downriver from Burks Falls, which was now the transfer point from the trains to the steamers. The village rapidly sprouted three hotels and several stores, and was incorporated as early as 1890. Magnetawan, now robbed of its north-south trade along the Nipissing Road, did not fare so well, though it remained the chief distribution centre on the waterway. Ahmic Harbour developed into a neat little village boasting a church, a planing mill, a few shops and a large hotel; unfortunately, its lack of water power and close proximity to the neighbouring village of Dunchurch tended to dampen its development. The importance of the steamers to the commerce of these communities is suggested by the fact that road communications between them lagged for many years. Not until 1899 was a good road opened south of Lake Cecebe from Magnetawan to Burks Falls.

Though the Muskoka Navigation Company at first monopolized the traffic on the Magnetawan, it was not very pleased with the results. Traffic on the new division proved disappointing, largely because so many of the settlers were despairing of the Ontario free-grant lands altogether and moving away. Hastening the process were agents of the C.P.R., who were assiduously spreading "Manitoba fever" by painting a rosy picture of life on the

Cataract House, Burks Falls
Courtesy, Mr. Merrill Dunbar, Sundridge

Burks Falls, Ont. — Steamer Wanita leaving Town.

Burks Falls, on the Magnetawan.
S.S. "Wanita" leaving town.

Steamers at Burks Falls.
S.S. "Wanita" (left) & S.S. "Wenonah".

prairies. Among those so enticed was the reeve of Chapman Township; upon boarding the *Wenonah* at Magnetawan to catch a train from Burks Falls, the gentleman slipped on the gangplank and fell into the water, thus soaking his sendoff. (The man consequently spent the whole cruise in the engine room, with his trousers draped over the boiler to dry.) So serious did the exodus become that the Navigation Company had to discontinue running the *Cecebe* after 1890; the little vessel lasted until about 1896, when she was finally broken up. Captain Kennedy meanwhile transferred to the *Wenonah*, as Captain Templeman retired to open a feed store in Burks Falls.

From the pen of a visiting clergyman engaged in mission work in 1896, we are given a glimpse of a typical cruise on the *Wenonah*. To quote him,

> . . we passed on to the neat, prosperous little town of Burk's Falls, where we took a substantial-looking steamer with good accommodation, and commanded by Captain K. for A [hmic] Harbour. The trip down the Magnetawan River, through Cecebe and Ahmic Lakes, was one long to be remembered. The stream, though narrow, was quite deep, and so winding and with such sharp turns that it required great skill upon the part of the commanding officer, who nearly always took the wheel while in the current, to avoid running into the shore. Such was the efficiency of this functionary, however, that an accident rarely happened.
>
> In many places along the banks the branches of trees touched the water, and all through on either side was the beautiful fringe of green, broken here and there by a clearing, containing farm buildings, which seemed to mar the original beauty of the scene, instead of improving it; thus showing the imperfections of man's work when placed alongside the work of the Divine Architect.
>
> There were one or two wharves — or, more correctly, landings — between B[urks Falls] and the first lake through which we were to pass, at which the vessel stopped to land passengers or freight, thus giving all who desired an opportunity of going ashore for a time. As they usually took a supply of wood on board at these points, sometimes a whole hour would be at the disposal of those on the vessel. . . .[1]

As the above account suggests, navigating on the Magnetawan waterway was often a difficult matter. Some of the channels were so narrow that a brisk crosswind could easily blow a large vessel sideways onto a shoal. This was especially true at the approaches to the Magnetawan lock. Every spring the rising waters made the currents unusually strong. In May of 1888 the runoff was so high that no one dared to lock the *Wenonah* through until the floods subsided. Later that season, a reverse hazard was created when the dam at Knoepfli Rapids partly gave way, draining away much of the water of Ahmic Lake. Log drives by the lumbermen posed additional problems. On one occasion the *Wenonah*, while pushing her way through a sea of logs bound for the mills at Byng Inlet on Georgian Bay, was shoved sideways onto a sunken shoal by rebounding timbers in the river below Magnetawan, and remained caught for two or three days. Not until the drive had passed did a local tug come to pull her off. In November of 1892, the *Wenonah* was holed by a deadhead near Ahmic Harbour and began shipping water rapidly. Captain Kennedy steered for the shore, intending to beach her, but soon the boiler fires went out and the crew had to take to the lifeboat. The steamer, sunk in shallow water, was later pumped out and repaired.

The vessel also had her share of freak accidents: one such occurred in May of 1891. The steamer had a tall mast and a hinged bowsprit, with a rope running from the tip of the bowsprit to the top of the mast. Every time she went through Magnetawan the mast had to be lowered to avoid hitting the overhead telegraph wire. On this particular occasion, the crew forgot to lower the mast. Unluckily, a gentleman from Toronto happened to be sitting on a chair on the foredeck, directly in front of the pilot-house. The mast, of course, struck the wire and snapped it; worse still, the impact flipped the bowsprit up and backwards, where it came to rest squarely on the head of the Toronto gentleman, crushing his high silk hat and giving him a nasty cut. The man flew into a rage and threatened to sue the Company, but the captain did his best to mollify him, and paid for the ruined hat, and the Toronto man sensibly dropped the matter.

These were not the only problems faced by the Navigation Company on the Magnetawan. There was the added problem of competition, as the Walton family was about to enter the steamboat business on the waterway.

The Waltons were of English descent, and originally of modest means. Arthur Walton, head of the family, lived originally at Little Britain, near Lake Scugog in the Kawartha Lakes. In his youth he engaged in fishing and working on some of the local steamboats, and never had the time or the opportunity to acquire any formal education, beyond what he learned from experience. Nevertheless, he and his family soon won the respect of their neighbours for clean living, tireless energy, and unfailing integrity. It was said that Mr. Walton never made a promise he did not intend to keep. By 1879 the family moved to the Parry Sound district, where Arthur took up residence for a time at Katrine, a newly emerging hamlet located where the Muskoka Road passed the east end of Doe Lake, itself on the south branch of the Magnetawan, about four miles from Burks Falls. Arthur's brother Henry meanwhile settled at Magnetawan, and eventually built a number of steamboats.

Exactly how the Waltons got started in steamboating is uncertain. In 1879 Arthur Walton, in partnership with S.E. Best, the Crown Lands agent at Magnetawan, is said to have been running a steamboat between Magnetawan and Burks Falls. This sounds like the aforementioned *Pioneer*, which Henry Walton built for E.A. Morris, but there is no record that the Waltons were ever in partnership with Morris, though that is possible. What is certain is that the Walton brothers had a steamer of their own on Doe Lake in 1885. This craft was the *Lady Katrine*, a single decked 40-foot vessel displacing 10.91 tons. Why she was placed on Doe Lake can only be surmised, since the lake is only about eight miles in length. Perhaps she was used to tow logs for the Jones Lumber Company of Katrine, which was once engaged in moving timber from a flume built across the lake at Beggsboro.[2] By 1885 the lumber could be shipped out from Katrine, which was on the railway. It also seems likely that the steamer carried some of the local settler's grain to be ground at the Beggsboro gristmill, which for many years was the only one in the area. A family tradition says that the Waltons charged 10¢ a bushel to transport the flour.

It would appear that the Doe Lake service did not pay very well, since Captain Walton, who won his certificate in 1887, soon decided to move the *Lady Katrine* to Burks Falls, and his own residence to Magnetawan. By 1888, if not earlier, the *Lady Katrine* was on her new route. According to the Muskoka Herald she was nearly swamped by high waters that spring while trying to lock through at Magnetawan with 100 bags of flour on board. The *Lady Katrine* plied on the Magnetawan as a freighter and tug until 1891, when she was broken up.

By that time the Waltons already had another tug in service. This vessel was the *Emulator*, built at Magnetawan in 1890. She was 49.7 feet in length, 10.2 feet in beam, and registered 17 tons. Old-timers recall her as a white-hulled, pot-bellied tug with a round stern, a short black stack, and a steam exhaust pipe running up from the engine room cabin to make up for her lack of a condenser. Most of the merchants of Magnetawan helped put up the money to pay for her. Commanded by Arthur Walton, the *Emulator* was used to tow booms of logs to the mills at Magnetawan and Ahmic Harbour, and also to haul scowloads of freight to all points on the waterway. She served the region for 20 years.

Business must have been good, because in 1891 Captain Walton and his sons, along with a number of partners, organized the Magnetawan Navigation Company Ltd., which lasted officially until 1898. They also built another steamer that year, probably to replace the *Lady Katrine*. Their new vessel, the *Glenrosa*, was a larger craft of 42.97 tons and a length of 66.5 feet. Powered by a two hp. high-pressure engines, the *Glenrosa* had a single deck and a round stern, and as befitted her name, she had a dark reddish coloured hull. Unlike the *Emulator*, she sometimes carried passengers as well as freight, being licensed for 40 people. (The *Wenonah* was licensed for 100.)

Like the *Emulator*, the *Glenrosa* remained in service for nearly 20 years. After the turn of the century, when new passenger ships were being built, she was used exclusively as a towboat, hauling freight and provisions as well as rafts of logs. One spring, probably about 1904, she was engaged by Walter and Henry Knight of Burks Falls, to collect a tow of logs on Goose Lake, an arm of Ahmic Lake, for the Knights' sawmill. Young Ed Knight, son of Walter, then a youth in his teens, was at the wheel, and with youthful exuberance he rang for full speed ahead and ran the vessel into Goose Lake at full throttle. Failing to appreciate that boats do not have brakes, he ran her right up onto the beach, with her bow high up out of the water. It is said to have taken the combined efforts of two other tugs to pull her off. As they say boys will be boys.

In 1904 the Waltons decided to add a third steamer to their fleet. The new ship was the *Glenada*, a 70-foot screw steamer built at Magnetawan. Apparently she started out as a single decker, used largely for towing and scowing, yet she was also a part-time passenger ship in the summertime. In that respect she was meant as a replacement for the smaller *Glenrosa*, which lapsed into the role of a workboat about that time. The *Glenada* had a long life, but she really came into her own about 1911, when she was rebuilt as a passenger steamer.

Until after the turn of the century the Waltons did most of the towing on the river, while the Muskoka Navigation Company was still running freight and passengers on the *Wenonah*. The early 1890s, however, were not good years, and it was only in 1896 that economic conditions across Canada as a whole really began to improve. The Magnetawan district shared some of this new prosperity. Lumbering and tanning were flourishing, and tourism was also on the increase, as a sort of overflow from Muskoka. More and more venturesome visitors, mostly doctors, college professors and businessmen from the United States, were discovering the charms of the lakes and establishing cottages and summer camps on them. A few resorts were also opened, notably Forest Nook and Cedar Croft on Ahmic Lake, and Rockwynn Lodge on an island in Lake Cecebe. Every resort, camp and cottage expected the steamers to call, and all built wharves for them. The government in turn rebuilt the docks at Burks Falls, Magnetawan and Ahmic Harbour around the turn of the century, while a railway spur, sponsored by A.P. Cockburn and most of the merchants of Burks Falls, was built from the main line to the town waterfront in 1902. That same year, the Muskoka Express extended its runs from Scotia Junction to Burks Falls. By 1903, through trains were running from points as distant as Baltimore, Maryland, connecting

S.S. "Glenada" at Burks Falls.

G.T.R. train connecting with the S.S. "Wanita", Burks Falls (around 1905).

S.S. "Wenonah" (left) and S.S. "Wanita" at Burks Falls, around 1900.

with a Pullman which ran overnight from Toronto and reached "the Falls" by 4:00 a.m. Passengers were allowed to sleep on the train for a few more hours, before boarding the steamer at 7:30.

As business improved, the local steamboat proprietors responded by building new vessels to handle the inflow. In November of 1897 the Muskoka Navigation Company decided on a running mate for the *Wenonah*, and purchased the new steamer *Cyclone*, which had been built at Ahmic Harbour the previous year for a local lumberman. The *Cyclone* seems to have started out as a tug with only a single deck; if so, the Navigation Company had her completely remodelled into a double-decked screw vessel of 30.14 tons. Her name was changed by Order-in-Council to the *Wanita* on June 20, 1898. The *Wanita* was a small and narrow ship, just 64 feet in length by a mere 12 in beam, which made her dangerously tipsy when carrying large crowds. Her silhouette was rather tall for her size, and on at least one occasion the wind blew her sideways right across Magnetawan Bay and onto a mud flat.

The *Wanita*'s deficiencies were, however, even more pointedly highlighted at a regatta held at Rockwynn Lodge on Lake Cecebe around the turn of the century, when spectators on her upper deck all surged over to one side to watch a procession of small boats go by. The steamer at once started to roll over and only the lines securing her to the wharf saved her from capsizing. Prudently, the Navigation Company decided to put her in drydock and have false sides added to her hull to make her more stable. In the winter of 1900-1901 the *Wenonah* was given a complete refit at Burks Falls. As the railway services improved, the *Wanita*, by 1903, was put on the morning run from Burks Falls, leaving at 7:30 a.m. after the arrival of the Muskoka Express. The *Wenonah*, apparently based at Ahmic Harbour, usually connected with the afternoon trains at 5:00 p.m.

In the fall of 1905, the Muskoka Navigation Company, then in the process of reorganization, decided to sell all its assets on the Magnetawan, including the *Wenonah* and the *Wanita*: apparently the new board of directors felt that the Magnetawan division was too small and too remote from the Company's main scene of operations to be worth retaining. Only a few years later the Walton enterprise also came to an end. In the spring of 1908 the *Glenrosa* was dismantled and set on fire in the river below the locks at Magnetawan. Later even the hulk was hauled out and burned. The *Emulator*, too, was dismantled and sunk in the river in 1909. Their last steamer, the *Glenada*, changed hands about 1912, while Captain Walton and his sons left to found a new steamboat service on the Pickerel River in northern Parry Sound.

FOOTNOTES

[1] Rev. W.W. Walker, 'By Northern Lakes', Toronto, 1896.
[2] The old village of Beggsboro almost disappeared after 1896, when the Canada Atlantic Railway bypassed it for Sprucedale.

S.S. "Waubuno", Flagship of the Beatty Line.

S.S. "F.B. Maxwell", Georgian Bay.

CHAPTER 9
The Muskoka Navigation Company's Expansion
to Georgian Bay
(1886-1893)

Still trying to retrieve its fortunes in the spring of 1886, and frustrated by its relatively meagre profits from the Magnetawan, the Muskoka and Nipissing Navigation Company turned its attention to Georgian Bay.

There was nothing novel about running steamships on "the Bay" at that time. A steamboat had been built at Penetanguishene as early as 1836 to ply on Georgian Bay and Lake Huron, but seemingly it was the Beatty family who, among their countless services to the town of Parry Sound in the early days, first inaugurated a regular steamship service from Collingwood. In 1865 the firm of J. & H. Beatty started out with a fine 200-ton sidewheeler called the *Waubuno* to keep Parry Sound in touch with "civilization". By the early 1880s the Company had at least five steamers in commission, but the Beattys had been having a lot of bad luck. On November 11, 1879, the *Waubuno*, while returning from Midland to Parry Sound, was caught in a blinding snowstorm, failed to find her way to the entrance of Parry Sound harbour, and was wrecked with the loss of every soul on board. Some of the wreckage from the ill-fated vessel was found, but not one body. The ship, valued at more than $10,000, was uninsured. In 1880 another of their boats, the *Simcoe*, was also lost. Again in 1882 their newly acquired steamer *Manitoulin* was destroyed by fire, and that same season the steamer *Asia* foundered near Byng Inlet with a heavy loss of life; there were, in fact, only three survivors. This succession of disasters must have benefitted other companies competing with the Beattys, and invited newcomers to try their hand.

An actual invitation was extended by some of the Georgian Bay communities to the Muskoka and Nipissing Navigation Company to provide a good daily steamer service from Parry Sound to Midland and other ports on the southern half of "the Bay". The Muskoka company expressed interest, but took no action for most of a year. However, by the summer of 1886, when the Company was starting to feel its losses at home rather keenly, the proposal from Georgian Bay was suddenly seen in a more favourable light. In August they purchased a new cabin steamer for the Georgian route. In 1889 the shift of emphasis was made official, in that the Company changed its name to the Muskoka and Georgian Bay Navigation Company.

The Company's new Georgian Bay service had a history strikingly similar to that of its Lake Nipissing division: a rapid rise and growth, followed by a lamentable string of blunders leading to an equally rapid decline and collapse. The full story is not known, but the basic facts are these.

The firm started out with the paddle steamship *F.B. Maxwell* which was easily the largest vessel the Company had ever owned, being 137.5 feet in keel, 23.5 in beam, not counting the paddle-boxes, and registering 271.90 tons. Built at Sorel, Quebec, in 1877, the *F.B. Maxwell* had a single low-pressure engine generating some 75 hp. She assumed a route from Collingwood to Parry Sound, calling at Penetanguishene, Midland and Waubaushene and sailing through the 30,000 Islands. Unlike the new *Wenonah*, the *Maxwell* earned a handsome profit, and for the next several years the Georgian Bay division was by far the most remunerative branch of the Company's operations.

Encouraged by this promising start, the Company proceeded to buy a second steamer in 1887. Their choice this time was the *Telegram*, a screw driven ship then in service around Sault Ste. Marie. Built at Collingwood in 1885, the *Telegram* was much smaller than the *Maxwell*, having a length of only 108 feet and a tonnage of 134. For one season the *Telegram* gave good service on the northern half of Georgian Bay, plying as far as Byng Inlet and the French River estuary. Schedules were interconnected with trains on the Northern Railway to Collingwood, and the Grand Trunk Railway to Midland; sometimes the boats plied west as far as Meaford. "Greatly Reduced Fares during the Excursion Season", proclaimed a Company advertisement in 1887.

S.S. "Imperial"
Courtesy, Mr. Robert Ireland, London

It would appear that the *Telegram* was acquired only as a stop-gap measure, since at season's end the Company sold her to good advantage to an individual from Romney, Ontario, on Lake Erie. She remained in service on the Great lakes until 1907. Meanwhile, a successor was required, and at first the Company proposed to charter a new, larger vessel for the Killarney run. Only one suitable ship, a paddlewheeler, could be found, and the owner was willing to sell outright, but would not charter. A proposal to buy this vessel was voted down by the Company board of directors, and, as a last resort, a 109-foot passenger screw steamer, the *Imperial*, was purchased instead and taken from Oakville to Parry Sound in the spring of 1888. The *Imperial* was only three years old, and proved very speedy, punctual and seaworthy on her new route, but she was scarcely larger than her predecessor, and the patrons of the line had desired a larger ship. Convinced that they would not be satisfied until they got one, the Manager of the Company, A.P. Cockburn, persuaded the President, J.S. Playfair, to call a shareholders' meeting to consider a more vigorous policy on "the Bay". To continue in Mr. Cockburn's own words,

. . I [then] went to work . . and with the office assistance at Gravenhurst, we wrote out about fifty notices of a meeting to the shareholders, and were in the act of posting the letters when a wire was received from the . . president countermanding the calling of the meeting. After a lapse of twelve months he again consented to the calling of a shareholders' meeting, which was held, and unanimously decided in favour of building a suitable boat for the Byng Inlet, French River and Killarney route; but procrastination had already proved fatal, as our chief patrons had, one day previously, let a contract for the building of the fine steamer "City of Midland" for our intended route. This step led to our ultimate withdrawal from the Georgian Bay route to my intense regret.

The *City of Midland* made her début in the spring of 1891, and rapidly won over much of the patronage on the Georgian Bay route. Again the Muskoka line felt the squeeze of sharply diminishing revenues. The Board of Directors' reaction was one of austerity, trying to cut the costs of operations to a minimum. This led to a well-meaning but suicidal policy of decreasing the wages of its employees, particularly on the Georgian Bay run. Naturally, the employees resented this, and many of them resigned. Reduced pay meant hiring poorer crews, which led to debased service and even lower revenues, in a vicious chain reaction. The new men installed on the *F.B. Maxwell*, now renamed the *Manitou*, neither attracted business nor ran the vessel with safety. The inevitable happened. Early in the fall of 1891 the *Manitou* piled up on the rocks and sank, and, though salvaged and repaired she never again ran in the interests of the Muskoka and Georgian Bay Navigation Company. In March of 1892 she was sold at a heavy loss to the Company's chief rival, the North Shore Navigation Company, which owned the *City of Midland* and was eventually to outlast all its competitors on "the Bay". The *Imperial* ran a little longer; then in August 1893 she, too, was sold, to the Kingsville and Pelee Island Navigation Company, at a loss of $3,000 on the original purchase price. So ended this branch of the Muskoka and Georgian Bay Navigation Company's operations. One more failure.

Before we proceed further with the internal affairs of the Company at this time, let us return for a look at events on the Muskoka Lakes after 1885.

S.S. "Telegram"
Courtesy, Mr. Robert Ireland, London

Four Steamers at Beaumaris, Circa 1896.
S.S. "Muskoka" (left), S.S. "Medora", S.S. "Nipissing" and S.S. "Oriole". All four wear the colours of the Muskoka and Georgian Bay Navigation Company.
Courtesy, Port Carling Pioneer Museum

CHAPTER 10
The Muskoka Steamer Fleet
(1886-1896)

The years 1886 to 1896 might almost be termed the dismal decade, both for the Muskoka Navigation Company and the country in general. On the whole, they were difficult, frustrating years. Business was sluggish, population growth was marginal, and the nation seemed to be going nowhere. Crop failures and a panic on the stock markets in 1893 made matters worse. Only in 1896 did conditions begin to improve.

The extension of the Northern Railway beyond Gravenhurst in 1886 dealt a staggering blow to the lakes trade in Muskoka, and it took several years for it to revive. As if this wasn't bad enough, disaster struck again that year. Around 4:00 o'clock, on the morning of August 3, 1886, while lying at her overnight berth at Port Cockburn, the flagship *Nipissing*, the largest, oldest, and seemingly the most popular of the Company's steamers, somehow took fire around the boiler room, and by the time it was noticed, the whole amidships was ablaze. Rudely awakened crew members barely had time to abandon ship; some, finding the gangways already a mass of flames, climbed out the nearest window and jumped overboard in their nightclothes. Nothing was saved. Fearing that the freight sheds and perhaps the Summit House as well might catch fire, the men hastily cast off the lines and pushed the burning ship away from the wharf. Now a roaring inferno with flames shooting a hundred feet up in the night skies, the doomed sidewheeler slowly drifted away toward Fraser Island, where she grounded, burned to the waterline, and finally sank. No lives were lost, but it was said later that the blaze cast a red glow that could be seen from as far away as Redwood, at the other end of Lake Joseph.

News of the tragedy was telegraphed to Gravenhurst from the Summit House. Receiving the grim tidings, A.P. Cockburn wired the Rosseau steamer (probably the *Kenozha*) to proceed to Port Carling, while he himself took the nearest steamer to the village to meet her. From here the Company manager proceeded to Port Cockburn to see for himself the listing, burned-out hulk of the ship he had launched so proudly sixteen years earlier. The engine of the *Nipissing* was salvaged, but the skeleton of the old sidewheeler still lies on the bottom of Lake Joseph, near Port Cockburn. Presumably the vessel carried some insurance, and plans were made immediately to replace her, but for the balance of the season, service on the lakes was somewhat curtailed.

By the spring of 1887, however, the fleet was restored to its normal size. Another *Nipissing* had been launched at Gravenhurst. The new steamer, also a sidewheeler, had a length of 128 feet, a beam of 21 feet, not including the paddle-boxes, and drew about six feet of water. She was, in effect, almost exactly the same size as her predecessor. Her engine, a walking beam paddle type generating 22.53 hp., was built at Kingston about 1872 and almost certainly came from the earlier ship. Pictures of the second *Nipissing* show her as looking so much like the original that it is difficult to distinguish them, though the stack of the new ship was shorter than that of the original, and the paddleboxes and pilothouse were styled differently. The new *Nipissing* featured one major innovation. Her hull, up to the main deck, was made of Welsh iron, fabricated in the Clyde shipyard of Davidson and Doran in Scotland and shipped across to Canada in sections, where they were assembled and rivetted together at Gravenhurst. Another novel feature about the new ship was an exquisite wood carving of a phoenix in the midst of a fire, which was soon mounted atop her wheelhouse. This, like the pickerel on the *Kenozha* and the bird on the *Oriole*, was the work of Captain Bailey, who became the first master of the second *Nipissing*. The carving was meant to salute the new ship, and to symbolize the fate of her predecessor. A new *Nipissing* had arisen from the ashes of the old.

The *Nipissing*, like her precursor, proved a most popular steamer, and could carry over 300 passengers. Her upper cabins were not entirely completed until 1888, owing to a disagreement between the contractor and the Company. Tourists and native Muskokans alike loved the ship for her paddlewheels and her pleasant, three-tone whistle. Officers liked her for her maneuverability, and her rapid rate of acceleration and reverse. For short runs she proved the best boat in the fleet. It was only when struggling against stiff winds in open water that she was at a disadvantage compared to her screw-driven sisters.

As a rule, until 1893 the *Nipissing* was on the Lake Joseph run, leaving Port Cockburn at 6:30 or 7:30 a.m. and meeting the incoming train at Muskoka Wharf at 12:25. Within an hour she would set sail again for Beaumaris, Port Carling, Ferndale, Minett, Port Sandfield, Redwood, Hamill's Point and Yoho Island, arriving again at Port Cockburn by 7:00 p.m. The *Kenozha*, under Captain Henry, would meanwhile ply from Rosseau to Gravenhurst and back, calling at Windermere and Juddhaven on Lake Rosseau, and sometimes taking in Torrance and Bala on Lake Muskoka as well. The steamer *Muskoka*, which was steadily evolving from a tug into a passenger ship, would provide a morning service from Gravenhurst to Rosseau on Mondays, Wednesdays and Fridays, and to Port Cockburn Tuesdays, Thursdays and Saturdays, with Captain Hans Peter Larson of Gravenhurst in charge. The once vital Muskoka River run to Bracebridge, which had formerly required two steamers, was now assigned solely to the little *Oriole*, under Captain McAlpine, who would take his vessel twice daily downriver to Point Kaye, Milford Bay and other ports of call on eastern Lake Muskoka, joining the *Kenozha*, *Muskoka* and *Nipissing* at Beaumaris to transfer freight and passengers.

Captain Bailey experienced a number of adventures during his tenure as Master of the second *Nipissing*. One of the most celebrated incidents took place on September 5, 1891, while the steamer was heading down the lake from Port Cockburn. A lady passenger up at the bow spotted what looked like a big snake in the water, ahead of the ship. The mate, Ralph W. Lee, soon perceived that it was a large black bear, and notified the captain, who was then below having breakfast. Within moments Captain Bailey was on deck with a Winchester. As the steamer drew up close to the beast and slackened her speed, the captain, who was an excellent marksman, took aim and fired twice, but the motion of the vessel nullified his accuracy, and he missed both times. By now the ship was right on top of the bear, and one of the paddlewheels actually caught him and rolled him under. Far from quitting, though, Bruin surfaced, snorting and shaking his head, and still swimming as strongly as ever. They were now quite close to the shore; the captain took another shot, and missed, and meanwhile shouted to Lee to reverse engines. Again the steamer ran over the bear, which again came up unhurt, but one more shot finally took effect. The bear's head went under and he stopped swimming. Warily, the crew lowered a boat, carefully slipped a rope around his neck, and finally hauled him aboard.

The bear was a magnificent specimen, all of 300 lbs. in weight and seven feet three inches in length. A passenger bought the creature, proposing to skin it near Muskoka Wharf and sink the carcass. That was fine with the captain, but it did not end the matter.

By a bizarre turn of events, that bear actually got his revenge on Captain Bailey. Two weeks later, as the *Nipissing* was approaching the little island near Muskoka Wharf, the captain noticed something unusual in the water. It proved to be the bear's carcass floating. Upon docking, the captain arranged to go out with a man in a boat to make certain of sinking the bear. Even that was not the end of it: about a month later, when the *Nipissing* was again approaching the Wharf, there once more was the bear's carcass, now swollen up like a balloon to about twice its former size. Muttering under his breath, Captain Bailey again secured a boat and rowed out to it, taking with him some scrap iron, some wire and a butcher knife. Then, while trying to figure out some way of fastening the sinkers to the thing, it occurred to him to try deflating the carcass with the butcher knife to reduce its size. He would have done better to use the Winchester again. The carcass exploded, bespattering the captain's uniform with pieces of decomposed bear. The stench was so nauseating that it was weeks before Bailey could really feel clean again.

S.S. "Nipissing" (Original Version).
Lithograph from a Muskoka Navigation Company Letterhead (1888).

The loss of the S.S. "Nipissing" at Port Cockburn, Lake Joseph, on August 3, 1886.
Pen and Charcoal Sketch by the Author

S.S. "Nipissing" docked at Port Cockburn, Circa 1888.

Captain Bailey was such a superb wheelsman that it almost seems derogatory to record that he once had an accident with the second *Nipissing* II. One time during the 1890s he was taking his vessel down through Lake Muskoka to Gravenhurst when a dense fog set in. It was soon impossible to see beyond the point of the bow. Speed was reduced to dead slow, but visibility remained almost nil. Presently the captain relinquished the wheel to a deckhand, while he himself stepped out of the pilothouse to take a look around. Just at that moment, ominous dark shadows were perceived up ahead, and before they could reverse engines the bow of the steamer ground on the rocks and tree branches began sweeping the forward deck. The ship had grounded on Old Woman Island, near Walker's Point. Happily, there was very little damage done, but it is said that she was so firmly caught that another steamer had to be brought in to drag her off. Captain Bailey was so humiliated by the mishap that he left the ship immediately after docking at Gravenhurst without stopping at the navigation office. He had every intention of resigning his command, but A.P. Cockburn soon talked him out of it and persuaded him to stay.

Despite the success of the new *Nipissing*, an air of stagnation still hung over the lakes trade for several years. The major exception to this trend was in scowing and log towing, but even there, all was not well for the Navigation Company. The numbers of small local tugs, sometimes dubbed the "mosquito fleet", was starting to grow into a swarm, with each new vessel after a share of the business.

The new tugs can be grouped roughly into three categories, depending on ownership. Some of them belonged to the tanneries in Bracebridge. Others were owned or leased by some of the lumber companies. The remainder belonged to free-lance boatmen who towed and scowed on contract. Some, of course, shifted from one category to another. A few were aging pleasure yachts that had passed their prime. We begin with the tannery tugs.

The Beardmore tannery, which passed to the Muskoka Leather Company in 1882, used a total of five tugs. Two of these, the *Jennie Willson* and the *Chateau*, we have noted earlier. In the spring of 1884 the firm also purchased the steamer *Rosseau* from the Navigation Company for $3,000. In June of 1885 the *Jennie Willson* was sold to Robert Stroud of Milford

Str. "Rosseau" at Port Carling.
Courtesy, Mrs. Joyce Schell, Barlochan

Steam Tug "Southwood", on the Muskoka River.
Courtesy, Mr. Alldyn Clark, Bracebridge

Bay, near Beaumaris, who would soon establish the Milford Bay Temperance Hotel. The *Rosseau*, meanwhile, remained with the tannery until 1899, when she was again sold.

In 1891 the Muskoka Leather Company found itself with competition on the river, in addition to J.D. Shier's sawmill and Singleton Brown's shingle mill. A Toronto leather manufacturer, David Watson Alexander, decided to take advantage of a $2,000 bonus offered by the Town of Bracebridge (plus a guarantee of a ten year tax exemption) by building a second tannery, on the south side of the Muskoka River. The new tannery, later acquired by the firm of Shaw, Cassils and Company of Montreal, was completed in October. Since boats were bringing in almost all the tanbark, the new tannery management decided that they, too, must have a tug. Their choice was the steamer *Southwood*, a fine screw tug built at Barrie in 1884 as the *Ella Alice*. Her length was increased from 41.6 feet to 67.5 and the name changed in 1888. The *Southwood* registered 13 tons and was powered by a 1.92 hp. high-pressure engine. Her special feature was a "modock" whistle, which was usually used in foggy weather and could let out a resounding wildcat screech. The vessel arrived at Gravenhurst on a railway flatcar in the spring of 1892, and was promptly put to work scowing tanbark, frequently from Rosseau Falls and vicinity. It is said that she could tow three or four barges instead of the usual two, each loaded with 100 cords of tanbark. She towed for the tannery until 1908, usually under the command of Captain George Parlett of Bracebridge, a former mate on the *Nipissing*.

Keen rivalry soon sprang up between the crews of the *Southwood* and the *Rosseau*, which was then commanded by Captain Ken Morrison. Whenever the two tugs found themselves on the same course, heading for the Muskoka River estuary with scows in tow, the result was always a race. Captain Levi Fraser has vividly described one such contest that took place on a Saturday in 1894. The *Southwood* had just locked throught at Port Carling, with the *Rosseau* following on the next lockage. Upon reaching Lake Muskoka, Captain Morrison soon noted that the *Southwood* was not too far ahead, and immediately called for more speed. The engineer and fireman promptly worked up a big fire and built up as much steam pressure as the boiler could generate. Passing Horseshoe Island, the *Rosseau* soon pulled ahead, while a jubilant Captain Morrison waved goodbye to the *Southwood* and offered her a tow. But he laughs best who laughs last. The smaller tug still had a little more power to deliver, and to Morrison's acute dismay the *Southwood* began to pound harder, narrowing the space between them. Short of screwing down the safety valve on the *Rosseau*, which was illegal, there was nothing more that Engineer Woodhouse could do, and soon the *Southwood* was steaming triumphantly past, with a broom now lashed to her masthead. Captain Morrison had to wait until the following year to get even, but by then the Muskoka Leather Company had a fast new tug for him to command.[1]

The new arrival was the beautiful steamer *Queen of the Isles*. Built at Orillia in 1885 as a pleasure boat, she had a clipper bow, a fantail stern, and the lines of a sailing yacht. With a length of 72 feet and a 15 hp. high-pressure engine, she was built for speed, and was initially used as a passenger boat on Lake Simcoe. By 1890 she had been transferred to Toronto, and plied for a few years between Trenton and Brighton, through the Murray Canal. (Rumour had it that she was also engaged in smuggling and rum running at that time.) In the fall of 1892, however, the *Queen of the Isles* was purchased by a Toronto speculator named William Odell Whiting, who brought her up to Lake Muskoka to serve as an adjunct to the Brighton Beach Hotel, which he was then building near Torrance. Unfortunately, Whiting's schemes had a way of not working out. In July of 1895 the Brighton Beach Hotel, which had cost $15,000, burned down and became a total loss. Assailed by a swarm of creditors, Whiting scuttled the *Queen of the Isles* in shallow water: submerged property cannot be seized. But she was too valuable to be left on the lake bottom, and before long the Bracebridge "old tannery" (Beardmore's) bought her and gave her a thorough refit at Gravenhurst as a tug. Among other things she received a much larger new propeller. The *Queen of the Isles* proved an excellent scowboat, and could easily outrace the *Southwood* by half an hour on a course from the Indian River to the Muskoka. Her owners used her for the occasional pleasure cruise, such as a free employees' picnic to Shanty Bay on Lake Muskoka to gather blueberries. One of the tannery scows would be temporarily fitted out with seats for the hands and their wives and sweethearts. With her splendid woodwork, plush seats in the aft cabin and well-

Str. "Queen of the Isles", scowing tanbark.

Str. "Queen of the Isles" with scow, passing through Port Sandfield.
Courtesy, Archives of Ontario Acc. 14777-14

Steam Tug "Theresa"
Courtesy, Mr. Arnold Groh, Gravenhurst

Steam Tug "Comet".
Sketch based on a photograph of the vessel in derelict condition. The bow was enclosed while Walter Fowler owned the boat.

160

equipped galley, the *Queen of the Isles* was, as Captain Fraser put it, the "most luxurious tug on the lakes". Fraser himself eventually bought the vessel from the Tannery in 1925, and found her the most useful craft he ever owned.

The usual procedure for scowboats, whether owned by the tanneries or by the lumber companies, was to haul two or more loaded scows to the tannery or railhead, and there, pick up two or more freshly emptied scows and tow them back up the lakes to be refilled. Scows were to be seen everywhere. Some totalled 100 feet in length by 21 in beam. Usually it took a crew of four, a captain, engineer, cook and fireman, to staff a tug and manage the scows, with extra help to load and unload. The scows were very prone to leak, and since steam siphons were scarce until 1900, many an unfortunate young deckhand could be sure of having to spend regular intervals of gruelling work at the pumps. Because of the leaky seams in the scows, skilled caulkers were very much in demand, and, being few in number, they were very well paid.

Some of the lumber companies in Muskoka grew tired of depending on the Navigation Company for their log towing, and began buying or building their own tugs. This was so, despite the generally depressed state of the national economy throughout most of the 1880s and '90s, largely because of the almost insatiable demand for wood products in American cities. In 1883 the American government abolished its tolls on lumber passing through the Erie Canal, with the result that Buffalo and North Tonawanda replaced Oswego as the principal receiving ports for Muskoka lumber. Gradually the needs of urban Canada also grew as cities expanded, and there were still markets in Europe and South America. Under such conditions it was natural that the Canadian lumber trade should continue to prosper. Professor Lower has estimated that only the upper portion of Georgian Bay and the Ottawa Valley exceeded Muskoka as suppliers of white pine during this period.

One of the first firms to acquire a private tug was the Snider Lumber Company. Founded by William Snider of Waterloo, Ontario, this company started off by building a sawmill at Rosseau Falls in 1877. In 1886 it purchased the little *Jennie Willson* from the Stroud family of Milford Bay, and used her to tow timber rafts to the mill, and scowloads of lumber to the towns. Later, in 1895, the firm transferred its activities to Gravenhurst, having bought out the interests of the bankrupt Taylor Brothers Lumber Company a few years before. The Snider Company did fairly well, and in 1899 it also purchased the old steamer *Rosseau* from the Bracebridge "old tannery" to assist the much smaller *Jennie Willson* with her work. Early in the present century, however, the timber limits were giving out, and in 1910 the mill had to shut down. During its last few seasons it had to rely on local residents for logs. Before that time both the *Rosseau* and the *Jennie Willson* were sold to local entrepreneurs. The *Rosseau* lasted until about 1915; the *Jennie Willson* only until 1909. In 1900 Peter Mutchenbaker, who had taken over the mill at Rosseau Falls, built his own tug, the *Theresa* (17.74 tons), a 49.5-foot vessel with a second-hand engine. Shortly afterwards the Mutchenbaker firm also ran out of logs, and in 1904 the *Theresa* was loaded onto a railway flatcar and shipped north to the Magnetawan, where we will find her again.

Although the Muskoka lumber trade was booming late in the nineteenth century, some companies, like that of the Taylor Brothers, failed to flourish. Some simply had more than their share of bad luck. The Woodstock Company of Gravenhurst, for example, was twice stricken by fires which destroyed first the mill proper, and later the whole mill yard, and consequently its days ran short. Other firms failed because of unwise planning. The Longford Lumber Company, controlled by William Thomson of Orillia, ran into trouble in Muskoka because it overestimated the timber capacities of the District. Thomson took over the Taylor mill around 1890 and developed it into the largest in Muskoka, with a cutting capacity of 80,000 to 100,000 feet per diem, when the average cut was then only 30,000 to 60,000 feet. The trade was now past its prime, and in 1901 the Thomson "White Mill", as it was called, had to be sold, to the powerful Rathbun Company of Deseronto, which had several mills elsewhere in Ontario, and already owned what was called the "Red Mill" at the south end of Muskoka Bay, the site of Peter Cockburn's old mill of 1876.

Included in the sale of the "White Mill" was the steamer *Comet*, a 60-foot, 13.66-ton tug which had been built in 1877 by Robert Stroud and his sons at Milford Bay as a replacement for the *Jennie Willson*. In 1896 the Strouds sold the vessel to Thomson, who moved her down to Lake St. John, east of Lake Couchiching, where the Longford Company had extensive operations. In 1902, however, her new owners, the Rathbuns, had her shipped back to the Muskoka Lakes, where for about eight more seasons she was a familiar sight, towing logs from the Company's limits in Cardwell Township to Gravenhurst. Like most tugs the *Comet* was occasionally used for running picnics and fishing trips on some of her days off.[2]

The *Comet* was the only tug ever used by the Rathbun Company in Muskoka. Previously the firm seems to have hired one of the Navigation Company's tugs to do its towing. As the timber stands became depleted, however, the Rathbuns also had to shut down their mills, in 1910 or shortly thereafter. About that time, the *Comet* was sold to Walter Fowler, a contractor from Milford Bay, who remodelled her into a general workboat, used chiefly to haul stone and timber for the construction of docks and boathouses. Around 1914, thoroughly worn out, she was dismantled, her engines removed, and the hull beached and left to fall to pieces.

It was the powerful firm of Mickle and Dyment which owned by far the largest number of tugs. In a previous chapter we noted how Charles Mickle of Cargill moved to Gravenhurst in 1877 and soon had two sawmills in operation near Muskoka Wharf, with more in other communities around the province. Soon the "M.-D." empire controlled vast timber limits, including one of 200 square miles, located deep within what is now Algonquin Park. Moving the logs out took months, and required a whole fleet of tugs, many of which were named after members of the Mickle family.

This was true of the Company's first tug, the *Bertha May* (13.50 tons), a small 43.5-foot boat built at Gravenhurst in 1886. Three years later the firm built a sturdy 18 ton tug at Kawagama or Hollow Lake, east of Dorset. It was named the *Herbert M.* and together with the *Bertha May* served the Company until 1908.

The next addition was the *Wawonaissa*, a small 36-foot tug built in 1897 by Robert J. Stroud of Milford Bay, apparently as a successor to the *Comet*. The Mickles bought the little craft in the winter of 1901-02, lengthened her to 50 feet (and 6.08 tons), and gave her the more pronounceable name *Nishka*. The *Nishka* doubled as a tug and pleasure boat for a decade, when she was sold and moved, first to Sparrow Lake, and then to the Lake of Bays. In the spring of 1905, by which time the firm was cutting an average of 14,000,000 feet of lumber every year, another tough little tug was built for the Company at Gravenhurst: the *Grace M.*, named for one of Charles Mickle's daughters. Listed at 27 tons, the *Grace M.* was 68.5 feet in length, 14 in beam, and drew 7½ feet of water. With her turned-up bow and gray (later black) hull with salmon-coloured superstructure, the *Grace M.* had an enormous five-foot eight-inch wheel, which, in the words of one of her captains, "could really pull". She served until about 1927.

Steam Tug "Grace M.", of the Mickle-Dyment Company.

Steam Tug "Bertha May"
Courtesy, Mrs. Joyce Schell, Barlochan

Steam Yacht "Nishka"

Some of the smaller sawmills were entirely dependent on free-lance captains who towed and scowed wherever they could get a contract. Many of these mariners, including Harper Walker of Walker's Point, the Croucher brothers of Craigie Lea (Lake Joseph), and Peter Campbell of northwestern Muskoka Township, were settlers or sons of settlers who combined steamboating with farming, contracting and lumbering. Others, such as Charles William Henshaw of West Gravenhurst, Albert F. Leeder of Bracebridge, Wesley D. Hill of Gravenhurst, and Levi Fraser, all started to work on the boats in their teens and made lifetime professions of it. Many at times worked for the tanneries and sawmills. A few independent mill owners, such as Andrew Boyd and Singleton Brown of Bracebridge, also owned various tugs and hired others to crew them.

We have already met Captain John Rogers, who built the little steamer *Pinafore* in 1876. To the Port Sandfield skipper, taking freight and passengers proved so profitable that during the winter of 1883-84 he built a larger boat called the *Sunbeam* which was 31.6 feet in keel, registered 2.41 tons, and had a four-horsepower high-pressure engine.[3] The *Sunbeam* was used for towing and scowing into the 1890s; in the event of large excursion parties the passengers were taken in a barge lashed alongside the tug. Business soon outgrew the *Sunbeam* too, and in 1887 Rogers designed and built a third steamer, the *Edith May*, which he named after his wife. With a length of 64.5 feet and a displacement of 30.52 tons, the *Edith May* was an attractive, yacht-like vessel, several times larger than the *Sunbeam*, with large, roomy cabins and two high-pressure engines. She was used successfully for eleven seasons, carrying supplies and provisions to settlers, campers and hotels. Frequently she was chartered for excursions from the Prospect House and other summer resorts.

Several other tugs and dynasties of tugs can be catalogued from this period. In 1884 Captain William Thomas Jones of West Gravenhurst and his neighbour, Henry Readman, built the *Dauntless*, a 44.6-foot screw vessel grossing 7.93 tons, and used her both for fishing and towing logs for some of the local sawmills. In 1892 the *Dauntless* was sold to Captain Windsor of Callander, and spent her remaining years on Lake Nipissing. At Walker's Point, Captain Harper Walker seems to have carried on with his tug, the *Ontario*, until about 1897. The *Ontario* had a number of later owners before she was finally beached and abandoned near Port Carling around 1916. In 1897 Captain Walker and his brother-in-law, Charles J. Smith, built a larger tug called the *Allena May*, which was 47.5 feet in length and registered 10.83 tons. Named for a favourite niece of the captain, the *Allena May* served around Walker's Point until 1901, when she was sold to Walter Fowler of Milford Bay. Fowler used the vessel primarily as a scowboat, until he obtained the *Comet* from the Rathbun Company.

Sometime before 1898 Captain Walker also obtained from Fowler the little steamer *Kate Murray*, which had once been Charles Vanderburgh's yacht at Port Carling. A story is told of the *Kate Murray* in November 1898, when Captain Walker and his wife and several neighbours arranged to take the little craft to Gravenhurst to stock up with provisions to help last the winter. Like numerous other Muskoka settlements, Walker's Point did not get a decent road to connect it with the outside world until the 1930s, and consequently winter was like a long, cold siege that ended only when the spring breakup heralded the reopening of navigation every year. On this occasion, the *Kate Murray* reached Gravenhurst without difficulty, allowing her passengers to complete their shopping, but on the way back during the late afternoon, having passed the Gravenhurst Narrows and reached the open lake, she encountered a snowstorm and it became almost impossible to see. The boat soon wandered off course and grounded on a small rocky island, where she almost turned turtle. The occupants all groped their way out through the gangway onto the island, where they were safe for the moment, but their plight was still an unenviable one, especially with the darkness setting in. Eventually one of the men volunteered to try paddling to shore on a driftwood log to get help. It was a perilous undertaking, and not accomplished without a few duckings in the freezing water, but he made it, and presently boats came to rescue the castaways.

As it happened, Harper Walker was the last owner of the *Kate Murray*. He seems to have scrapped her in 1902-03, at which time he built the new steamer *Sharon*. Listed at 9.42 tons, the *Sharon* was essentially another tug, with a length of 46 feet, and she may have inherited one of the engines from the *Kate Murray*. She was named after the Sharon Fishing and Social

Str. "Edith May", at Port Sandfield.
The pilothouse atop the cabins is a late modification.

Steam Tug "Dauntless" with Houseboat.
This picture shows the vessel during her later years on Lake Nipissing.

Club, a friendly fellowship of American sportsmen from Sharon, Pa., who had been camping and cottaging on Tondern Island, near Beaumaris, since the 1880s. On frequent occasions the Club used to charter the tug to take its members out to their favourite fishing grounds for a day, often with a string of rowboats in tow. Those were the days before motor launches became common. In 1906 Captain Walker sold the *Sharon* to his brother-in-law, Charles J. Smith, and soon replaced her with the Mickle tug *Bertha May*, while Smith and his partner, George Gillan, continued to accommodate the Fishing Club. Otherwise the *Sharon* remained a tug. In the spring of 1910, for example, she helped the *Southwood* tow a log boom containing 350,000 feet of timber from the mouth of the Indian River to Gravenhurst. After the season of 1913, however, the *Sharon* was drydocked at Gravenhurst, and never sailed again. Smith meanwhile bought the hull of the old *Bertha May*, which was now engineless and unfit for further service, and rebuilt it piece by piece, copying every timber, and fitted it out with the machinery from the *Sharon*.

While Smith and Captain Walker were busy towing around Walker's Point, their neighbour, Captain Peter Campbell, who had his home where Campbell's Landing Marina now stands, was erecting a portable sawmill of his own at the head of Shanty Bay. In 1899 Captain Campbell bought the tiny steamer *Siesta* (2.35 tons) from Donald Burgess of Bala, who had imported her from Lake Simcoe a few years earlier, and used her to tow logs to his mill and sawn lumber around the lakes. Finding her too small for the purpose, Campbell sold the *Siesta* in 1901 and built a larger vessel, the *Gravenhurst* (19.80 tons), which was 52 feet in keel and powerful enough to tow 1,000,000 feet of timber at a time. The *Gravenhurst* accepted towing contracts all over the lakes, and in 1904 came to the aid of the *Oriole* when it ran into trouble on the Muskoka River. In 1908, however, Captain Campbell bought another vessel, the *Nymph*, from the Stroud family, and bequeathed her to his sons after his death in 1912. The *Gravenhurst*, meanwhile, followed the *Theresa* to the Magnetawan River.

Another prominent local merchant who built or purchased a succession of steamboats was Alfred Mortimer, whose father William founded the community of Mortimer's Point on the west arm of Lake Muskoka and subsequently built a tourist hotel, the Wingberry House, sometime before 1892. Just about that time Alf Mortimer obtained his tug master's certificate, and was soon in business with a little tug called the *Wasp*. In 1895, however, Captain Mortimer arranged to exchange the *Wasp* for the *Ethel May*, an aging 30-foot vessel that had previously been used to peddle farm produce on Lake Rosseau. The *Ethel May* lasted only two more years before she wore out and had to be replaced, by the second *Ethel May*.

The second *Ethel May* was a larger, less elegant craft, some 46.5 feet in length, with a square stern and a tonnage reckoned at 8.80. Her engine came from the earlier boat. On her first trip into Bracebridge in 1897 with a few neighbours aboard, the second *Ethel May*, to everyone's astonishment, was impounded by the authorities for nearly four months on a complaint by one of the Navigation Company captains, who alleged that Captain Mortimer had no right to be carrying passengers. Technically speaking, this was true, and the captain was forced to pay a very stiff fine before he got his vessel back, but at least he had the satisfaction of giving his accuser a black eye! Sometime later, Captain Mortimer did obtain a passenger certificate.

The second *Ethel May* remained with the Mortimers until 1903, when she was sold and converted into a laundry delivery boat. Then, after a period of idleness, she was resold to Charles Woodroffe, who owned a sawmill at Foot's Bay. Woodroffe ran the vessel until 1914, when he scrapped her. After a stint overseas, he returned and imported a new tug called the *Voyageur*, a peculiar steel hulled craft of 30 tons, with a round bottom and a steeple compound engine, built at Montreal in 1895 and used until the 1940s. As for Captain Mortimer, he and his sons built still another steamer in 1901. We shall meet him again when we resume our discussions of the passenger ships.

Just a few more tugs from this period should be mentioned. One was the *Linnia* (3.32 tons), which was imported by Thomas and Alfred Croucher of Craigie Lea in 1892 and used as a work boat for a dozen years. Another was the *Dee*, which was in service from around 1899 until the war years, towing for Thomas Clarke's sawmill on the Dee River, near Windermere: the vessel's neat little high-pressure single-cylinder engine long outlasted the boat itself. Also during the 1890s Thomas Orgill of Orgill's Point, Lake Joseph, bought a

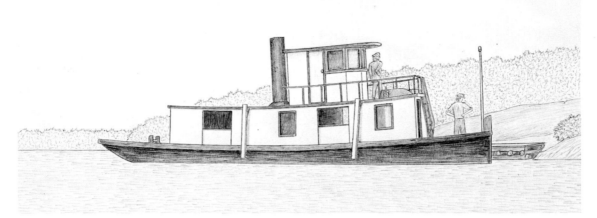

Steam Tug "Ontario" (Reconstruction Sketch).

Steam Tug "Sharon"
Courtesy, Mrs. Joyce Schell, Barlochan

Steam Tug "Siesta".
The side panels are a modification.
Courtesy, Mr. Peter B. Campbell, Campbell's Landing

Steam Tug "Gravenhurst"
Courtesy, Mr. Peter B. Campbell, Campbell's Landing

Steam Tug "Voyageur".
From the Collection of the late Mr. Lester Turnbull, Dundas

Str. "Albion" (Original)
Courtesy, Mr. Charles Orgill, Bracebridge

Str. "Albion" (Second)
Courtesy, Mr. Charles Orgill, Bracebridge

small steamer called the *Albion*, which was used for towing, contracting-work and family outings for several years. Once she wore out, the family rented the much larger steamer *Spray* from Lake Muskoka, kept her a couple of years, then sold her and built the handsome steamer *Albion* sometime around 1910. Both the second *Albion* and *Spray* were used variously for scowing, picnics, collecting laundry, and sometimes taking passengers to and from the railway station at Barnesdale.

Another tug from this interval was the *Maple Leaf*, which was built in Toronto in 1892 and owned by Singleton Brown, a merchant and shingle-mill owner who for many years was very prominent in the affairs of Bracebridge. The *Maple Leaf* was 37 feet in length, registered 8 tons, and towed on the river until 1899, when the mill shut down. On August 8, 1897, she was credited with rescuing the steamer *Muskoka*, which had gone aground near the river-forks in an effect to avoid a drive of logs. That year Mr. Brown took the unusual step of building a houseboat — actually a roofed-over passenger scow called the *Vladmir* (42.74 tons) in order to run excursions down to Lake Muskoka in tow of the tug. The idea was perhaps inspired by some of the "palace scows" that Brown may have seen during his younger days on the Kawartha Lakes. The *Vladmir* was licensed to carry 100 passengers, and the *Maple Leaf* 25. After Singleton Brown's death in the spring of 1900, his widow sold both the tug and the scow to an individual from the Windermere area: the *Maple Leaf* probably went to the Lake of Bays in 1902.

In the meantime the Navigation Company tug fleet was gradually shrinking, from three vessels to two in 1884, and from two to one in 1893. In 1896 its last tug, the *Lake Joseph*, now fifteen years old, was sold to Andrew Boyd, another very prominent Bracebridge lumberman who opened a sawmill at what is now Cedar Beach, near Milford Bay. It was used to tow cribs of logs from all around the lakes to the mill at night, when the winds were usually low, and to scow sawn lumber to Gravenhurst by day. Because of this crews were often on deck 24 hours a day, but this was considered normal. Overtime was unknown, and pausing for a rest when there was a job to be done was unthinkable; after all, if the tug failed to deliver, the mill would have nothing to cut and no product to sell. The only days off ordinarily were Sundays, though occasionally a strong headwind or ice, or fog, might afford the men a few hours of rest. Those days of hard work at long hours for low wages were prosperous times, according to Captain Fraser, and there was then a mark of permanence and security about steamboating.

Thanks to Fraser, who ran the boat for Boyd, a number of stirring reminiscences of the *Lake Joseph* have been preserved. He assures us that nearly every shoal in the Muskoka Lakes came in contact with the its keel at one time or another — probably a safe assertion about any Muskoka tug! He tells us how, on his first trip up to Foot's Bay to collect several cribs of logs, after spending a day helping the rafting gangs to assemble the cribs and running overnight to Port Carling, and then downriver to Lake Muskoka the following morning non-stop, he relinquished the wheel to a subordinate and retired to get a little sleep. He woke up suddenly a few hours later to find the boat absolutely still, the lake as calm as a millpond, and the entire crew sound asleep at their posts. And then, upon arrival at the mill late that afternoon, to be complimented by the foreman for having made such good time! He recalls another time, in April of 1898 or '99, when the weather was still windy and cold, that he and his men collected a block of cedar logs near Juddhaven on Lake Rosseau, only to encounter fresh ice off Tobin's Island that night, forcing them to wait until the following day, when the wind rose and the steamer *Kenozha* arrived from Rosseau to break up the ice. Vividly he recounts how, just one week later, having spent 21 hours a day on deck for the past several days, he fell asleep for a few minutes at the wheel one night, while taking the *Lake Joseph* and a crib past St. Elmo to Gravenhurst — and awakened with a start to find his boat bearing down rapidly on a small island, only a few yards ahead. He describes the horror of that moment, when his whole career and reputation were hanging in the balance, and his vessel was about to be wrecked, and the lives of his crew were entirely in his hands, and it was already too late to avoid a collision. He instantly rang to reverse engines, but such maneuvres take time and there was no time left. Just at the last moment he spotted a log by the shore of the island, half out of the water and just in time he swung the bow over, so that

Captain Levi R. Fraser
Courtesy, Mrs. Allan Fraser, Bracebridge

the boat struck the log rather than the rocks, softening the impact. The *Lake Joseph* climbed up on the island and rolled to port, but then the propeller, now in reverse, began to take effect, and after much bumping and rolling she finally slipped back into the water. Incredibly, she had not been damaged. It was an extremely close call.

Captain Fraser has also left an account of the tragic end of the *Lake Joseph*. It happened on a windy, rainy August night in 1899 when the old tug was at work just south of Milford Bay. A fire started in the boiler room, and before the hands could get it out, it spread to the woodpile, filling the room with smoke. The captain cast off the tow and headed the boat toward shore, intending to give the men a hand, but soon the flames were shooting out of all the forward windows. About 30 feet from shore the burning boat grounded. The captain rang the clearance bell for the last time, and the men prepared to abandon ship. The cook led the way with the lifebuoy, and the others followed. Once ashore, the men helplessly watched the old *Lake Jose* burn to the waterline, then wandered through the bush for a few hours until they reached a local home. Here they were given a meal, and later taken to Bracebridge. Andy Boyd had to arrange with the new tannery people to borrow the *Southwood* to tow his logs after that. She became Captain Fraser's new command.

Were all these Muskoka tugs of any real importance? On the local scene, overwhelmingly so: they were essential to most of the District economy. The fact that the tanneries and sawmills depended on them is obvious, and besides all the jobs created by the boats themselves, hundreds more were created by the lakes trade developed by the boats. Thousands of cords of slabwood had to be piled up on the lake shores to fuel the steamers. Thousands more cords of tanbark had to be cut and peeled for the tanneries. This, plus the filling of tourists ice houses, provided work for hundreds of men and horses every winter. The old tugs, in short, did almost all the work that trucks commonly do today, and much more besides. Many of the boats were grimy and poorly maintained by their owners, yet together they once represented a total investment of hundreds of thousands of dollars. Possibly no other inland waterway of comparable size in Canada ever hosted so many workboats.

Not surprisingly, the Navigation Company did not appreciate all these rival tugs which steadily cut deeper and deeper into its towing revenues just at the time that it was also losing so much of the transport business to the railway. During the late 1880s no dividends were issued, and the Company faced an uncertain future. As we have noted, its attempts to expand onto other waterways did not work out very well: the Magnetawan traffic proved disappointing, and the Georgian Bay division, after an excellent start, collapsed by 1893.

It is hard to be objective about what resulted from all this, since events are known only from the viewpoint of A.P. Cockburn, who, whatever his faults, was a plain dealing, honourable gentleman, thoroughly dedicated to the Company that he had founded. Few of his fellow directors devoted much time to Company affairs, and the President, J.S. Playfair, was seldom seen in Muskoka. Thus Mr. Cockburn was in a class by himself on the Board, and, human nature being what it is, perhaps we should not be surprised to find resentment and jealousy of the Manager, especially since Cockburn had more than once committed the unforgivable sin of knowing better than the others. He had urged acceptance of the Booth contract on Lake Nipissing. He had pleaded for a more vigorous policy on Georgian Bay at a time when such a policy might have saved the Company's business there. On both occasions his pleas had been disregarded, and both times it had cost the Company dearly. No wonder, then, that when the Manager was proved right, some members of the Board were disposed to blame him for everything that went wrong.

Early in 1891, for the first time since the Company was formed, Mr. Cockburn was taken ill and was bedridden with a severe attack of influenza. This seemed like a good time for his enemies to strike. A conspiracy involving the President, J.S. Playfair, the Secretary-Treasurer, Alexander Link, and one of the Company directors, was soon afoot to have him accused of incompetence and summarily ejected from his post. This fresh source of alarm probably did not speed the Manager's recovery very much, but it aroused his ire, and he struggled for all he was worth to retain his position, feeling, as he did, that he himself was "the truest and most valuable friend the Company possessed". On the basis of the available evidence, one is not inclined to argue with that assessment. Mr. Cockburn had devoted 25 of his 54 years to the Company's well being, despite intense worries, hard work and low pay. He was, in fact, its soul. After a severe struggle he succeeded in holding his own, and largely recovered his health, while Alexander Link resigned as Secretary-Treasurer. The following year, as if to justify Mr. Cockburn, a dividend — the first in six years, albeit a small one — was declared, and in the years that followed they kept appearing, rising to five, six, eight, and eventually ten per cent. The ordeal, however, probably undermined the Manager's sturdy constitution, and no doubt shortened his life. One wonders why he did not use his power as majority shareholder to get rid of his detractors once and for all.

How did the Navigation Company manage to retrieve its losses over those difficult years? The answer lay in the expanding passenger and freight business engendered by the tourist industry in Muskoka. The tourist trade had never ceased to grow since the early 1880s, and during the 1890s the advent of industrialism in the United States and to a lesser extent in Canada, concentrating corporations and capital in the cities, gave tourism an added impetus. The City of Toronto, for example, had 100,000 people in 1881, but this figure doubled over the next decade, and many of the new city-dwellers yearned for the occasional visit to the more congenial countryside. Hitherto it had largely been well-to-do Americans who flocked to Muskoka for sport, fresh air, and a chance to "get back to Nature". Now Canadians were also getting in on the act. On July 17, 1890, the Toronto Daily Star observed that

> .. now regions are being opened up .. and new treasures of forest and stream are laid bare for gun and rod. Those fields were formerly left to Americans of means, but this year Canadians themselves are becoming alive to the facilities of enjoyment that lie ready to their hands, and with increasing leisure they have begun to take advantage of them.

The Maplehurst Hotel, near Rosseau.
The S.S. "Nipissing" is in the foreground.

All this, despite the generally depressed state of the economy in both countries. In 1883 Muskoka had about fifteen hotels and summer boarding houses around the lakes. Several more had been built since, including Ernescliffe House, founded by Alfred Judd of Juddhaven on Lake Rosseau; the Maplehurst (near Rosseau) in 1886; the Fife House, built at Windermere in 1888; Wingberry House, opened at Mortimer's Point around 1892; and the Milford Bay Temperance Hotel, built by the Strouds about the same time. The splendid Elgin House, on Lake Joseph near Port Sandfield, also started to emerge in 1893. Its founder, Lambert Love, was another settler who had discovered that there was more money in entertaining summer visitors than in ploughing among the pine stumps. Over the years the Elgin House has grown to huge proportions, and today it is the largest surviving resort on the lakes and still doing well. In September, 1892, the Huntsville Forester claimed that railwaymen, hotel men and steamboat men were all in agreement that 1892 had been the best tourist season on record. Business was good at Rosseau, Ferndale, Clevelands House, Bala, Beaumaris, Milford Bay, Stanley House and Port Cockburn. Only Windermere business declined because of overcrowding the previous season, a problem that was already being rectified. It may be that the stock market panic of 1893 caused some interruption to this trend, but if so, it proved only temporary.

Several of the resorts began to acquire their own steam yachts as added attractions for their guests. Such craft could be used for picnics and pleasure cruises, or for towing fishermen in rowboats to their favourite fishing-spots. In a pinch, they could also ferry guests to and from Muskoka Wharf. Charles Vanderburgh was one of the first to obtain a yacht when he imported the trim little *Kate Murray* for his Vanderburgh House at Port Carling in 1878. In 1884 Hamilton Fraser of the Summit House, Port Cockburn, followed suit by purchasing the 47.2-foot steam-launch *Onaganoh* (12.74 tons) from Kingston. The *Onaganoh*, which had her own private boathouse, served as an adjunct to the Summit House for over 20 years, and would often accompany the *Nipissing* or the *Kenozha* down the lake from their overnight berth at Port Cockburn. In 1889 Enoch Cox of Port Sandfield imitated Fraser and bought the steamer *Edith May* from his son-in-law, Captain Rogers. The *Edith*

The Milford Bay House, Milford Bay
Courtesy, Archives of Ontario Acc 9939

The Elgin House, Lake Joseph

Steam Yacht "Onaganoh", at Port Sandfield.
Prospect House is in the background.

Steam Launch "Flyer", Circa 1910.

Str. "Edith May" at Port Sandfield.
Prospect House is in the background.
Courtesy, Archives of Ontario S. 1876

May remained with the Prospect House until 1896, when she was sold and converted into a supply boat. For some years afterward, the hotel engaged Captain Rogers' last steam vessel, a beautiful 39.2-foot launch called the *Flyer* (3 tons) for the benefit of its guests. The *Flyer* was built at Kingston in 1892, and was apparently so named because she could reach the amazing speed of sixteen miles per hour. She lasted for about a quarter of a century, until destroyed by fire. This by no means completes the list. Other hotels often chartered steam yachts for their patrons, or arranged excursions on the ships of the Navigation Company.

Encouraged by the upward trend in freighting and tourism, and noting the downward trend in towing, the Navigation Company itself was having alterations made to the steamer *Muskoka*. Sometime during the 1880s the old tug evidently had an extra cabin added to the bridge, plus a hurricane deck covering both the new cabin and the pilot house, making her look quite unusua. In 1893 the second deck was extended the full length of the vessel, the bow enclosed, and the upper deck cabin rebuilt. These changes greatly increased her interior space. Very shortly afterwards she was entirely enclosed between decks, and began to look more like her sister ships. In 1895 the upper deck cabins were again rebuilt, and the pilot house raised to the hurricane deck. Over the winter of 1897-98, as ever-increasing demands were being placed on her carrying capacity, the old *Muskoka* was drydocked and lengthened some sixteen feet at the stern (from 94 feet to 110), and for good measure she was also given a new boiler, purchased from the Grand Trunk Railway. This not only increased her speed from eight to twelve miles per hour, but also left her with far more space on the main deck, since the new boiler fitted in underneath it. Her upper deck was fitted out with a handsome new lounge cabin. By June she was ready to resume her runs between Bracebridge and Bala, as a regular passenger steamer. Registered now at 133.78 tons and licensed to carry 200 people, the *Muskoka* no longer bore much resemblence to the original version of 1881. She was not a particularly handsome vessel, but she was still immensely sturdy, with a reinforced bow, and was long considered the safest ship in the fleet.

Leaving daily from the Bracebridge "old wharf" at the foot of Dill Street at 7:00 a.m. (a route she now shared with the *Oriole*), the *Muskoka* was a familiar sight around Bracebridge for several years, banging her way through the logs both ways and wooding up from a huge stockpile of slabwood maintained downriver near "the Cut". Long after her timbers rotted away at the Gravenhurst dockyards, people would fondly recall watching her come quietly chugging home in the moonlight once her daily runs were through, the cabins dimly lit by coal oil lanterns.

By 1892, with its fortunes now clearly on the upswing, the Company soon perceived that four passenger ships were not going to be sufficient for the upcoming season, and resolved to build a new steamer for 1893. This was the stately *Medora*, a screw driven vessel registered at 202.99 tons. Slightly smaller than the *Nipissing*, the *Medora* was 122.6 feet in length at the waterline and 25.4 in beam — about the maximum the old lock-chamber at Port Carling could handle — and was powered by a single 29.06 hp. fore and aft compound engine. She was also the first composite steamer in the Muskoka fleet; which is to say that she had a wooden hull built around a steel frame. One long time officer with the Company, the late Captain Reg Leeder, once remarked to this writer that the *Medora* was "the most ocean-liner-like of all the Muskoka steamers."

The *Medora* was launched one rainy day in June 1893 at the Mickle and Dyment lumber dock near Muskoka Wharf. A large crowd of school children and their teachers had been let out for the day to watch as Miss Medora Playfair, for whom the vessel was perhaps named, broke the customary bottle of champagne over her bow. According to the late Captain Wesley Hill, who witnessed the event, the new steamer managed to get stuck on the ways while sliding into the water, but with the help of a cable and engine from Muskoka Wharf she was soon safely floating. That was not the last of her troubles during trials, however. On her maiden trip up Muskoka Bay on June 28th., she proceeded only a short distance when the wheelsman felt a slight jolt at the stern, after which the propeller failed to get any purchase. A block of timber caught under her hull during the launching had worked its way

S.S. "Muskoka" (Second Version) at the Canal at Port Sandfield.

S.S. "Muskoka" (Second Version) at Port Cockburn.

S.S. "Muskoka" (Third Version) near Torrance, Ca. 1893.
Courtesy, Mrs. Gertrude Johnston, Torrance

S.S. "Muskoka" (Fourth Version)

S.S. "Muskoka" (Fifth Version)

Crew of the S.S. "Muskoka", Circa 1894.

Launching of the S.S. "Medora" at Gravenhurst (June 1893).

S.S. "Medora" (Original Version)
Courtesy, Port Carling Pioneer Museum

loose and broken the screw. There was nothing to do but to tow the disabled ship back to the marine railway and order new blades. After this unlucky start, the *Medora* soon proved a most valuable addition to the fleet.

The new steamer commanded by Captain Bailey, was at once assigned the Lake Joseph route, plying from Port Cockburn to Gravenhurst and back, while the *Nipissing* was shifted to the Rosseau run. Both vessels would usually rendezvous at Port Carling with the *Kenozha*, coming north from Gravenhurst to the upper lakes, while the *Muskoka* and *Oriole* now looked after Bracebridge and the ports on Bala Bay. During the off-seasons, when there was much less traffic, the *Medora* and *Nipissing* would be tied up, leaving the smaller steamers to take over, with curtailed service. Trying to please all the lakeside communities was almost impossible, since each felt it deserved calls at least three times a day, with good connections to all other places. In July of 1888 the 'Muskoka Herald' complained harshly that Bracebridge was being short-changed by the Navigation Company, which was running daily visits by the *Oriole*, *Muskoka* and *Rosseau*, which the editor felt was not enough. (The Bracebridge 'Gazette' was more understanding, noting that the west sides of the lakes were also clamouring for better service.)

Sometimes, despite the best will in the world, cruise arrangements could backfire. On August 16, 1888, the Bracebridge Masonic Order was planning to take a cruise to Bala on the *Muskoka*, but on the appointed day, which was drizzling rain, the crowd learned that the *Muskoka* would not be coming; only the tannery steamer *Rosseau*, which was too small to carry everyone. Many were bitterly disappointed, although the *Rosseau* managed to take some of them downriver to Alport for a picnic and a game of baseball, by which time the weather had improved. Two weeks later, A.P. Cockburn formally apologized in a letter to the press, explaining that a group in Windermere had placed a prior request for a cruise that same day, that the *Kenozha* had been busy, and that consequently one party or the other had to be denied. Cockburn also reminded his readers that he had warned the organizers that the *Muskoka* might not be available, and that they should keep the *Rosseau* on standby, just in case. Compounding the mess, the Company manager had been called away to Penetanguishene the day before, and by the time he returned it was all over. Whether or not his readers were mollified is impossible to say. Just a few weeks later, the 'Herald' damned Mr. Cockburn again for cancelling another cruise to Bracebridge set for August 30th., omitting to mention that fog was the reason for the cancellation, or that Cockburn had wired Bracebridge as soon as it was evident that the cruise could not be held.[4]

Sometimes cruises could be complicated by other factors. On Dominion Day, 1893, several hundred Bracebridge residents joined the Order of Foresters for a grand excursion to Port Sandfield. The weather was lovely, the food excellent, and there was a good band along. The problems were with the boats. First, the *Medora* was still tied up with a broken propeller, and since the *Nipissing* was busy, the Company sent both the *Muskoka* and the *Kenozha* to pick up the crowds. Then the troubles started. The *Kenozha* somehow broke two propeller blades at Gravenhurst, and consequently made a very slow trip to Port Sandfield, where she underwent repairs. The *Muskoka* did better at first, leaving Port Sandfield at 3:30 p.m., but upon reaching the Muskoka River her rudder broke, and her passengers didn't make it home until shortly before midnight. The *Kenozha* in turn was not ready to leave Port Sandfield until 6:00 p.m., and her patrons did not fare much better. Everyone voted the outing a great success — except for the amount of time they had spent on the boats.

A really horrible mixup on August 2, 1897 left scores of people fit to be tied. The occasion was a grand regatta being held up at Rosseau, at which crowds converged from all the towns and resorts around the lakes and some even came from Toronto. This involved a lot of improvised scheduling, which to be effective, demanded close co-operation among the steamers. The *Kenozha* was instructed to take some of the crowds to Rosseau in the morning, while the *Nipissing* was to remain above the Port Carling locks in case the *Kenozha* could not handle the rush. As it happened, the *Nipissing* failed to connect at Port Carling, having many calls to make on Lake Rosseau, hence the *Kenozha* locked through and went up to meet her. Near Windermere she joined the *Nipissing* and the *Medora*, both of which were laden with passengers, and the three ships drew alongside for a conference in mid-lake, at which it was

S.S. "Kenozha" (Second Version) at Port Carling.

agreed that the people going to the regatta would be transferred to the *Medora*, while the *Kenozha* would return to Gravenhurst to meet the early afternoon train. The *Kenozha* was then to return to Port Carling by 5:00 p.m. to connect with the *Medora* (which would head back to Port Cockburn), and later the smaller ship would return again to Port Carling to meet the *Nipissing* and collect the southbound passengers who would be leaving the regatta in the late afternoon. All that was fine, but then A.P. Cockburn was requested to delay the *Medora's* departure from Rosseau from 4:00 p.m. to 6:00 p.m., so that the spectators wouldn't miss anything. Accordingly he wired the *Kenozha* not to wait at Port Carling, but to meet the *Medora* later on, near Windermere. Instead of doing so, the *Kenozha* headed off to Lake Joseph for some reason, ignoring whistle signals from the *Medora* to come alongside. The best the *Medora* could do was take her people to Port Carling, where they were left stranded for hours. Eventually the *Oriole* was alerted, and shuttled them as far as Beaumaris, where some of them were again stranded. Some Bracebridge residents did not get home until 1:00 a.m., and others not until 5:00 a.m. They were furious and demanded an explanation. A.P. Cockburn assigned almost all the blame to "the disobedience and bad judgment" of Captain McAlpine of the *Kenozha*, who was demoted for the rest of the season.

Mishaps and accidents to the steamers were a continual problem, though they were generally kept to a minimum by the care and vigilance of the crews. One incident on the Muskoka River on the night of September 11, 1895 nearly ended in disaster. The steamer *Muskoka* was returning to Bracebridge well after dark, when she met the tannery tug *Rosseau* coming downstream, just below town. As the two vessels drew closer and closer together the *Rosseau* swerved away, then blew two toots on her whistle. The *Muskoka* replied and reversed engines, but they were now too close. The *Muskoka* struck the *Rosseau* directly opposite the boiler room, dislocating some of her steam pipes, and the smaller steamer had to be towed back to the tannery dock. She was only slightly damaged, but it was an extremely close call: had the *Muskoka* been going faster, the *Rosseau* would have been cut in half. By the next day the *Rosseau* was back in service again.

S.S. "Kenozha" (Second Version, left) & S.S. "Nipissing".

S.S. "Nipissing" at a private dock.

S.S. "Nipissing"

S.S. "Oriole" (Original Version)

Another encounter, on the foggy night of June 30, 1889, ended in tragedy. The steamer *Oriole*, then under Captain McAlpine, was pushing through flood wood near the Gravenhurst Narrows around 12:30 a.m., when the skipper spotted what looked like a clump of debris directly in his path. Then he realized that it was a small boat full of people, who in their excitement had turned across his bow. He rang for reverse and swerved to starboard, but it was too late, and the steamer cut partway through the little boat, spilling its occupants into the water. The steamer's crew threw life preservers to them and managed to rescue four adults and one child, but two women and one little girl disappeared from sight. The *Oriole* continued searching for the bodies until 3:00 a.m., but then the crew decided they could do no more. By the next morning there were nearly 40 boats from Gravenhurst engaged in the search. Two bodies were recovered. Captain McAlpine was much upset by the tragedy, but in a sense he made up for it (if he was to be considered blameworthy at all) when as Master of the *Kenozha* on the morning of July 30, 1901, he promptly and speedily came to the rescue of a sailboat that had capsized on Lake Rosseau, picking up all six of its occupants safely. The grateful sailors afterwards presented him with a pair of binoculars in appreciation.

A never-ending nuisance to the navigators continued to be floating logs. In 1891, some 23,000,000 feet of timber were sent down the south branch of the Muskoka River alone, and often a steamer would be delayed for hours trying to reach Bracebridge — or worse, would break a propeller trying to bump her way through the logs. The Indian River to Port Carling was frequently just as bad. Interestingly enough, the Town of Bracebridge, rather than the Navigation Company, seems to have led the fight to keep navigation clear on the Muskoka River, since her merchants stood to lose a great deal if provisions were not delivered, or, more importantly, if tourists were prevented from reaching town on the boats.

In 1892, matters came to a head. Warned by A.P. Cockburn in the spring of that year that the river was low, and that logs might prove unusually troublesome, the Mayor, James Dollar (himself a lumberman), agreed to go to Ottawa and talk with the Minister of Marine and the Minister of Justice. When he returned in May it was to report that both gentlemen were agreed that nobody had the right to obstruct navigation on the Muskoka River, and that the Government would take action if there were any more complaints from Bracebridge. Much of the abuse was aimed at Charles Mickle, of Mickle and Dyment, who was running a goodly portion of the offending logs. It was sometimes argued that there would be fewer problems if the logs were bagged directly below the timber slides at Bracebridge and Muskoka Falls, but the lumbermen preferred to let the logs float free downriver and boom them at the estuary, which was where so many of the problems with the passenger steamers took place. For his part, Mr. Mickle, who was an affable civic-minded man, had no personal desire to create difficulties for the boatmen. He suggested that the steamers should use the cut at the river mouth, leaving the main channel for the river drivers. The cut, however, was no longer deep enough for the Navigation Company ships, nor did the authorities feel much inclination to redredge the passage just to suit Mickle. Furthermore, the Minister of Justice, Charles Hibbert Tupper, had informed Mayor Dollar that the steamers could quite legally cut through the log booms if they found their way blocked.

Charles Mickle; Gravenhurst lumberman.

Sometimes that very thing happened. Once, about the year 1897, Captain Charles Edward Jackson of Gravenhurst, who had recently joined the Navigation Company, was taking the steamer *Muskoka* to Port Carling at the usual time, when he found the river blocked by a huge raft of logs. Angered, the captain came out on deck and shouted to the river drivers that they'd better clear a path for his vessel soon — or else! The lumbermen, in effect, replied by telling Captain Jackson just where they thought he could go, and took their time. Less than a week later, when the captain was again returning to Port Carling, he found another drive of logs obstructing his way to the wharf. This time he threatened to break the boom. The lumbermen laughed at him and dared him to try it. The captain obliged; he reversed engines, then rammed the timbers just where two of the boom logs were chained together, snapping the chain. Then, as the logs rapidly spilled loose, he forced his way through them and reached the wharf. There the crew faced a very angry group of river drivers, and a fight might have broken out, but Captain Jackson reminded the drive foreman that he had warned them to leave a passage clear for the steamers. Threats followed by direct action were something the lumbermen could understand, and after that the captain had much less trouble with log booms blocking the river.

Despite meetings and hearings and inquiries and resolutions, the problem of the logs remained. On June 14, 1898, when the *Medora* and *Kenozha* were engaged to take 700 visitors from Bradford and Newmarket to Bracebridge for a picnic and lacrosse match, A.P. Cockburn himself made special arrangements with Mr. Mickle to make certain that the river would be clear of logs that day. Two years later, on August 18, 1900, a tour by the Minnesota Editorial Association through the lakes had to be curtailed somewhat, because the *Medora* found her way blocked by a timber raft at the Gravenhurst Narrows. However, in fairness to the lumbermen it should be added that the train from Georgetown was late that day, and no one could have foreseen just when the steamer would be coming.

In 1896 a new period in Canadian history began. On the political scene the Liberals under Wilfrid Laurier were swept into power in Ottawa with a comfortable majority, ending eighteen years of increasingly moribund Conservative rule. The new government speedily tackled the nation's problems with vigour and enthusiasm. At the same time the depression of the nineties lifted, business revived, new immigrants were soon pouring into the prairies, transforming them into one of the world's great bread-baskets, and a new wave of transcontinental railway fever was gripping the country. In London, Queen Victoria was celebrating her Diamond Jubilee, the British Empire seemed mightier than ever, and all those benighted souls not fortunate enough to be counted as British subjects were only to be pitied for it. Progress seemed inevitable and irreversible: telephones and electric lighting were coming in; anything appeared possible. Amid so many opportunities, and so few doubts, no wonder people felt optimistic. Nowhere, perhaps, did this new buoyant mood find greater expression than in Muskoka, but before we carry on with that portion of our story, let us pause for another look at the lakes of North Muskoka.

FOOTNOTES

[1] Captain Morrison was tragically killed by a train near Utterson in January 1904.
[2] In 1905 the *Comet* nearly went to the bottom of Lake Muskoka as a result of a collision with the *Southwood* during a picnic at Browning Island. Fortunately, there were no injuries either to the boats or their passengers.
[3] The *Pinafore*'s engine was meanwhile installed in another tug of 1.98 tons called the *Jubilee*, which was built for a merchant in Port Carling in 1887.
[4] It might be noted that the 'Muskoka Herald' was then an ardently Conservative newspaper.

Captain Charles Edward Jackson

Crew of the S.S. "Muskoka", Circa 1894.

S.S. "Gem" on Mary Lake (Second Version).

CHAPTER 11
Rise of the Huntsville Navigation Company
(1886-1906)

We left the North Muskoka Lakes in 1886, just when the navvies were busy ballasting the new railway line through the region. At that time there were only two steamers on the Huntsville lakes, and two or three more on the Lake of Bays. The former waterway was dominated by Captain Alfred Denton, who had pioneered by building the steamer *Northern* at Port Sydney in 1877. In 1884 the captain consolidated his position further by arranging to build at Huntsville, a second, smaller screw steamer called the *Florence*, primarily to carry passengers. The *Florence* was 54 feet in length, registered 5.73 tons, and is said to have had one deck, a small rectangular wheelhouse, a large bank cabin behind it, a short stack and a round fantail stern. She had a single high-pressure engine, built in 1880 and capable of generating 2.94 hp. Her master was the amiable Captain Lorenzo McKenny, who had been working for Captain Denton since 1879 and continued to do so until failing health forced him to retire around 1895.

In 1886 the long-expected railway extension came through, though not without a great deal of controversy over its projected route. At one point the line was expected to go through Parry Sound and north past Georgian Bay, and even after the more easterly inland route was adopted, there was still a lot of bitter wrangling as rival communities sought to entice the tracks their way. There was a serious struggle between Port Sydney and Utterson over the issue, and an even more bitter contest between Huntsville and Hoodstown as to which would become the focal point for all of north Muskoka. Having decided the former case in favour of Utterson, the railway planners at first appeared to favour Hoodstown, which was on a fairly direct line to the Magnetawan country — to the extent of actually surveying a line through the budding village. In the end, however, it was decided that Huntsville made a better sawmill centre, and besides, Dr. F.P. Howland was throwing his very formidable weight, both political and physical (he weighed 300 lbs!) behind the claims of Huntsville. Thus Huntsville secured both the honour and the benefits; furthermore, it was the only point on the waterway where the railway tapped the lakes.

The chosen route had momentous consequences on the local scene. Port Sydney lost forever its only chance of becoming one of the really important towns in the District, like Gravenhurst or Bracebridge, although it eventually achieved the status of an incorporated village in 1934. In retrospect, though, its people today are probably thankful that the railway did not pass through their little community, disturbing the quiet of its scenic charm. Ironically, the failure of the railway to touch Port Sydney probably helped keep it alive as a steamer port. Had the line gone through both Port Sydney and Huntsville, there would have been no further need for a boat service between the two places. As for Utterson, one is tempted to speculate that this little hamlet would have lost its raison d'être and disappeared from the map, had it not been on the railway. Today, of course, it no longer has a station, and only the occasional summer train stops there.

Unlike Port Sydney, Hoodstown lost everything when the railway bypassed it. Once its people realized that fact, they began drifting away; some of them to Huntsville. A fire which destroyed its sawmill and several of its homes only hastened the decline. By 1891, so few residents remained that the post office was closed, and Captain Hood was forced to give up his dream of a prosperous town at the site and return to Toronto. In time, nothing remained except the bridge, and today there is only one permanently occupied residence on the old Hoodstown property. It has become Muskoka's most celebrated ghost town.

S.S. "Northern" with passengers.
Courtesy, Mr. George Johnson, Port Sydney

Vernon River at Huntsville, Ontario Circa 1896.
S.S. "Empress Victoria" rounding the bend.
Courtesy, Archives of Ontario Acc. 9939

What Hoodstown lost, Huntsville gained. The latter community was now confirmed as the hub of all the local lakes and a major transshipping centre. In recognition of the new state of affairs, the steamer *Northern* at once made Huntsville its new home port, and was soon connecting with the local trains. Huntsville also became a major lumber town: in no time at all it had three new sawmills on the Vernon River or Hunter's Bay, collectively employing 250 men and cutting up to 160,000 feet of lumber every day. Soon there were six mills in town, plus several new stores and hotels. Huntsville was now exporting huge quantities of lumber, railway ties, pulpwood, cordwood, tanbark and shingles. After 1890, sole leather was added to this list when the Shaw family arrived to open their tannery. By 1896 the Huntsville tannery was reckoned to be the second largest in Ontario. As early as 1886 the thriving community was formally incorporated as a village, with a population of 400. By the turn of the century, that figure had swollen to 2,000. Today the Town of Huntsville is the most populous in Muskoka.

Little is known of the day-to-day operations of the Huntsville steamers during the 1880s, but we can surmise what they could have been. The *Northern* continued to carry freight and passengers to various points on Fairy Lake, and to Port Sydney, and also to Ravenscliffe and Hoodstown, but the Lake Vernon traffic steadily tapered off until the route was abandoned altogether, except by tugs. Of course, there were also huge log drives down the Fox and Big East Rivers, requiring to be boomed and towed into Huntsville, plus cordwood and tanbark to be scowed. We hear of the *Florence* towing on Lake Vernon in May of 1888, and the following year she was also used to restock the lakes with fingerlings from the Newcastle Fish Hatchery. There would also have been recreational cruises at times, but despite the efforts of Captain Denton few tourists were yet attracted to Huntsville.

In 1890 the captain decided to build his third steamer, a 65-foot screw vessel launched at Huntsville in May of that year. He called her the *Erastus Wiman*, in honour of the co-founder of the Dwight-Wiman Sporting Club, some of whose members had been coming annually to the Lake of Bays to hunt and fish since 1863. (He may have wished he had chosen another name, when in 1894 the controversial Mr. Wiman made headlines by being sent to Sing Sing for forgery!) Listed at 36 tons, the *Erastus Wiman* was licensed for 34 passengers, and apparently assumed most of that portion of the business. The *Northern* meanwhile spent her last few years as a tug. She is last listed in 1893, and there is no record of her being in commission after that time. A few older residents of Huntsville still recall seeing the hulk of the old sidewheeler, dismantled down to the main deck and stripped of everything of value, sunk in shallow water next to the Fairy Lake dock, just east of town. The remains are still there.

While Captain Denton was consolidating control of the boat business on the Huntsville lakes, another individual was doing the same on the Lake of Bays. George Francis Marsh of Marsh's Falls, near Dwight, was eventually to accomplish for the North Muskoka Lakes what A.P. Cockburn had already done on the lower lakes. In many ways the career of Captain Marsh was to run remarkably parallel to that of Cockburn. Both men were Scottish in background and Presbyterian in religion. Both were born in a semi-pioneer environment in Upper Canada. Both tended to migrate from "civilization" towards the frontier. Both were staunch Reformers in politics. Both became involved for a time in lumbering. Both developed steamboat lines operating on several lakes in conjunction with the railways. Each showed a patient, perservering spirit enabling him to overcome grievous losses and setbacks. They were born and died within a year of each other. There were differences of course. Captain Marsh did not become involved in steamboating until he was 48, nor did he ever take an active part in politics, though he was sometimes invited to do so. The captain's manner was also markedly different from that of the South Muskoka manager. Whereas A.P. Cockburn was very much the affable, cultivated gentleman, Marsh was more like a labour foreman, husky, rugged, outspoken and used to giving orders, yet good-humoured and genial. Whereas A.P. Cockburn liked to devote his leisure hours to reading and study, Marsh was quite at home in a machine shop. Traits of character that the two men shared were unfailing integrity, a strong sense of public spirit, and tireless energy. Both lived long enough to accomplish their respective life-work.

S.S. "Erastus Wiman".
A reconstruction, based on two half-tone photographs in the Toronto *Mail*, July 9, 1892.

Captain George Francis Marsh,
founder of the Huntsville Navigation Company.

Captain Marsh's Sawmill, Marsh's Falls (1900).

George Francis Marsh was born at Richmond Hill, Ontario, on March 16, 1838, and spent his earliest years there. Having a certain flair for business, he took on a number of enterprises in Cannington, Woodville and Bolsover. For a time he also worked as a conductor on the Toronto and Nipissing Railway, which was completed from Toronto to Coboconk in 1872. Conceivably, he may have met A.P. Cockburn at some point when the latter was still living at Kirkfield. What is certain is that Marsh paid a visit to Muskoka in 1873, accompanied by Cockburn. The following year he was back, this time with his family. They settled initially at Baysville, where they cleared some land and did a little farming and lumbering, besides building a wharf and storehouse. Before long, however, the Marshes moved again, up to the Oxtongue River in Franklin Township, where Mr. Marsh bought a block of land and the water power rights at the Oxtongue Falls, now known as Marsh's Falls. By 1878 he had a sawmill erected, and was doing a thriving business selling lumber to the local settlers. Nearby stood his home, which eventually boasted bay windows and a lath and plaster coating.

George Marsh was not content just to be a lumber merchant. Steamboating was beckoning as an additional prospect. Perhaps Marsh was hoping to expand his lumber business by acquiring a tug. Perhaps he had become dissatisfied with the service and fares charged by Captain Joseph Huckins, who had hitherto monopolized the boat business on the Lake of Bays. Whatever his motives, over the winter of 1883-84 Marsh and his three sons laid the keel for their first steamboat at the mill yards at Marsh's Falls. The new vessel was 68 feet in length by 15.6 in beam, and when completed totalled 43.27 tons, more than any earlier steamer on the Lake of Bays. Building such a craft in such a remote location posed formidable difficulties. According to local stories, the engine and boiler had to be hauled on sleighs during the dead of winter from Bracebridge to Baysville, and thence across the ice to the head of the lake. Two teams of horses were required to move the boiler. The launching took place in the spring, and we may imagine that Mrs. Marsh was given the honour of breaking the bottle. after all, the new boat bore her name, Mary Louise. The *Mary Louise* was a sturdy vessel with a 30-hp. engine, two decks and a round stern. She did not get a protective hurricane deck until 1895.

S.S. "Mary Louise".
Captain Marsh's first steamboat, on the Lake of Bays.
Courtesy, Mr. John Baker, Rockwynn

Her launching was bad news for Captain Huckins, who had just completed his own new steamer, *Excelsior*, at Baysville. We do not know the details of what followed, but probably there was a rate war between the two steamers, which must have been injurious to both of them. Captain Huckins had the advantage of operating two boats (the *Excelsior* and *Helena*) from the port of Baysville, which was then the gateway to the Lake of Bays. Yet within two years it was he who had to call quits. In October of 1885 he "sold" the *Excelsior* to the Doty Engineering Works in Toronto, to whom he had mortgaged it in order to pay for the engine, and left the District. The Doty Company in turn resold the steamer in 1886, but the new owners kept her only one season before selling her to Captain Marsh. With the *Helena* apparently gone, Marsh now controlled the boat business on the Lake of Bays. By 1888 he was using the *Excelsior* primarily as a towboat, while the *Mary Louise* looked after passengers and pleasure cruises, running daily from Baysville. On July 11, 1889, the *Mary Louise*, having just broken a propeller blade on a sunken log at Dwight, also grounded on a sandbar at the Dorset Narrows, and had to be rescued by the *Excelsior*.

The main problem for the Lake of Bays region was still its frustrating isolation and remoteness. The nearest railway station, at Huntsville, was about twelve miles away; that at Bracebridge was even further. The local residents obviously wanted improvements in transport facilities, while many outsiders, noting the scenic and timber resources of the area, agreed that this was a potential market of considerable value. How best to exploit it? As early as 1889 there was talk in Bracebridge about building a railway from Muskoka Falls to Baysville, a proposal warmly applauded by Captain Marsh. But this was not the only scheme in contemplation. Huntsville was also eyeing the region as a possible source of trade, and in 1886-88 its chances of building up influence there were greatly increased when the Ontario Government agreed to dredge the marshy creek meandering from Peninsula Lake into Fairy Lake. The task, utilizing the dredge from Lake Nipissing, took about two years, but by 1887 the canal was passable. In August of that year a correspondent reported to the 'Toronto World' that:

At the extremity of Fairy Lake, four miles from Huntsville, the boat arrived at the 'cut', a channel nearly a mile long, which has been deepened by the . . Government at an expense of $25,000, giving boats an access to Peninsula Lake, another turquoise surfaced gem, upon whose north shore is the little village of Grassmere. It cannot fail to be observed of how great a service the little steamers have been in the development of the country, to merchant, farmer and tourist alike, and Captain Denton who has sacrificed much to maintain them, should now be rewarded.

At first glance, the opening of this canal, which added about six more miles to the eastward route of Captain Denton's steamers, seems of trivial importance. Yet its implications were profound. The canal also extended the influence of Huntsville to cover Peninsula Lake, which in turn comes to within a mile of the Lake of Bays. If that one-mile gap could be overcome in some way, preferably by something better than a dirt road, then Huntsville, through its steamers, could more or less add the whole Lake of Bays region, including the four townships fronting on it, to its "territory". Already Huntsville interests were contemplating a second canal across the Portage to the Lake of Bays. Such an undertaking, though, was not as simple as it sounds, because the Lake of Bays happens to be over 100 feet higher than Peninsula Lake. Bracebridge partisans naturally pooh-poohed the idea of a "ditch" across the Portage and continued to press for a railway to Baysville. As it turned out, neither scheme ever came to fruition, but in the end Huntsville was to emerge the victor in the struggle for the Lake of Bays.

Hitherto the Huntsville steamers and the Lake of Bays steamers had been operating strictly separately, and thus there was no cause for a quarrel between them. Possibly there was even a degree of co-operation after Captain Denton's steamers began to ply on Peninsula Lake: he may have arranged an interlocking schedule with Captain Marsh's boats across the Portage. Amicable relations, however, depended on neither the Marsh nor the Denton interests trying to invade the other's territory. Such an incursion by either side could only spell war.

Within just a few years, war broke out. From the record it is impossible to say who started it, or when. All we know is that by 1891 the *Florence* had been moved across the Portage to the Lake of Bays, where she began taking passengers in competition with the *Mary Louise*. By 1892 the *Excelsior* had been transferred to the Huntsville lakes to compete with the *Northern* and *Erastus Wiman*. On August 12, 1892, the Lindsay 'Canadian Post' speaks of the *Excelsior* racing from Huntsville to the Portage in the record time of 40 minutes with two surgeons aboard to save the life of a man critically injured by a circular saw at the Portage sawmill.

Captain Alfred Denton.
Founder of the Huntsville Steamer Service.
From a photograph published in the Toronto *Mail* July 9, 1892

By that time the battle for the lakes was already near its height. Captain Marsh summoned reinforcements by importing another steamer, the *Lady of the Lake*, from Lake Muskoka. The *Lady of the Lake* was a former supply-boat, originally built near Bala in 1886. She was 49.6 feet in length, registered 7.04 tons, and in general was very similar to the *Florence*.[1] She, too, was added to the Huntsville route. The pressure on Captain Denton was intensifying. In November of 1893 Captains Denton and McKenny found themselves being prosecuted for violating certain sections of the Steamboat Inspection Act, apparently following accusations by Captain Marsh. They were found guilty and fined $90.00 plus costs. Denton retaliated the following summer by complaining that Marsh had illegally used the *Lady of the Lake* and a scow to take some passengers to the Portage: she was not licensed for that. This time Captain Marsh ended up paying $50.00 with costs.

By 1893 Captain Denton's position was weakening, and in the spring he found it expedient to sell the *Florence* to Newton Langford of Baysville, a venturesome speculator who was always ready to dabble in something new. (Langford kept the vessel for only two years.) At the end of the 1893 season the old *Northern* apparently completed her last trip. This left Captain Denton with only the *Erastus Wiman*, which he continued to operate between Huntsville and the Portage, and also on picnics and pleasure cruises, during the season of 1894. But the end of the struggle was close at hand. In the spring of 1895 Denton sold the *Erastus Wiman* to his rival and left for Rat Portage, now the Town of Kenora. Subsequently he returned to Huntsville, where he engaged in building wharves and other public works, and for a time ran the Fairy Glen Tourist Resort. But his days as a steamboat captain were over.

Captain Marsh had emerged the victor in the contest to control the North Muskoka Lakes, but not without troubles of his own. In 1894 he had arranged to import a small steam-yacht called the *Zetta Bruce* from the Kawartha Lakes to supplement his fleet, but the yacht burned at Lindsay before she could be taken north. By an odd coincidence, on the same day as the *Zetta Bruce* fire (April 18, 1894) he also lost the *Excelsior* at Huntsville.

The largest steamer on the Huntsville lakes, the *Excelsior*, had left her winter quarters at the Fairy Lake locks early that year to resume her duties of freighting and towing. She was at the Huntsville wharf at mid-day between trips, without a head of steam up, when disaster struck. Uptown, behind Harry A. May's hardware store, someone was carelessly burning rubbish close to the shed containing several drums of coal oil. The coal oil ignited and burst into flame, setting the nearest stores ablaze. Rivers of burning kerosene ran down the streets and alleys, spreading the fire to other stores, which, built mostly of wood, burned like tinder. Even worse, there was a wind to fan the flames. The fire brigades of Gravenhurst and Bracebridge answered the call for help, but they arrived too late. Altogether 35 businesses were burned out in Huntsville that day, entailing losses then estimated at $100,000.

As palls of smoke rose over the community and a series of explosions shook the downtown area, a few of the merchants hastily secured permission to load some of their merchandise on board the *Excelsior*, which appeared to be in no danger. Then, amid the alarm and confusion, someone noticed that burning coal oil was running down a drain towards the river. Quickly the steamer was cut loose and pushed away. She drifted out onto Hunter's Bay, away from the fire, which was now blazing partly on the water surface, but then the eddies in the river slowly carried her back, right into the holocaust. She burned to the waterline, along with all the goods stowed aboard. The loss appeared total, but Captain Marsh, refusing to consider himself licked, made plans to rebuild. Within weeks he had a team of shipwrights at work on the vessel, but for the balance of the summer the boat-service was curtailed.

By September, the new ship was ready, and by common agreement she was quite a beauty, easily the finest ever seen at Huntsville. Framed with tamarack, she was 76 feet in length by 17 in beam, and listed at 72.23 tons, considerably more than the old *Excelsior*. She was powered by a rather noisy Doty high-pressure engine, and could go about fourteen miles per hour, if necessary with only three men to crew her. On September 14, 1894, the Huntsville Forester reported that the new steamer *Empress Victoria* had completed her

S.S. "Excelsior" (1894).
The only known photo of the "Excelsior", showing her just after the fire of April 18th.

maiden trip to the Portage on the 10th., and was now plying daily, although the hurricane deck was still unfinished. Within a few more weeks she was formally certified as Class A, and licensed for 300 passengers. For the next ten years she was, in name as well as fact, the queen of the North Muskoka Lakes.

The *Empress Victoria* arrived too late to do much business in 1894, but her appearance may have been the last straw in Captain Denton's decision to sell out. The following spring she was back in service, gaily liveried in red, white, blue and black paint, and running regularly to the Portage, usually under the command of Captain Marsh himself. She carried most of the passengers and freight, assisted by the smaller steamer *Erastus Wiman*, which sometimes took the Port Sydney run since the *Empress Victoria* had some difficulty rounding the numerous sharp bends in the North Muskoka River. On May 9, 1895, Captain Marsh took some of the advocates of a proposed electric railway at the Portage on a cruise to Peninsula Lake aboard the *Empress Victoria*, free of charge: the gentlemen were thus given an opportunity to survey the site and take a look around. On June 28th. we find the *Empress Victoria* running a moonlight cruise for the Sons of England, from Huntsville to Port Sydney; on Dominion Day, 1896, Captain Marsh took her downriver to Mary Lake, through the locks and booms and drifting logs, for a mammoth picnic at Port Sydney. A band was aboard, many residents at the Port joined the festivities, and to most people, the only thing wrong with the day was that it was too short. Because of the intricacies of navigation, the *Empress Victoria* had blown her departure whistle at 4:00 p.m. to get her patrons home to Huntsville by 7:00. One week later, the people of Port Sydney had their turn, when the *Erastus Wiman* collected 250 villagers and took them upstream through the locks to Fairy Lake: here the *Empress Victoria* picked them up and ran a cruise to the Portage. However, it required a certain amount of promotion and publicizing, to say nothing of good service, to get people into the habit of taking steamship cruises.

S.S. "Empress Victoria", Docked at Huntsville.

S.S. "Empress Victoria".
Courtesy, Mr. Owen Swann, Huntsville

On the Lake of Bays, the *Empress Victoria* and *Erastus Wiman* ran in conjunction with the *Mary Louise*, which usually sailed every morning from Baysville to the Portage. A local resident named Arthur Osberne ran a stage (actually a democrat with a canvas cover) to complete the connection, but the road was dreadful. Not until July of 1897 was it macadamized, at a cost of $500, allowing the Huntsville Forester to assure its readers that stilts were no longer necessary! Schedules by the steamers were not guaranteed in those days, especially in the spring, since log drives were often known to block the way to the Portage. On the Huntsville side the *Lady of the Lake* and the *Erastus Wiman* did most of the towing, while on the Lake of Bays everything — towing, freighting and passengers — was left to the *Mary Louise*, which was commanded by Captain Marsh's son Fred. In the spring of 1895 the *Mary Louise* was thoroughly overhauled and rebuilt at Baysville, and fitted out with a new hurricane deck. Weeks later, she was towing again for the Gilmour Lumber Company, before resuming passenger runs to Dorset.

One incident around the fall of 1902 helps illustrate the casual informality of the boat service at that time. Mr. W.E. Hutcheson, one of the leading merchants of Huntsville, had left to go hunting near Dorset, intending to return home on the steamers. On the appointed day, his son took the *Empress Victoria* to the Portage to meet him, but upon arrival the elder Hutcheson was not there! Upon crossing the Portage to investigate, the men found the *Mary Louise* docked on the other side, but no Mr. Hutcheson. The crew had forgotten to wait for him at Dorset. Captain Marsh sent the *Mary Louise* back to get him, but she proceeded only a short distance before she encountered a canoe, containing a livid Mr. Hutcheson and his guide. They were picked up, and the *Mary Louise* swung her bow around towards the Portage once again, blowing four whistle blasts as a signal to the *Empress Victoria* to wait. She was still at the portage, and the Hutchesons were able to return home with no further trouble.

S.S. "Mary Louise" at Dorset.

Predictably, Captain Marsh was not permitted to keep the upper lakes all to himself. A few independent operators were building or acquiring steamboats of their own, usually for towing or freighting, seldom for passengers. In 1895 William Sutherland Shaw, manager of the Huntsville tannery, ordered a tug called the *Sylvester* built to scow tanbark to his plant, rather than continuing to rely on Marsh and Denton. The *Sylvester* was 45 feet in length and registered 18.09 tons. She served the tannery for five years, with little trouble worse than that of the night of August 1, 1899, when one of her scows sank while under tow near the Huntsville wharf, forcing her crew to gather up and boom the tanbark the following morning.

Elsewhere, a few more steamers were appearing on the Lake of Bays. In 1889 a pair of Dorset businessmen, dissatisfied with the service their community was getting from Captain Marsh, built a small yacht called the *Swift* to handle freight and passengers. Apparently she was too small to be registered, but old-timers recall her as a 35-foot launch with curtains around the cockpit. She was launched at Dorset, and completed her first trip to Baysville on July 28. Nothing more is heard of the vessel until 1897, by which time she had become the property of James E. Fisher, co-owner of a Huntsville dress goods store. Fisher used the boat to travel to his cottage, on an island in Vernon Lake, and also to take guests on cruises, until about 1902, when she was again sold and spent her remaining years as a tug.

Meanwhile, the old steamer *Florence* was still active on the Lake of Bays. Captain Denton had sold this craft to Newton Langford of Baysville in 1893, and since then she had been used chiefly for log towing. On May 23, 1893, the *Florence* was caught in a violent windstorm on the Lake of Bays and spent two hours bucking four-foot waves. Those on board donned life preservers and wondered if they were all heading for Davy Jones's locker. The same storm carried a large timber raft four miles back towards Dorset and blew away the sign on the Colebridge Hotel. Later, in the fall of 1895 Langford sold the *Florence* to Matthew McCaw of Dorset, who had just imported a steamer to the Huntsville lakes with the idea of establishing his own boat line between Huntsville and Dorset.

McCaw's second steamer was the *Equal Rights*, a 3.90-ton screw yacht imported by rail from Penetanguishene. Old-timers recall her as a "tidy little lady", some 36 feet in length, with a bowsprit and clipper bow, a hinged stack, and a round, fantail stern. Her colour was grey with green trim, and her cabins were trimmed with oak. In September of 1895 McCaw announced that the *Equal Rights* and the *Florence* would carry freight from Huntsville to Dorset for as little as 15¢ per cwt.

The scheme did not prosper. Over the winter of 1895-96 the *Equal Rights* sank at her wharf at Huntsville. Her owner was convinced she was sabotaged, though this proved not to be the case when she was refloated. Nonetheless, she spent the winter on the bottom, and could not be raised until the ice went out. Mr. McCaw gave her a thorough overhaul, adding a new awning and fenders, but he used her for only one more season. In the spring of 1897 she went to Captain William Grieves Robson of Birkendale, a "roustabout" boatman who worked at various jobs on the upper lakes. The transfer did not proceed without an uproar. When Captain Robson came to collect the accessories for the steamer from McCaw's storehouse at the Portage, McCaw accused him of stealing certain items from it. The magistrate hearing the case declared the question insoluble and threw it out of court. McCaw's other steamer, the *Florence*, was likewise sold in March 1897 to Captain Marsh, who had entrusted her to Captain William A. Marsh another of his sons, to tow timber and tanbark, thus taking some of the pressure off the *Mary Louise*.

As for the *Equal Rights*, Captain Robson soon arranged to bring her across the Portage to the Lake of Bays, where he used her to peddle merchandise of all sorts from Dorset, accepting produce or cash in return. Apparently this plan did not pay very well because in 1898 Robson sold the craft to Edward J. Gouldie, who ran the store and post office at Dwight. Dwight was still a very tiny village, but it had a church, school, blacksmith shop and sawmill as well as a cluster of homes, and for a year Mr. Gouldie used the *Equal Rights* to tow and take passengers. He soon discovered, however, that she required a certified captain to carry out all these functions, and the amount of business done did not seem to justify the expense of hiring one. The *Equal Rights* then went to Newton Langford, who now owned a store in Dorset, and for a few more years she was again used as a supply boat. In 1903 she was sold to George Robson, an older brother of Captain Robson and the owner of a small sawmill at Paddle Point, near Birkendale. By that time the Robson family home had developed into the Birkendale summer resort, and between the hotel and the local mills the trim little steamer had plenty of work to do, primarily running excursions. Captain Robson, when not engaged on other boats, frequently resumed command of the vessel for his brother. The *Equal Rights* continued to run until midsummer of 1909, when she burned at Birkendale wharf.

The only other commercial steamboat operating on the North Muskoka Lakes in competition with the Marsh fleet was that of Albert Sydney-Smith, the presiding genius at Port Sydney. Though Utterson was now the central distribution point for the region (thanks to the railway), Port Sydney, despite the occasional fire, had managed to cope with the change quite nicely. The village still had several saw and shingle mills, plus Mr. Smith's gristmill, a number of shops, and two stores, and around the turn of the century it was reckoned to have a population of 215. A new planing mill built in 1897 added further to its prosperity. In the meantime Sydney-Smith had been running a small steamer on Mary Lake for his own and the community's convenience, towing logs and running Sunday School picnics, but the name of the vessel is unknown.

Early in 1897 the residents of Port Sydney decided, as a community co-operative venture, to build a cheese factory beside the river. By July it was turning out about 300 lbs. of cheese every day, and providing an important market for the local farmers' milk. Partly as a result of this development, Sydney-Smith decided to build a new, larger steamboat, whose duties would include gathering cans of milk at all the local landings, as well as towing timber rafts to the various sawmills and running regular market trips to Huntsville. The new steamer was built on skids on the east side of the river, just north of Sydney-Smith's sawmill, close to the spot where the old *Northern* was launched twenty years before. She was supposed to be ready by June, but the work took much longer than expected. Not until July 15th. did she actually hit the waves. She was christened the *Gem*, which seemed oddly comical, since she was a stubby little craft with a distinct tendency to roll as she puffed along. Immediately after the launching, Mr. Smith treated his neighbours to a free cruise around Mary Lake. Shortly afterwards, on August 9th. she ran a complimentary moonlight cruise for the people of Utterson.

S.S. "Gem" (Original Version) approaching Port Sydney.
Courtesy, Mr. George Johnson, Port Sydney

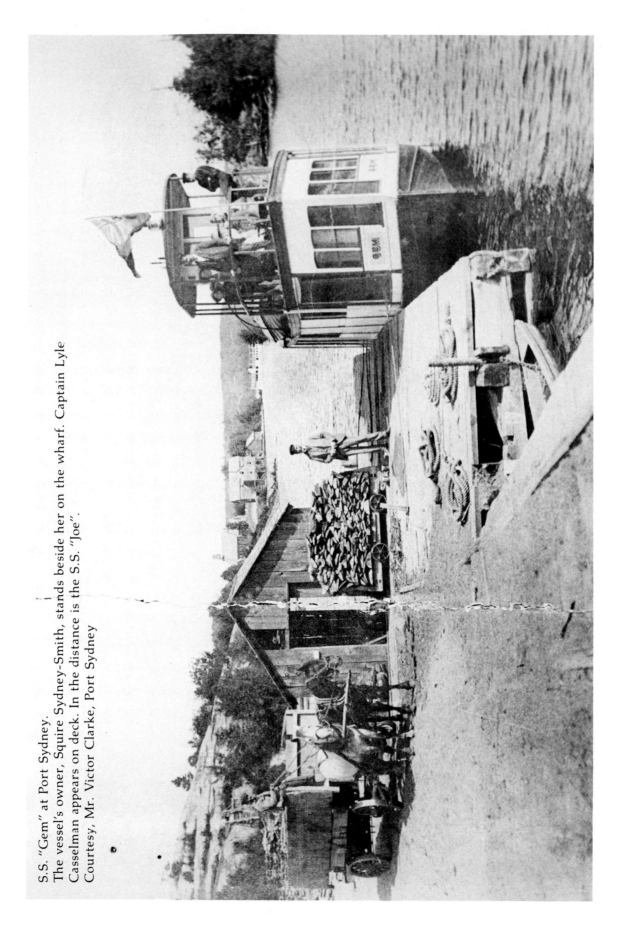

S.S. "Gem" at Port Sydney.
The vessel's owner, Squire Sydney-Smith, stands beside her on the wharf. Captain Lyle
Casselman appears on deck. In the distance is the S.S. "Joe".
Courtesy, Mr. Victor Clarke, Port Sydney

The *Gem* was 35 feet in keel by 10 feet in beam, and registered 6.12 tons. Every Saturday she would take the householders of Port Sydney to Huntsville to do their weekly shopping, departing about 9:00 a.m. and leaving Huntsville around 4:30. The trip generally took about one-and-a-half hours, depending on the number of stops she had to make on the way: passing through the locks alone required fifteen to twenty minutes. On weekdays the vessel combined towing logs, slabs and tanbark into Huntsville or Port Sydney, with collecting cans of milk on alternate days. In 1899 the cheese factory consumed 500,000 lbs. of milk, most of which was transported by the *Gem*. She was also available to run picnics and pleasure cruises, sometimes by moonlight, and as the tourist industry became better established, she was sometimes chartered by the resorts to tour the lakes or attend regattas.

From time to time Sydney-Smith made improvements to his vessel. In the spring of 1900 the *Gem* was fitted out with a new fore-and-aft compound engine to give her greater speed and power. Further improvements followed in 1902. Altogether the *Gem* was to serve for over 30 years and became a regular institution at Port Sydney.

Throughout this period, the lumber trade was busily laying waste the remaining stands of virgin timber in North Muskoka. Most of the industries of Huntsville were then oriented towards the timber trade, including the Huntsville Lumber Company, the Riverside Lumber Company, the Huntsville Planing Company, and the Muskoka Wood Manufacturing Company. The latter firm, organized by R.J. Hutcheson in 1902, once owned or controlled up to seventeen sawmills. Most of these companies ran camps north of Huntsville and floated their logs down the Big East River to Lake Vernon, where the tugs took over. On the Lake of Bays the principal operators were the Shier Lumber Company of Bracebridge and the Mickle-Dyment Company of Gravenhurst, both of which had extensive limits around Kawagama Lake, east of Dorset, and within what is now Algonquin Park. Another firm active in this area after 1890 was the Gilmour Lumber Company, which was now pushing inland nearly 200 miles from its headquarters in Trenton in its continuing search for logs. Establishing a depot at Dorset, the Gilmour Company bought some very desirable timber limits around Canoe Lake — for which it paid dearly — and was then faced with the problem of how to transfer the sawlogs from the Muskoka watershed to the Gull River system, which feeds into the Kawartha Lakes. In 1894-95 the firm tried to solve the problem by building an elaborate set of tramways and steam-powered jackladders to cross the height of land from the Lake of Bays to Raven Lake, but the tramway proved too slow. It could handle only about 15,000 logs per day, and reputedly it took all of the seasons of 1895 and 1896 to move out the cut of 1894. Luckily for Gilmour, however, J.R. Booth of Ottawa built a branch of his private railway, the Canada Atlantic, to Depot Harbour, opposite Parry Sound in 1896; primarily to exploit the pineries of the Nipissing and Parry Sound Districts. The Gilmour Company abandoned the tramway (which collapsed about ten years later) and eagerly came to terms with Booth. Pulling out of Dorset, the firm built a new "town" beside the railway, complete with sidings, a mill, a post office, hospital, warehouses and boarding houses at Mowat, on Canoe Lake . Sixteen years later, after the Gilmour Company itself had gone bankrupt, Mowat became a ghost town.

Life was much the same in all the lumber camps, no matter which company owned them. Lumberjacks often spent months at a time in the bush camps (which they seldom saw in the daytime), and each logger was expected to cut down about 110 trees a day — or be ready to explain to the foreman why he had not! In the spring the logs were sent down the local lakes to the Oxtongue and Hollow Rivers, and thence to the Lake of Bays. There was always intense rivalry among gangs of river drivers, as each company tried to get its logs down to the Lake of Bays first. Fights were frequent, especially at Dorset, where there was plenty of liquor to be had at McIlroy's Hotel. On one occasion when the "river-hogs" were raising an even worse ruckus than usual, the Dorset Council tried swearing in constables to restore order, but "the jacks", getting wind of this, simply grabbed the constables and put them in their own jail.

Getting the logs to the Lake of Bays was only half the battle. There was then the problem of moving them across the lake to Baysville or the Portage. A common technique for moving booms of logs across still water, when tugs were not available, was the process of "warping" them along, using a scow or crib fitted out with a winch and cable, to which an

Gilmour Company Tramway, near Dorset Circa 1894.
Courtesy, Mr. Brad Robinson, Dorset

McKay Sawmill, Dorset, Ontario.
Courtesy, Mr. Brad Robinson, Dorset

Gilmour Company Alligator near Dorset Circa 1896.
Courtesy, Mr. Brad Robinson, Dorset

Steam Alligator "Hamilton H.".
The craft appears above winching herself ashore at Norland, Ontario.
Courtesy, Mr. Verne LeCraw, Norland

anchor was attached. The scow would be propelled ahead of the tow for a half-mile or so, depending on the length of its cable, and the anchor dropped. Then it would return to the tow, playing out the cable as it went. The flukes of the anchor, being at an angle, would always catch on the bottom. A short line would then be attached to the tow, and the crews would reel in the cable by an endless treadmill action, thus winching both the scow and the tow along. Then the process would be repeated. It was gruelling and monotonous work, and if the weather was cold that only made it worse. In time horses were substituted for men, and later steam engines for horses. This led to the invention of the "alligator".

The alligator, or warping tug, was a squat, ugly scow powered by a noisy steam engine and boiler, which were used both to power a pair of paddle wheels and to reel in a cable, but not both together. These craft were sometimes preferred to conventional steam tugs because they were cheap, easy to build, and could move huge quantities of logs. Since they always towed by winching, they were relatively unaffected by head winds and bad weather. They also had the major advantage of being amphibious, which is to say that they could winch themselves overland from one lake to another by anchoring their cables to a tree, hence the name "alligator". Sometimes on an uphill grade, rollers might be placed under the tugs to help them along, and usually the bottoms were protected by skids. Their only drawbacks were that they were very slow and cumbersome. Some could not exceed half a mile an hour while under tow.

The first alligators appeared on the back lakes around 1893. At first they were exceedingly crude, but later models began to exhibit a few refinements, such as protective paddle-boxes, engine room cabins and wheelhouses. For a time a few foundries and factories in Ontario — at Lindsay and Simcoe, for example — even made a specialty of building such craft, which naturally could be transported by rail. Alligators were unknown on the Muskoka Lakes, although we hear of one being built on Pine Lake in 1893 by Francis Baker, owner of one of the Gravenhurst sawmills. The tugs were also a rare breed on the Kawartha Lakes, although relatively common on the small lakes of Haliburton and Nipissing. A few were used on the Magnetawan, and several on the Huntsville lakes: on May 17, 1895, the 'Huntsville Forester' noted that three alligators were then at work near the Portage, having recently been imported by the Gilmour Company.[2]

In 1907 the McCrea foundry of Lindsay received an order for an alligator from the Huntsville Lumber Company and around 1910 the Mickle-Dyment Company would build a huge 'gator, called the *John Bull*, on the Lake of Bays to tow logs to Baysville for itself and the Shier Company: at Baysville, of course, the river drivers would take over.

Meanwhile, with characteristic energy Captain Marsh was busy securing a sizeable share of the towing business for his own steamers. In November of 1899 for example, he obtained a contract from the Shier Company to scow 500,000 feet of lumber from the Portage to the Huntsville station wharf, and managed to get it all done before the winter freeze-up. The tannery was constantly consuming more tanbark, and the captain had to build more and more scows to cope. In 1898, taking a cue from A.P. Cockburn, he decided to expand his operations beyond Huntsville and the Lake of Bays by purchasing an elderly steamboat called the *Enterprise* (99.27 tons) to carry freight and passengers on Lake Simcoe. Marsh believed strongly in the prospects of Lake Simcoe, and dreamed of building a huge palatial excursion steamer on it. For the moment, however, he contented himself with upgrading the *Enterprise*. This venture was probably a mistake. Lake Simcoe lacks the wild, rugged scenery and countless picturesque islands so typical of Muskoka, and consequently it never became much of a resort area. Besides that, there was a fair amount of competition on the big lake from rival steamers, none of which were making very much money. The *Enterprise* struggled along until 1903, but then the leaky old vessel finally gave up the ghost and sank at Barrie. There were no casualties, but the sinking effectively spelled the end of the Lake Simcoe division of the Huntsville Navigation Company.

Until 1896 almost all the summer resorts in Muskoka were on the three lower lakes, but there were a few exceptions: Archie Gouldie had established the Gouldie House at Dwight to cater to campers and sportsmen even before 1884, while the Lake View House had been opened at North Portage, facing Peninsula Lake, as early as 1889. On the Lake of Bays, B.H. Cunnington, an English settler, had been entertaining guests at his home at Port

S.S. "Enterprise", Captain Marsh's only ship on Lake Simcoe.

Cunnington since 1892. All these, however, were mere drops in the bucket. North Muskoka was not yet tourist country, and Captain Marsh demanded to know why it shouldn't be. What did the Muskoka Lakes have that the Huntsville lakes did not?

One answer was immediately evident: superlative railway connections. Since 1888, the Northern Railway system had been absorbed by the Grand Trunk Railway, which thus assumed all rail service through Muskoka. By the 1890s the Grand Trunk was running several passenger trains to Gravenhurst every day during the warm season, but places further north continued to get just one train per day each way. The Huntsville 'Forester' complained repeatedly about this neglect. Over the winter of 1896-97 Captain Marsh continually lobbied the Grand Trunk to extend its "Shoo Fly" trains from Gravenhurst to Huntsville, and appealed to the Huntsville Council for support, which was forthcoming, but the railway declined, alleging that it would not pay. This caused great indignation in Huntsville and led to some nasty insinuations, voiced by the paper that the real reason for the refusal was the G.T.R.'s cozy relationship with the Muskoka Navigation Company, which presumably did not want any competition from Huntsville. Irritated by this accusation, A.P. Cockburn sent a letter of denial to the 'Huntsville Forester' on April 10, 1897. He protested that the above innuendoes were unjust, and that the Muskoka Navigation Company never presumed to tell the Grand Trunk how to run its business. He reminded the editor that the "Muskoka Line" had been luring tourists to the District long before the railway reached Gravenhurst: without the Muskoka steamers there would never have been a significant tourist industry in the region. Cockburn termed Huntsville's drive for tourism "both legitimate and commendable", but he insisted that his Company was not trying to thwart it. He agreed, too, that earlier train arrival times at both Huntsville and Burks Falls would benefit both travellers and boatmen.

Apparently the letter achieved its purpose, because the paper ceased its attacks and A.P. Cockburn remained a popular man around Huntsville. However the problem of unsatisfactory rail accommodation remained. The Grand Trunk might have complained that one of the key requirements to a viable tourist industry — good quality resort hotels — was manifestly lacking around Huntsville, but this situation, fortunately, was starting to change. Encouraged by the example of South Muskoka, where 70 resorts were said to be in business, attracting some 10,000 visitors in 1894, Mr. Charles W. Waterhouse of Aspdin, near Lake Vernon, purchased a fine, elevated property on the north side of Peninsula Lake near the Canal in 1895, and made plans to develop a summer hotel there. Construction began the following April, as soon as it became possible to deliver the first scowloads of building materials. The new hotel, called Deerhurst, was ready in August, and soon the first tourists arrived from Rochester, N.Y. The *Empress Victoria* was calling twice daily, but for the first few years business was slow. Nonetheless, the proprietor persisted, and the advantages of a lovely setting amid shady groves and grassy lawns, combined with fishing, bathing and tennis facilities plus an excellent table, began to have their effect. The new hotel, fortunately, was built at an auspicious moment, just when the depression of the mid-1890s was lifting and the Laurier era was starting. By 1899 Mr. Waterhouse had to turn away some of the crowds flocking to his resort, and by 1900 he took care to improve and enlarge it.

The success of the Deerhurst Hotel triggered a rush of imitators. In the spring of 1899 Mr. Charles J.C. Crump of Fox Point, near Port Cunnington on the Lake of Bays, announced plans to develop another resort, which he christened "Ronville". Work must have proceeded very rapidly, because the hotel was opened that same June. Nestled in a grassy valley at the foot of a lofty, rugged hill, and featuring a 200-yard bathing beach, Ronville boasted acetylene gas lighting, broad verandahs and tasteful furnishings. Soon it was the largest resort on the Lake of Bays, taking 200 guests, even more than Deerhurst. Mr. Crump himself seemed the very image of an English country squire, which in a sense he was, cultivating a farm of 198 acres to supply fresh food for his guests. It is gratifying to be able to state that both Ronville and Deerhurst are very much in business today.

Elsewhere around the lakes, new resorts, large and small, elaborate and simple, were springing up like mushrooms. In 1899, William Hollingshead of Fairy Lake, whose pretty farm had become the scene of several picnics by steamboat over the years, decided to enlarge his premises into a small tourist home, which he called Springfield Farm. Around the same time the Robsons of Birkendale developed their home into another small resort, the Birkendale House. Their neighbour, W.E. Irwin, turned his farm on Ten Mile Bay into the Bay View Villa, which was rechristened "The Hemlocks" in 1901 to avoid confusion with the Bay View Farm, also on the Lake of Bays. In 1900 Louis Keown purchased and rebuilt the Lake View House at North Portage, which he renamed the Hotel La Portage. By 1902 Dorset had two hotels, the Fairview and the Algonquin, soon to be joined by the Alvira House. Nor was Mary Lake forgotten. Before 1901, in response to popular demand, James Jenner and his family replaced their old log farmhouse on the southeast side of the lake with a new hotel, which they called the Clyffe House after a home Mrs. Jenner had known in England. This hotel still stands. Somewhat more celebrated, but much less long-lived, was Grunwald, built on the opposite side of the lake, facing the rising sun, about two miles north of Port Sydney. Opened by William Gall of Huntsville in 1902, Grunwald, with its two distinctive corner towers, was designed to look like a castle in the Black Forest of Germany: the name "Grunwald" in German means "greenwood". This hotel could take 123 guests, and for a dozen years it was the scene of countless concerts, dances and regattas, but during the First World War, when anything even remotely German was distinctly out of favour, Grunwald had to close. Rather mysteriously, on the night following the armistice that ended the War, the hotel burned to the ground.

Many more names could be added to the list: the Riverside Resort at Huntsville (1901), the Belleview Hotel at Port Sydney (1906), Edgemere resort on Mary Lake, plus Sea Breeze near Birkendale, Fox Point Lodge, Port Cunnington Lodge and Point Ideal Lodge, all on the Lake of Bays, and more besides. All, needless to say, became calling points for Captain

Deerhurst Hotel, Peninsula Lake.
Courtesy, Archives of Ontario Acc. 9939

Grunwald Hotel, Mary Lake.
Courtesy, Mr. George Johnson, Port Sydney

Clyffe House, Mary Lake.
Courtesy, George Johnson, Port Sydney

Marsh's steamers. For its own part in 1897, the Huntsville and Lake of Bays Navigation Company — as Captain Marsh was already calling his operation — was lending a hand by distributing thousands of tourist brochures featuring photos and a neat map of the North Muskoka Lake, showing all the resorts, to places all over Canada and the United States.

This publicity began to pay off. In 1898 the Huntsville Line sold about 550 passenger tickets, but this figure jumped to 1,099 the following year.[3] Such figures looked quite satisfactory, both to the boatmen and the G.T.R., which now became more sympathetic to Huntsville's appeals for a larger piece of the action. In the spring of 1899 Captain Marsh and his son Peter C. Marsh met with A.P. Cockburn and various railway officials in Toronto, and agreed that the trains running to Muskoka Wharf from June to September would henceforth continue to Huntsville, arriving at 4:25 p.m., while the Huntsville steamers in turn would depart at 5:00 p.m. Captain Marsh followed up this 'coup' by arranging a triumphal tour of the North Muskoka Lakes for a delegation of G.T.R. passenger agents in June. The Huntsville Board of Trade co-operated, and everything came off without a hitch — almost.

The G.T.R. train pulled into Huntsville early on the morning of June 14th. The visitors were treated like royalty. A throng of Huntsville well-wishers were on hand to greet them at the station as they detrained and boarded the *Empress Victoria*, herself gaily decked out with British and American flags and now commanded by the genial Captain John Fraser, a son-in-law of Captain Marsh. At 7:15 a.m. the *Empress Victoria* gave a deep-throated roar from her whistle signifying "All aboard!" as the lines were cast off and the vessel gracefully backed out into Hunter's Bay amid the cheers of the crowd. The steamer then glided past the tannery and sawmills of Huntsville, where activity was just beginning to stir in the morning, before she erupted with three more blasts to signal the bridgemaster to open the swing bridge to let her pass. Minutes later she was out on the lovely expanse of Fairy Lake, where green fields in the springtime formed a mottled mosaic amid the darker greens of the forest. As befitted a good host, Captain Marsh was out on the deck, ready to point out items of special interest or answer questions from his guests. Within an hour, the lake began to contract into a narrow river, framed on both sides with leafy green shrubbery and second-growth trees whose branches almost brushed against the steamer as she wended her way through the canal. As the ship emerged onto Peninsula Lake, the new Deerhurst Hotel overlooking the water quickly came into view off the port bow. The gentlemen had time for

S.S. "Empress Victoria" at Hunter's Bay Wharf, Huntsville.

S.S. "Empress Victoria" at Huntsville Wharf.
Courtesy, Mr. Owen Swann, Huntsville

Baysville, Ontario (1908).

a tour of inspection here, up the winding gravel path through a grove of trees to the hotel itself, set amid its tranquil lawns, before another blast from the *Empress Victoria* summoned them back to resume their cruise. After passing a few islands, some of which were already embellished with new cottages, the steamer sounded her whistle three times more as she approached the wharf at North Portage. Here they found a landing with a freight shed, a small hotel commanding a lovely view of the lake, a number of homes, a shingle mill, and huge quantities of shingles and tanbark waiting to be scowed to Huntsville. Also on hand was Arthur Osberne with his teams to take the group across to the Lake of Bays. Captain Marsh explained the plans to build a railway of some sort to bridge the divide.

At the South Portage on the Lake of Bays side, they found the *Mary Louise* waiting with a full head of steam up. It was now 9:15 a.m. Boarding the boat, the men luxuriated in the cool fresh air as the morning sun lit up the little green islands set like emeralds amid the sparkling lake, while the steamer ran a 13-mile trip south to Baysville, now a busy little burg of about 110 inhabitants. Here the main attraction was the high dam at the rapids, plus George Howard's big hotel, which catered largely to shantymen. Leaving Baysville, the steamer entered the east arm of the lake, calling at Ronville at 1:00 p.m. Mr. Crump was expecting them, and had two dining rooms set for lunch. Toasts were proposed, photographs taken, and a chorus of "For They Are Jolly Good Fellows" sung, followed by plenty of applause. The party then embarked for Dorset, but here, alas, no one had been forewarned to welcome them. At 3:15 the *Mary Louise* left Dorset for the Portage, arriving at 5:00 p.m. at Huntsville where the gentlemen were wined and dined at the Reid House hotel. Some of them made impromptu speeches extolling the beauties of the North Muskoka Lakes, which were said to be lovelier than Scotland. All that was needed, they added, were more cottages and hotels to bring out its potential. Finally, after more cheers for the G.T.R., and for Captain Marsh, the visitors boarded their train for Scotia and Parry Sound, with the local band on hand to see them off. On days like that, the life of a railway passenger agent could be pleasant.[4]

Those years were good years for the Huntsville steamers, and presaged even better times to come. When the boats were not towing and scowing or running their regular routes, they were sometimes chartered for special events. Moonlight cruises on the *Empress Victoria* and *Erastus Wiman* to Lake Vernon, which had been abandoned by the passenger boats for a decade, now came back into favour. Accidents or near-accidents happened occasionally but they were rare and usually unimportant. For example, the *Erastus Wiman* managed to break a shaft near Huntsville on July 27, 1896 but she was going again within a few days. There were also a few close calls involving small boats. In May of 1897 three boys out fishing in a rowboat tried cutting between the *Erastus Wiman* and a scow she was towing on the Vernon River. The boat capsized, two of the occupants grabbed the towline and were hauled aboard, but the third was run over by the scow. Quick thinking by an onlooker ashore saved the day: he seized a rowboat and fished the lad out, unconscious but alive. Another time, on an evening in July 1899, eight ladies who were out rowing near the entrance to Fairy Lake were nearly run down by the *Empress Victoria*. Twice they crossed the bow of the approaching steamer; Captain Fraser reversed engines and avoided a collision by a few scant feet.

Other incidents were less harrowing. On the evening of November 15th. 1899, the *Empress Victoria* was unable to return from the Portage because of fog, and the crew had to adapt the lounge cabin into a makeshift dormitory for the passengers. Just a few nights before, the *Mary Louise* had grounded on a sandbar near Dwight, and two of the crew were forced to walk all the way to Peninsula Lake to get help.

The first really serious disaster for the Huntsville Navigation Company, since the *Excelsior* fire, occurred on the night of December 15th., 1899, a week after the season of navigation closed. The *Erastus Wiman* and the tannery tug *Sylvester* were both being laid up at the Locks for the winter, when fire broke out aboard the former apparently from a lantern in the boiler room. By the time help arrived the blaze was completely out of control, and a strong wind soon spread the fire to the *Sylvester*, which was moored alongside. Sparks from the holocaust threatened a nearby sawmill, hence both vessels were hastily towed downstream out of range. They were completely gutted, and to make matters worse, the insurance on the *Erastus Wiman* had been allowed to lapse just two weeks earlier as an economy measure. The sole consolation was that the machinery of the two steamers was later salvaged.

This double loss immediately put both the steamer service and the tannery's operations for 1900 in jeopardy. But Captain Marsh was anything but a quitter. He soon announced that he would replace the *Erastus Wiman*, and he would replace the *Sylvester* too, with a new tug of comparable size. The captain was as good as his word: both vessels were under way by the spring, with priority given to the tug. Thus reassured, the new manager of the tannery, Charles Orlando Shaw, decided not to build a new tug of his own, at least for the next two years. The Navigation Company would henceforth tow for the tannery. Captain Marsh, however, was forced to postpone his plans to add new passenger ships to his fleet, and also

Main Street, Dorset, Ontario.
Courtesy, Archives of Ontario Acc. 9939

Steam Tug "Phoenix".
The vessel appears above scowing near Hoodstown, on Lake Vernon.

to delay dismantling the old tug *Florence* on the Lake of Bays. Thus reprieved, the *Florence* carried on until 1901.

The new tug, meanwhile, was being rushed to completion, and was ready to go by the first of May. Slightly larger than the *Sylvester*, she was 50 feet in keel by 11.2 feet in beam, and was listed at 19.59 tons. She had a good, deep draught, and inherited the steeple compound engine of her predecessor. There was much speculation as to what the new vessel would be called, but in the end she was christened the *Phoenix*, because parts of the earlier, burned-out boat were incorporated into the new.

Commanded initially by the popular, energetic Captain Daniel May of Huntsville, the *Phoenix* was put to work immediately, scowing tanbark, towing timber rafts, hauling scowloads of provisions for the lumber camps — in short, just about everything except taking passengers. The Huntsville Lumber Company, for one, regularly hired her as a towboat. In June of 1903 she was engaged to restock Fairy Lake with bass, while the *Gem* was doing the same on Mary Lake. Sometimes the *Phoenix* was called in to rescue a stranded steamer, and on one occasion she herself needed to be rescued. On July 24, 1903, she sank at the Canal as a result of a freak accident, when a badly loaded scow suddenly rolled over and punched a hole through her side below the waterline. The *Empress Victoria* was summoned and cleared the passage for navigation, and a few days later the *Phoenix* was raised with the help of the Navigation Company's new passenger steamer, the *Joe*.

The *Joe* was, of course, the successor to the *Erastus Wiman*. She was essentially an all-purpose boat, about the same size as her predecessor (65 feet by 13), but somewhat more modern, with tamarack framing, a double tow post, and a passenger cabin at the stern. Registered at 38.89 tons, she was named after the youngest daughter of Captain Marsh, Miss Josephine, who afterwards married and moved to Seattle. The new steamer was launched near John Whitesides' sawmill at Huntsville on October 14, 1900, before a large concourse of people. Little Archie Fraser, the five-year-old son of Captain Fraser, did the honours. The *Joe* was still unfinished at that point, and it was not until mid-April of 1901 that the shriek of her wildcat whistle was first heard at Huntsville. Her galvanized steel hurricane deck was not completed until the following July. Captain Marsh at first planned to put the *Joe* on the Lake of Bays to replace the unseaworthy *Florence*, but instead the new vessel was usually assigned the Mary Lake run to Port Sydney. Apparently the *Lady of the Lake* was taken across the Portage instead to substitute for the *Florence*, which was dismantled and sunk at the South Portage. Within about five years the *Lady of the Lake* herself, now worn out from towing, met the same end.

S.S. "Joe", at Clyffe House Wharf, Mary Lake.
Courtesy, Mr. George Johnson, Port Sydney

With the completion of the *Joe*, Captain Marsh had six steamers in his fleet, of which three — the *Empress Victoria*, the *Phoenix*, and the *Joe* — operated on the Huntsville lakes, while the *Mary Louise*, *Florence*, and perhaps the *Lady of the Lake*, plied on the Lake of Bays. In the spring of 1902, following the retirement of the *Florence*, he imported a small 15-ton freight tug called the *Maple Leaf* — perhaps the same *Maple Leaf* recently owned by Singleton Brown of Bracebridge — for service on the Lake of Bays. The new steamer was unloaded from a G.T.R. flatcar and taken in a scow to the Portage on May 12th., and launched on the Lake of Bays four days later, to begin towing, freighting and taking passengers. The following year she was lengthened from 37 to 50 feet, and was put on the Baysville route, between towing assignments, while the much larger *Mary Louise* continued to ply to Dorset. The *Maple Leaf* was a serviceable boat, but her time on the Lake of Bays proved brief. On the evening of July 26, 1906, the trim little vessel took fire at her dock at Baysville and burned to the waterline. Fortunately, by that time the Company had several other steamers available for the Lake of Bays division.

In the meantime, despite the occasional setback, such as bouts of bad weather, which tended to dampen the tourist trade, the Marsh interests were doing so well that in April 1902 his venture was formally incorporated as a limited joint stock company, officially called the Huntsville, Lake of Bays and Lake Simcoe Navigation Company. The new firm was capitalized at $100,000, of which $38,300 had already been sold, mostly to a number of Toronto capitalists. Its charter allowed it to build and operate hotels and shipyards as well as scows and steamboats. At its first directors' meeting, held June 2nd., 1902, Captain Marsh was elected president, while a newcomer, William Duperow, became Secretary-Treasurer and General Manager. It was an excellent choice. Born near Stratford in 1872, Duperow had spent nine years with the Grand Trunk Railway, mostly as a clerk and passenger agent in Toronto, before resigning to join the Huntsville Navigation Company. Hardworking, handsome and debonair, he had a quick, lively mind, a fine head for business, and a pleasant, courteous manner that speedily made him one of the most popular men in Huntsville. In 1903 he was elected Vice-President of the Company, and the following year he also became President of the Huntsville Board of Trade, where he served with great distinction. It was a pity for all concerned that his stay in Huntsville was not destined to exceed four years.

Under the leadership of Duperow and Captain Marsh, who still remained business manager, the Huntsville Navigation Company set to work with vigour. Within a few years it nearly doubled its fleet of scows, some of which were roofed over for the transport of such commodities as dried flooring. The Company secured or confirmed towing contracts with the Huntsville Lumber Company, the Rathbun Lumber Company, the Mickle-Dyment Company, and most of the local sawmills. In 1902 it scowed 4,500 cords of tanbark from the Lake of Bays, plus 2,500 more from the local lakes for the tannery. It lobbied the Government to rebuild or replace the wharf at Huntsville and in 1903, a new 200-foot dock was built northeast of Queen Street, at a cost of about $3,500. The Company then applied for, and got, a new freight shed on the wharf, part of which it occupied as an office in September of 1903. It secured the mail contract for such communities as Grassmere, Hillside, Peninsula Lake, Dwight, Fox Point and Birkendale. It appealed successfully to have lights installed on the Huntsville swing bridge, so that the boatmen could see whether or not it was open on dark nights. In the passenger line, the Company planned a new palace steamer for the Lake of Bays and a new $35,000 hotel at Dorset (which never materialized) and agents were appointed for Dorset, Dwight and Baysville. Captain Marsh and his sons continued to attend railway passenger agents' conventions in the United States, sometimes along with A.P. Cockburn, and never failed to distribute plenty of brochures and folders advertising their respective lakes. The Company also tried persistently to obtain financial backing for a railway to cross the Portage.

As a result of all these efforts, profits soared: in July of 1902 alone, despite much wet weather the Company handled 1,500 luggage items at the station wharf, and sometimes Manager Duperow had to come out and lend a hand to the porters. Schedules were laid out in four divisions, with the *Empress Victoria* running twice daily to the Portage, calling at Fairy Port, Springfield Farm and Deerhurst; the *Joe* plying two trips three to four days a week to Mary Lake, calling at Grunwald and Port Sydney; the *Mary Louise* running twice daily from

Dorset to the Portage, calling at Bay View Farm, Birkendale, the Hemlocks, Ronville, Edgewood, Norway Point and elsewhere; and the little *Maple Leaf* leaving Baysville every morning for Port Cunnington, Dwight and the Portage. Despite some local objections, the boats sailed on Sundays, partly to enable vacationing husbands to get back to the office safely on Monday mornings; though the bridgemaster at Huntsville insisted that the steamers must not blow their whistles on the Sabbath!

In the meantime, a new breed of steamboat was appearing on the Huntsville lakes: the steam yacht. These small corollaries of growing affluence became status symbols for cottagers and local residents during the days before the internal combustion engine: a few were used as adjuncts to the local hotels. The smaller launches were usually about 24 to 30 feet in length, with white hulls, fantail sterns, varnished decks, vertical boilers and canopied cockpits; some had steering wheels mounted at the side, so that one person could stoke the boiler, run the engine and steer the vessel. For the very well-to-do there were much larger yachts, sometimes 60 to 70 feet in length, equipped with lounge cabins and washrooms, but such craft were comparatively rare in North Muskoka.

The first known steam launch on the Huntsville scene was the little *Swift*, which we have already noted at Dorset in 1889, and on Lake Vernon after 1896. In 1899 Captain Marsh imported a beautiful pleasure steamer called the *Gypsy*, which he used briefly on the Lake of Bays in 1900 as an auxiliary to his fleet, before bringing her back across the Portage. In August of that year he treated the General Passenger Agent for the Lehigh Valley Railroad and his family to a cruise to Hoodstown. By 1901 Professor William K. Simpson, a science lecturer at the University of Toronto, fitted out a little steamer called the *Pinta*, with an engine he built himself, and used her to ply to his cottage at Wolf Island on Peninsula Lake. The *Pinta* was apparently in service for over a decade, and sometimes took part in local regattas. That same year a new steam launch called the *Star* was imported to Deerhurst, while in 1904 a well known missionary, the Rev. J.S. Leckie, brought the little steamer *Corinne* to his cottage on Peninsula Lake. Two other nameless steam launches are mentioned in the 'Hunsville Forester' during this period.

Better known is the steamer *Dolly Gray*, which was built at Dorset in 1900 and soon acquired by W.E. Irwin of Birkendale as an addition to his hotel, the Hemlocks. Registered at 3.11 tons, the *Dolly Gray* was 35.5 feet long, had a single cylinder high-pressure engine, and

S.S. "Empress Victoria" at Hunter's Bay Wharf, Huntsville.

S.S. "Gem" (left) & Steam Launch "Sea Bird".
Scene at Port Sydney, around 1905.

Steam Tug "Hildred".
The above is a detail from a scene of the Huntsville Tannery in early winter, around 1906.

could take about two dozen people. She had a white hull, built of red oak, unfortunately, plus a tiny boiler, a slender red and black stack, and a partially glassed-in cockpit. For about seven years she ran outings from Birkendale and Ronville, and in June 1904 she took a pair of newlyweds from Baysville to their new home at Norway Point. Unbeknownst to all, her hull was riddled with dry rot, and one stormy night around 1910 she suddenly split open along the keel while docked at Birkendale. The wreck was hauled ashore and burned, leaving thousands of nails on the beach.

A better launch was the *Seabird*, a 32-foot steamer imported to Huntsville in 1903 by Frank Kent, owner of the Kent Hotel. This trim little vessel could take 30 people, and was used both to entertain guests at the hotel and to run excursions by charter. On the evening of July 21, 1903, she took fire at her dock, but two boys spotted the blaze and raised the alarm, and the hotel staff quickly doused the flames. The *Seabird* proved a speedy boat and attended many a regatta, but around 1910 she was sold when her owner left Huntsville, and she spent her last few years as a tug. Finally, she grew waterlogged and was scuttled in the river about a mile below the locks.

Two more steam yachts appeared on the Huntsville scene around this time. One of these was the *Hildred*, a speedy 30-foot craft built in 1900 for Andrew Tait, a prominent Orillia lumberman, and occasionally used to tow logs on Lake Couchiching. In the spring of 1903 the Huntsville Navigation Company bought her and brought her in by rail to carry passengers and mail on the Lake of Bays. She served on this route only until July, when she was taken back across the Portage and used to carry special parties from Huntsville to Grunwald.

On August 12, 1903, Manager Duperow sent the *Hildred* to join the *Joe* and the *Empress Victoria* at the fourth annual regatta at Deerhurst. Though the weather was not ideal, the event drew nearly 1,000 spectators, some of whom came from the Lake of Bays on the *Mary Louise*. The usual lawn and water sports were held, but the climax for the day was something new: a race by the local steam yachts. Entered were the *Hildred*, the *Seabird*, and Professor Simpson's *Pinta*. The *Seabird* was using a special fuel, in the form of pine roots, but the engineer on the *Hildred*, Ernest Goldthorpe of Huntsville, who loved any type of race, had a trick of his own up his sleeve: he used split cordwood soaked in kerosene.

The course was set around a small island in Peninsula Lake. Late in the afternoon the three contestants lined up, the shot was fired, and the race was on. The *Seabird* took off like a shot, with the *Hildred* closely following. Spectators gasped as they saw flames twelve feet high shooting out of the *Hildred*'s stack; two or three times the *Hildred* actually caught fire, but the flames were always put out. The *Pinta*, hopelessly outclassed, trailed far behind and didn't bother to finish the race. The other two rounded the island, with the *Seabird* maintaining a slight lead until only 200 yards of the course remained. Then Goldthorpe threw some preheated water into the boiler around the firebox, and this final burst of speed carried the *Hildred* ahead to victory. It was an exciting day.

The *Hildred* resumed her runs to Mary Lake after this event and in September she was on hand to rescue the *Gem*, which had broken a shaft while towing logs. The *Hildred* towed her home, and also substituted for her on her regular market trip the following Saturday. This was not the worst to befall the *Gem* that season. At noon on Saturday November 20th., she caught fire while docked near the Navigation Company office at Huntsville. The burning boat was pushed away from the wharf, and by the time the Huntsville fire brigade arrived, she was too far away to be helped. The blazing steamer drifted over to the opposite shore, where she grounded and sank. Her patrons were left stranded as a result, but the *Joe* was engaged to take them back to Port Sydney. The loss was a heavy one to Sydney-Smith, whose insurance on the vessel had just run out. Actually, Smith had been planning to build a larger steamer anyway, but now he changed his plans. He had the hulk of the *Gem* pumped out and towed back to Port Sydney, where she was lengthened and rebuilt over the winter. Both her master, Captain Lyle Casselman and Captain Denton, assisted in the work.

The new *Gem* was ready by July of 1904. Now 51 feet in keel and registered anew at 18 tons, she was steadier and far more commodious than before. Soon she was back in service, towing, scowing, collecting milk, running to Huntsville, and conducting moonlight cruises, frequently calling at Grunwald. Sometimes she also attended regattas or ran pleasure trips to the Portage.

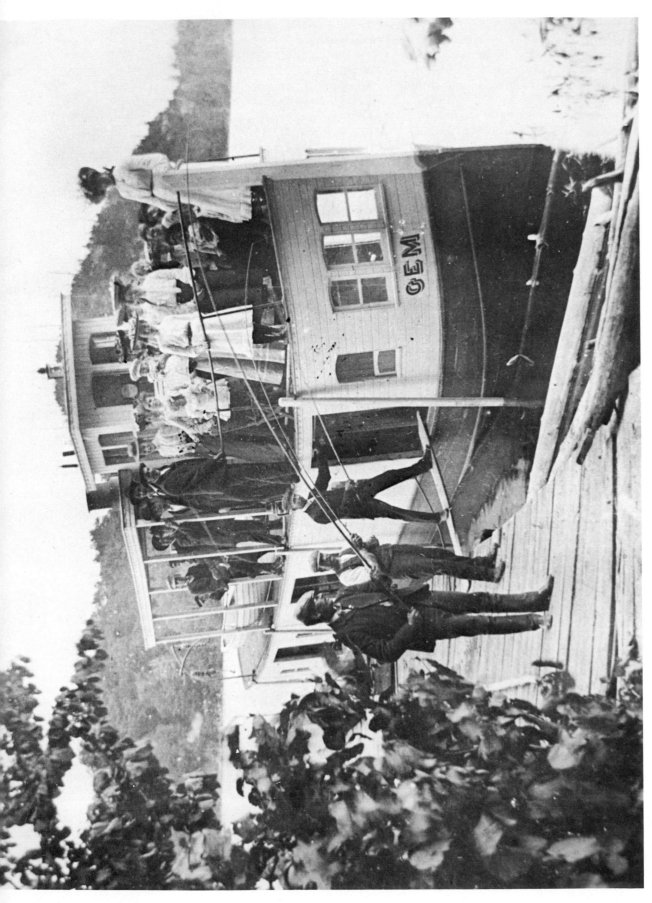

S.S. "Gem".
The vessel is transporting a Sunday School picnic at Hilarity Hall, on the south side of Mary Lake.

Steam Yacht "Sarona".

Before the *Gem* was relaunched in the spring, a most unusual new steamer arrived at Huntsville on a railway flatcar from the Great Lakes. This was the *Sarona*, a long, narrow, cigar-shaped yacht built of solid oak. With her two masts and portholes she looked almost like a gunboat. She was owned by Charles Orlando Shaw, the peppery manager of the Huntsville tannery, and even featured a tiny piano in her cabin, which was convenient, considering that Mrs. Shaw, who liked to entertain her friends on the vessel, was a former opera contralto. The *Sarona* also had a screeching wildcat whistle, and when she first sounded that whistle on her maiden cruise around Hunter's Bay, half the town of Huntsville came out to see what was causing the noise. Reputedly Mr. Shaw was instructed not to blow the whistle, and reputedly the indignant manager afterwards used his yacht as little as possible around Huntsville.

The *Sarona* proved a speedy craft, and was sometimes used to take large parties on luncheon cruises to the various resorts. Unluckily, she had trouble rounding some of the curves in the rivers on account of her 65-foot length, and with her round bottom she was distinctly tippy: sometimes those on board were known to get a little queasy! For reasons such as these, the big yacht was used less and less as the years went by, until she ended up spending most of her time at the tannery wharf.

There was, naturally, considerable speculation as to how the *Sarona* might fare in a race against some of the other steamers. It was agreed to put the matter to the test at a regatta to be held at Grunwald on August 10th., where the *Sarona* would race the Navigation Company steamer *Joe*; in addition, Frank Kent, smarting over his setback at Deerhurst the year before, again challenged the *Hildred* with his *Seabird*. The former contest was to have far reaching consequences.

Older residents still recall what happened, although they disagree somewhat on the details. A storm hit that day at 12:30, but the weather improved during the afternoon. Almost all the steamers were present, with the *Joe* bringing in the crowds from Huntsville, and the *Gem* and the *Empress Victoria* handling the throng from Port Sydney. The regatta proceeded as planned, with the steamboat races set for the last. The yachting race came first, with the hotel proprietor, Mr. Gall, running the *Hildred*, assisted by Mr. Duperow; while Frank Kent ran his *Seabird*, aided by the manager of the Dominion Bank in Huntsville. The match was close, but this time Ernie Goldthorpe was not at the controls of the *Hildred*, and in the end the *Seabird* won by just a few lengths. Then the big boats lined up to race a triangular course, with Captain Alex Casselman commanding the *Joe*, and Captain Dan May the *Sarona*. C.O. Shaw was also aboard. At the signal, the *Sarona* "took off like a scared cat", with the *Joe* in hot pursuit. During the race, the two steamers ended up on different courses, and the *Joe* crossed the finish line first and was proclaimed the winner. C.O. Shaw was not very pleased. Some say that Manager Duperow good-naturedly needled Shaw afterwards about who had the faster boat, but there is no doubt that Mr. Shaw denounced the outcome from the verandah of the hotel when the prize — a handsome silver service — was awarded to the crew of the *Joe*. He alleged that the *Sarona* had been shown the wrong course before the race, and that some of the signal flags had blown down, with the result that the *Sarona* had run a mile and a half farther than the *Joe*. Mr. Duperow, always a gentleman, agreed to disallow the race and suggested holding another, but the regatta committee persisted in awarding the prize to the *Joe*. Somewhat unwisely, the Manager afterwards set the prize out on public display at the Navigation Company office, and also awarded a gold locket to each member of the *Joe*'s crew to commemorate their victory. All this amounted to pouring oil on the flames. C.O. Shaw sullenly bided his time, but those who thought the whole affair had blown over were soon undeceived.

A few other incidents added the occasional touch of drama or excitement during those years. One evening in May 1900, the *Empress Victoria* grounded on a sandbar at the entrance to the Canal and broke her rudder chain, and Captain Fraser had to walk to Huntsville and summon the *Phoenix* to pull her off. The passengers arrived home at daybreak. Later that summer she broke her rudder shaft while backing away from the wharf at Springfield Farm and began drifting helplessly. Some of the passengers were picked up by rowboats, and presently the little *Gem*, coming in from Port Sydney, was alerted by whistle calls and took the *Empress Victoria* in tow. Following some makeshift repairs she was able to complete her usual afternoon run to the Portage. In November 1900 the Company flagship again got into trouble when she broke loose from her moorings at Huntsville one night during a violent windstorm: she drifted downstream and grounded near the town bridge. Fortunately, some of the crew were on hand to raise a head of steam, and got her free the following morning, little the worse for wear.

The Lake of Bays was not devoid of exciting moments either. On November 11, 1902, the men on the *Mary Louise* reported spotting two deer, both near Dorset, and since there were then no laws against shooting game in the water, the boat crew pursued the animals and caught them both. In 1903, no doubt following complaints from nervous passengers, the steamer *Joe* was rebuilt in drydock with false sides to make her wider and steadier, and later, during the fall of 1904, we find her going to the rescue of the *Empress Victoria*, which had broken her rudder on Fairy Lake and gone aground amid high winds.

The biggest remaining headache for the Navigation Company was the problem of the Portage, where traffic was building up to massive proportions. Thousands of feet of lumber, thousands of cords of tanbark, and thousands of tons of freight were crossing the one-mile divide every year, but despite the services of Arthur Osberne's stage and wagons the Portage remained a serious bottleneck. It often took more than twenty minutes to transfer passengers and their effects from one lake to the other. Scows of tanbark had to be laboriously unloaded by hand at the South Portage, hauled overland in wagons, and laboriously reloaded onto scows at the Peninsula Lake terminus. If something could be done to streamline operations, commerce and tourism would benefit enormously and Huntsville, through the Navigation Company, would totally dominate the Lake of Bays. The "ditch" or canal proposal had already been judged impractical, and this left only one viable alternative: a railway of some sort. Only Baysville stood to lose much by the scheme, which would leave the village as a mere dead end terminus of the boat route rather than gateway to the Lake of Bays region, and its people continued to plead for a railway spur to connect them with Bracebridge.

The first concrete move to build a railway over the Portage was taken in the spring of 1895, when the Huntsville and Lake of Bays Transportation Company Ltd. was formed to build an electric rail line across the divide, and to generate electric power. This firm had many influential backers, but it was inaugurated at a bad time. The depression of the 1890s had not yet lifted, and the tourist boom had not yet begun: as a result, capital was not forthcoming. In March 1900, when the business scene was brighter, an Act to incorporate the Huntsville and Lake of Bays Railway Company was tabled in the Ontario legislature, empowering the proposed Company to survey, equip and maintain a railway run by steam, compressed air or electricity, and requiring that it be started within three years and completed in seven. Captain Marsh, F.W. Clearwater of the 'Huntsville Forester', and

S.S. "Mary Louise", with Log Drivers, Lake of Bays.
Courtesy, Mr. John Baker, Rockwynn

several prominent businessmen and lumbermen of Huntsville were among the directors, but though the Act was passed, the Government neglected to budget any money for it, and little was accomplished. By 1902, when the charter was in danger of lapsing, the Navigation Company took it over. In September, Manager Duperow announced that negotiations were under way for 40-lb. steel rails, of a type used by streetcar lines, despite the fact that the money problems had not been solved. Nevertheless, surveys were finalized the following spring, and in May, President Marsh could present his Board of Directors with terms for the acquisition of locomotives and rolling stock. Four months later, he and Duperow were back from Ottawa with an invoice for the purchase of two engines and 24 cars from the E.B. Eddy Company of Hull, Quebec. In the meantime, both men appealed to the Ontario government for help, with the result that in April 1904 the legislature voted $10,000 for the Portage Railway.

Construction was already under way in the fall of 1903, under the supervision of Captain Marsh. A gang of about 40 Italian workmen from North Bay was employed (local labour being scarce), and by November the roadbed was completed and 23 tons of rail had arrived. Six flatcars and the two locomotives also left Huntsville aboard scows on November 16th. Work was suspended over the winter, but resumed again in April, and finally, on July 7, 1904, the 'Huntsville Forester' could report that the trains were running, though the terminals were not yet complete. Passengers services were not inaugurated until 1905, partly because the new line was not fully ballasted until then. Captain Marsh himself got to take his one and only trip across in November of 1904.

The Portage Railway, which became a veritable institution on the Lake of Bays for 55 years, was widely celebrated as the shortest complete railway system in the world. Its main line, excluding sidings, totalled a little less than one mile. From South Portage wharf it went inland a short distance before crossing the wagon road and skirting the east side of Osberne's Lake (now Little Lake), from which point it wound through the bush and then ran parallel to the road out to the Peninsula Lake terminus. Sidings were provided at both ends, plus a "Y" at North Passage to allow trains to back down to the wharf. It was, nonetheless, impossible for them to turn around, and the engines always had to return to South Portage running backwards. The tiny line was built to the unusually narrow gauge of three feet eight and one-half inches (later regauged to three feet six inches), in order to match the rolling stock, which had previously been used in the yards of E.B. Eddy's match factory. The two original locomotives were a pair of four wheel saddletank wood burners, sometimes fondly called "rambling cookstoves". First built by H.K. Porter and Co. of Pittsburgh in 1888, they were intended as switchers. Each weighed seven tons and both squealed a great deal on the curves of the Portage tracks. The four original coaches, which were fully enclosed, were obtained from the Toronto street railways and were originally horse drawn. They had to be fitted out with new trucks and undercarriages at the Portage. The coaches had wood-stoves on board, which were never used, since the trains did not run beyond the navigating season. In addition, the line had a fleet of flatcars and a few boxcars to carry freight.

As a rule, in the early days only one double header train was formed, combining both freight and passenger cars. In later years two trains were run, one for freight, the other for passengers, always in conjunction with the steamers. If the locomotives could not climb the grades, the passengers had to get out to lighten the load; most did so good-naturedly. During the winters the engines were kept in a roundhouse at South Portage, and the coaches under the local canopy, the sides of which were then enclosed to form a shelter. Basic maintenance and boiler work was done at the Portage; more serious jobs such as locomotive overhauls were carried out at the Company machine shop in Huntsville.

This funny, loveable little railway was like nothing else in the world, and it looked like something out of an amusement park. The employees dubbed it the "International Corkscrew Route"; others called it the "Hot Tamale Express". Comical though it looked, it was exceedingly useful in that it hauled incredible quantities of freight and passengers over the divide, and technically its proprietors, Messrs. Marsh and Duperow and their successors, were entitled to a status equal to such contemporary railroad tycoons as

E.B. Eddy Company's two yard switchers (Hull. P.Q.).
The "Ella C." and the "Nettie" later belonged to the Portage Railway.
Courtesy, Public Archives of Canada PA 12446

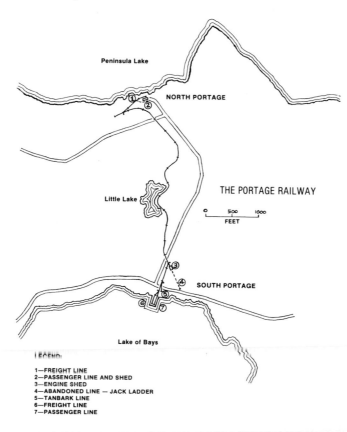

Peninsula Lake

NORTH PORTAGE

Little Lake

THE PORTAGE RAILWAY

0   500   1000
FEET

SOUTH PORTAGE

Lake of Bays

LEGEND:

1—FREIGHT LINE
2—PASSENGER LINE AND SHED
3—ENGINE SHED
4—ABANDONED LINE — JACK LADDER
5—TANBARK LINE
6—FREIGHT LINE
7—PASSENGER LINE

Cornelius Vanderbilt of the New York Central, or Charles Melville Hayes of the Grand Trunk. The Portage trains usually bumped along at about the speed of a slow trot, yet they were four times faster than the wagons they replaced. Hay, oats, camping supplies, canoes, groceries, cement and lumber were all in a day's haul, not forgetting tanbark, which was customarily piled on racks at South Portage and hoisted onto flatcars by means of a derrick. Later, a second derrick was added for unloading at North Portage. There were seldom any accidents: the only man known to have been injured on the railway was Arthur Osberne himself, who became mechanical superintendent after teaming was discontinued. Sometime around 1912, Osberne broke his leg jumping from a runaway flatcar, leaving him with a permanent limp and apparently hastening his retirement.

The Portage Railway consolidated the link between the Huntsville and Lake of Bays steamboat routes, and effectively laid to rest any lingering hopes of a rival line to Baysville. As such, it was the culmination of the work of Captain George Marsh. But the tireless old mariner, now 66, did not long survive its completion. As early as 1897 Captain Marsh had developed three malignant tumors in his lower lip: these were removed using strong drawing plasters and he seemed to be rid of the problem. However, the symptoms returned some years later, and in October 1902 he had to undergo an operation in hospital at Orillia. Again he was pronounced cured, but by the spring of 1904 the odious growth returned and spread to his jaw. This time he went to Milwaukee, Wisconsin, for specialized treatment. Once more he seemed better, but the session there only bought time. Another operation followed that August in Indianapolis, but by now no one entertained much hope for his recovery, although he remained active almost to the last. In September he was present to witness the driving of the last spike of the Portage Railway, and early in November he took his one and only trip on it. The end came at his home in Huntsville on November 18, 1904, at midnight; his sufferings partly consoled by the presence of his family, and by the knowledge that he had largely completed his life-work, and had done it well. His funeral was about the largest ever seen in Huntsville, whose debt to him was overwhelming, in that he had practically founded the tourist industry in North Muskoka. The Masonic Order, the International Order of Foresters and the workmen all gathered to pay their last respects. Was his old rival, Captain Denton (himself a Mason) at the funeral? We do not know, but in any case the co-founder of the Huntsville steamboat enterprise was destined to outlive Captain Marsh by sixteen years.[5]

The passing of Captain Marsh marked the end of the pioneer period in the evolution of the Huntsville Navigation Company, which had nearly another half-century ahead of it and was about to enter a new era. That discussion, however, we leave to succeeding chapters. Meanwhile, let us see how the South Muskoka steamers were faring during the interval of the "gay nineties".

FOOTNOTES

[1] The sale was made official in 1893, but the 'Toronto Mail' affirms that Captain Marsh already owned the *Lady of the Lake* by July of 1892.

[2] The Gilmour Company used at least six alligators in the Muskoka and Nipissing Districts, including the *Peck* (1894), *Nipissing* (1894), *Hunter*, *Trent*, *Muskoka*, and perhaps the *Alligator* (No. 13).

[3] Its counterpart, the Muskoka Navigation Company, meanwhile sold 11,527 tickets in 1899.

[4] Two days later they were out cruising through the Muskoka Lakes.

[5] Captain Denton died at Taber, Alberta, on March 24, 1920, at the age of 82.

North Portage, on the Portage Railway.
The picture was taken around 1905, shortly after the railway was built. To the right of the locomotive is a crate containing two Toronto street railway carriage-bodies. The S.S. "Joe" is at the wharf, while the tug "Phoenix" can be glimpsed behind the scows.
Courtesy, Public Archives of Canada PA 20597

Portage Railway train passing Osberne's (Little) Lake.
Courtesy, Archives of Ontario Acc. 9939

Steamers at Muskoka Wharf, Circa 1904.
In the foreground are the yachts "Wanda", "Mildred" and "Rambler". Behind these are the
Navigation Company steamships "Medora" and "Nipissing".

CHAPTER 12
The Muskoka Navigation Company Consolidates
(1897-1906)

The turn of the century seems to have been the "golden age" of the inland passenger steamers in Ontario. There were then more steamboat lines than there were railways, and some companies built beautiful ships. The Ottawa River Navigation Company was operating several palatial paddle-wheelers between Ottawa and Montreal. The Rideau Lakes Navigation Company had a pair of opulent cabin steamers plying from Ottawa to Kingston and Lake Ontario, along the historic Rideau Canal. The Calcutt Steamboat Line was conducting regular excursion cruises on the Otonabee River, between Peterborough and Rice Lake. Further north, the Stoney Lake Navigation Company was blossoming, while on the central Kawartha Lakes the Trent Valley Navigation Company was consolidating a service from Coboconk to Lakefield, using five steamers. Excursion steamships plied on Lake Simcoe, Lake Nipissing, the Magnetawan River and the Upper Ottawa, while to the north, the Lumsden Steamboat Line on Lake Timiskaming was busy transporting hundreds of hopeful settlers with their goods and chattels to the newly developing Clay Belt country of Northern Ontario. The Huntsville Navigation Company, as we have seen, boasted a fleet of seven steamers by 1903. Almost every waterway within settled regions seemed to have its steamers.

By far the most successful line of all was the Muskoka Navigation Company, which by 1900 had seven steamers in commission, and by 1907 had a total of nine. The general revival of prosperity after 1896 and the buoyant optimism of the Laurier era were to bring unprecedented prosperity to the Muskoka fleet, much as it did to the Huntsville steamers but on a much larger scale. Indeed, the parallels between the two boat lines during this period are striking. Both were reorganized and consolidated within a year of each other. Both rapidly expanded operations. Both contemplated going into the hotel business, and both forged close links with the Grand Trunk Railway. The main differences were that the Huntsville lakes were smaller and remoter than the Muskoka Lakes, the Huntsville fleet had been founded later, and the tourist industry was just beginning in North Muskoka, at a time when it was already well established in the South. In 1909, Baysville held its first regatta, while Port Sandfield was celebrating its 21st!

We noted earlier that relations between the Muskoka and Georgian Bay Navigation Company and the railway were quite friendly, and became more so as the years went by. We have also observed that the Grand Trunk Railway, having bought a controlling interest in the old Northern, formally absorbed it on January 24, 1888, just a few years after the line was extended from Gravenhurst to Lake Nipissing. The Grand Trunk continued the Northern's policy of publicizing Muskoka as a tourist paradise. For decades the railway and the Navigation Company interlocked their schedules, sold one another's tickets, and published joint advertisements. A minor setback occurred in April 1895, when fire destroyed the station and storehouse at Muskoka Wharf, but in a sense the loss was timely, in that it allowed for the construction of a much larger, handsomer and more ornate station. The new Muskoka Wharf Station became the gateway to the Muskoka Lakes for the next 53 years, and was soon the scene of frantic activity three times a day from May to October.

Meanwhile, the tourist resorts were doing famously, especially after 1895, when the inflow of summer visitors turned into a torrent. On the national scene, foreign tourists, most of whom were Americans, spent about $7,000,000 in Canada during 1900 alone; a figure that climbed steadily to a peak of $19,000,000 by 1914. During that interval we find whole sections of the Toronto newspapers' weekend editions devoted to chatty news about the regattas on Burlington Bay, Rice Lake and Lake Rosseau, or to the dances, picnics and

New Muskoka Wharf, Circa 1900.
This view shows the wharf station shortly after it was rebuilt in 1895. The S.S. "Medora" and S.S. "Nipissing" (rear) are at the dock to meet the train.

fishing trips involving well known people at or near the summer resorts. Muskoka, as always, was in the forefront. As of 1896 there were about 30 resort hotels around the Muskoka Lakes. By 1903 there were 57 or more, and by 1909 there were 76, with advertised accommodations exceeding 4,983. Of these, Milford Bay had two, Juddhaven three, Port Sandfield four, Rosseau five, and Bala and Port Carling about six apiece. Among the newcomers were Paignton House, near Minett on Lake Rosseau (by 1894); the Golfa House (afterwards Nepahwin), at Gregory, near the mouth of the Joseph River; Rostrevor, north of Windermere, which started out as a hunting lodge in 1896; and the Island F Hotel (afterwards Glen Echo). Many of the older hotels, including the Beaumaris, Windermere House, the Monteith House, the Prospect House and the Summit House, could each accommodate 200 guests. Others such as Ferndale, Woodington, Clevelands House, Ernescliffe, the Maplehurst, Stanley House, the Elgin House, the Windsor House at Bala, and Bala Falls Hotel, could take 100 or more apiece.

The resorts themselves were changing. Besides getting bigger and adding new amenities such as ballrooms, concerthalls, bowling greens, gas lighting, and (sometimes) golf courses and modernized sanitation, some of the larger hotels were becoming very "fashionable" and "first-class", and charging accordingly. By 1906 the Summit House at Port Cockburn was setting its rates at $2.00 per day or $12.00 a week and advising the public to make reservations in advance. In short, the strong social cleavage between the well-to-do and the ordinary citizen, which was already clearly pronounced in the cities, was extended to the resorts as well, and Muskoka was building up a reputation as a "rich man's vacation land". It seems only fair to add, however, that there were still a large number of small, unpretentious places taking only a few dozen guests at such rates at $7.00-$10.00 per

Rostrevor Lodge, Lake Rosseau.
This resort, commanding the finest beach on the lake, is still in business today.

Windermere House, Lake Rosseau.
Time for the steamboat to arrive! The hotel has been enlarged considerably since the 1890s.
Courtesy, Archives of Ontario Acc 9939

Elgin House, Lake Joseph, from the Wharf.

Clevelands House, Minett.
Numerous refinements have been added since
the 1880s.

Paignton House, Lake Rosseau.

Summit House, Port Cockburn, Circa 1897. Leaving the wharf is the S.S. "Kenozha".

Beaumaris Hotel, at its height.

week. Cruises on the Navigation Company steamers cost as litle as $6.00 on all three of the Muskoka Lakes, or $4.00 on Lake Muskoka alone. Such rates probably did not preclude humbler folk in Toronto or Hamilton from taking the occasional holiday in the North country.

From the pen of Lady Aberdeen, wife of the governor-general of the day, we derive the following impressions of the Muskoka Lakes in the summertime, when she and her husband took an extended cruise on the *Medora* in 1898; calling at Gravenhurst, Beechgrove Island, Beaumaris, Port Keewaydin, Port Carling, Windermere, Maplehurst, Rosseau, Port. Sandfield, Yoho Island, Stanley House and Port Cockburn. As Lady Aberdeen describes it,

> The Muskoka Lake region, where [we]..were entertained by the Muskoka Lakes Navigation Co. . . . is a much loved summer resort of Canadians but especially of Torontonians — & two or three islands with big hotels are practically colonies of Americans. . . . Imagine . . these three Muskoka Lakes (Muskoka, Rousseau & St. Joseph) dotted with hundreds of picturesque wooded islands, abounding with scenery of a quiet pretty type & giving infinite resources for boating, sailing, fishing & bathing. These islands were originally sold by the Government at a mere nominal rate of 50 cents an acre & any number of Toronto families possess one or part of one. Now they are nearly all taken up & it is hard to get one, but the other day one of 60 acres was sold for about $700. [!]

Lady Aberdeen goes on to mention such activities as swimming, boating, fishing and picnicking, adding that "Tents are .. largely used & so hospitality stretches itself indefinitely . . . in the evening they often have a "camp fire" which means a sort of impromptu concert, & to which the inhabitants of every island have to contribute in turn." She concludes by remarking, "I must not omit reference to our visit to Major Denison at his Buckgrove Island[1] a pretty little place where he lives in patriarchal Muskoka style."

235

The Earl and Countess of Aberdeen at Port Sandfield, 1898.

As on the Huntsville lakes, the growing influx of tourists and cottagers soon led to a proliferation of private steam launches and yachts. Apparently there were very few yachts in Muskoka before 1903, but afterwards there were dozens of them. As to private steam launches we cannot be sure, since most of them were never registered. Some are known only from passing references in contemporary newspapers; as for example the *Maggie Revel*, which according to the 'Muskoka Herald' met with a sad end on November 18, 1891. The little craft was being piloted down to Gravenhurst amid high waves and strong winds, which finally swamped her near the Narrows, forcing her sole occupant to make for shore in bitterly cold water, clinging to a small ladder from the boat. He reached Gravenhurst in the evening, very hungry and thoroughly chilled, after a long tramp through the bush.

Another small steam launch called the *Oz* met a similar fate in 1903, but under more tragic circumstances. The little vessel was on her way home from Bracebridge to the Island F Hotel on December 1st., with a load of hay and assorted groceries. She never made it. Somewhere off Empress Island on Lake Muskoka, she was lost during a windstorm with all hands. Captain Peter Campbell found a pail of lard and some bales of hay in the water near the scene a day or so later, and eventually he retrieved the boat itself, using grappling hooks. Only later did he learn that one of the victims was his eldest son, Dan. The body of young Campbell was recovered, but the other two men were never seen again. The *Oz*, meanwhile, was beached at Glen Echo.

Another handful of launches from this period are still dimly remembered. One was the *Pickerel*, owned and perhaps built by David Rose of Torrance, a master carpenter and sawmill owner who used the craft to peddle provisions and run picnics and fishing trips in the vicinity of Acton Island, around 1890-1907. Another, the *Narissa*, was owned by a contractor from Port Carling after the turn of the century. Three more that are known by name were the *Nellie*, which was acquired in 1893 by J.L. Fenn, a prominent Bracebridge merchant; the *Avon*, owned and constructed by I.H. Waltenbury, a Bracebridge contractor, in 1897[2]; and the *Ida May*, mentioned as having been overhauled in 1897. From Lake Joseph came a few more, including the *Dot*[3] (1890), owned by a minister from Reef Island for nearly two

Steam Launch "Pickerel", on Bala Bay.
Courtesy, Mrs. Margaret Jestin, Torrance

Steam Launch "Narissa" of Port Carling.
Courtesy, Mrs. Dorothy Duke, Port Carling

Steam Launch "Valda" at Gravenhurst Narrows.
To the left are a pair of pulleys used by the lumbermen to winch tows through the channel.
The cameraman taking this picture heard the whistle and thought he was photographing
the S.S. "Islander".

decades; the *Opeeche* ("robin"), which belonged to a judge who began summering at
Wegamind Island around 1895; and the *Midget* (1906-08), also owned by a vacationing
minister. Around 1900 an odd little steamer called the *Valda*, based at West Gravenhurst,
was often seen puttering about on towing jobs or fishing trips on Muskoka Bay. Other
steam launches are alluded to during the 1890s, but their names are not known.

The big yachts for the most part are much better documented. Aside from A.P.
Cockburn's *Helena* (1877) and various hotel boats such as the *Kate Murray* and *Onaganoh*, the
first known steam yacht on the Muskoka Lakes — and also one of the most celebrated —
was the lovely *Naiad*, a 68-foot craft built at Toronto in 1890 for Senator William Eli Sanford
of Hamilton. Senator Sanford, one of Canada's wealthiest wholesale clothing merchants,
developed the Sanford Manufacturing Company and was nicknamed the "Wool King of
Canada". He was a leading banker and philanthropist, and used the yacht to entertain
guests at his summer home at Sans Souci Island, Lake Rosseau. With a steel frame,
mahogany planking and a round stern, the *Naiad* registered 19.74 tons and looked like
something intended for royalty, featuring glittering British plate glass windows and a gilt
ornamented clipper bow. In 1894 she escorted Prime Minister Sir John Thompson on a
fishing trip, and also Lord and Lady Aberdeen in 1898. The sight of the graceful vessel
glidsing across the waters, with a little brass cannon on her deck and the Union Jack
fluttering at her stern, inspired envy in all who saw her, although from the captain's
viewpoint she was less than ideal. She was temperamental and hard to steer in a chop sea,
and the helmsman had no protection from spray flying over the bow. In July 1899 Senator
Sanford, aged 61, was tragically drowned while fishing near Windermere, but the *Naiad*
remained with the family for decades to come.

Steam Yacht Naiad"

Steam Yacht "Naiad" at Port Carling.
In the background is the yacht "Priscilla".

Steam Yacht "Priscilla" at Beaumaris.
Courtesy, Mr. Peter B. Campbell, Campbell's Landing

Steam Yacht "Llano" leaving Muskoka Wharf.
From the Collection of the late Mr. Lester Turnbull, Dundas

Steam Yacht "Hepburn", near Walker's Point.
Courtesy, Mrs. Joyce Schell, Barlochan

As we have seen, Captain Rogers of Port Sandfield built the *Flyer* in 1892, while sometime shortly thereafter another beautiful, silent running steam launch appropriately called the *Secret* (3 tons) was imported by some cottagers at Monyca Island, Lake Rosseau. Tradition says she was brought in to replace the much larger steamer *Nymoca*, which was built in 1892 but proved too unattractive to please her new owners. The *Secret* was often used to go puttering up the Shadow River, a well known beauty spot near Rosseau, until about 1908, when she was sold off to Georgian Bay. In 1895 the *Wapenao* (3.07 tons), a 40.7-foot steam yacht built at Kingston two years before, was imported to Lake Rosseau by Timothy Eaton, founder of the famed Toronto Department Store. This vessel was used by the Eaton family at their palatial summer cottage near Windermere until 1914, but before that time she had been converted into a gas boat. In the meantime, Mr. Eaton bought a larger yacht, the *Wanda*, from the Polson Works in Toronto in 1898. Registered at 7.87 tons, the *Wanda* had a length of 53.5 feet and a triple-expansion engine that made her, for a time, the fastest vessel on the Muskoka Lakes. Mr. Eaton traded her in on a new yacht when she lost her title in 1904.

Steadily the fleet grew. A steam launch called the *Viola* is mentioned on Lake Rosseau in 1896. Later she was sold to Captain Henry Wallace of Minett, who converted her into a motorboat and used her for pleasure cruises until about 1914, when she was replaced by a Ditchburn launch, the *Viola* (the second), which still survives. In 1897 the *Priscilla*, a splendid vessel of 13.72 tons, built at Kingston, was brought to Port Carling by Senator Miles Standish of Pittsburgh as an adjunct to his summer home. Similar to the *Onaganoh* but larger, the *Priscilla* was 53.2 feet in keel, had a triple-expansion engine, and cost a reputed $10,000. Like the *Naiad*, she had a miniature nickel-plated cannon on her foredeck, plus other trimmings of polished nickel embellishing her varnished cabins. For over a decade the natty little craft was a familiar sight on Lake Rosseau. In 1908, she was sold to Mrs. Emma Mickle, wife of the Gravenhurst lumber king, who kept her another fourteen years. In 1923 the *Priscilla* was again sold, and spent her last years taking passengers on Lake Couchiching and the Trent. Another yacht, the *Manolia* (4.08 tons), was imported from Toronto in 1898, apparently as a new attraction at Clevelands House, but this vessel was resold in 1903 to a farmer at Milford Bay, who turned her into a supply boat.

Three more private pleasure steamers are known to have appeared in 1900. One of them was the *Dawn* (2.34 tons), a tiny, 27-foot canoe-like craft with a .53 hp. high-pressure engine. Her owner, Joseph Cooper of Bracebridge, used her primarily for fishing trips, until the early morning of June 4, 1912, when she was destroyed by fire on the Muskoka River, along with her boathouse, another yacht, several gasboats, canoes and rowboats, and four additional boathouses. (The total loss was reckoned at $15,000.) Another 38-foot yacht, the *Kestrel* (4.62 tons), was likewise built at Toronto and imported to Gravenhurst by a lumber merchant from Midland, but after 1915 this vessel became a workboat. Much larger still was the *Llano* (9.38 tons), another 61.3-foot Polson yacht, used by a Toronto clergyman around Windermere for nine years before going to the Irwin family of Columbus, Ohio.

About a dozen more yachts call for brief mention. They include the *Alleghania* (1901), the first of three vessels owned by Professor John A. Brashear, an American astronomer who summered for many years at Urania Island, near Beaumaris; the *Fidelia* (5.82 tons), which arrived at Lake Rosseau from Kingston in 1901; the *Ina* (10 tons), which was 56 feet in length and built in Toronto the same year; and three vessels imported to Beaumaris in 1902; the *Hepburn* (10.05 tons), a 50.5-foot twin engined craft built at Racine, Wisconsin in 1901; the *Bella Vista* (2.74 tons but soon enlarged); and the *Osso* (3.97 tons), also from Kingston. Still another newcomer in 1902 was the *Anchora* (3.46 tons), which was used for twenty years, initially at Anchor Island, Lake Joseph, and later around Bracebridge and Browning Island. The following year saw a rush of new arrivals, mostly from Kingston, including the *Edith Ann* (7.15 tons), a 43.4-foot vessel owned by the Cassidy family of Pittsburgh and Beaumaris; the *Sky Pilot* (3.21 tons), used aroung Port Carling; the *Shamrock*, later to become a passenger boat; and the *Izaak Walton*, an unregistered yacht about 45 feet in length and named after the famous English angler of the seventeenth century. Both she and the *Hepburn* became the property of John Walker, another wealthy Pittsburgh steel magnate who purchased Buck Island, near Beaumaris, as a summer home in 1898. Also during this

Steam Yacht "Izaak Walton", opposite Rankin Island, Lake Muskoka.
Courtesy of the late Mr. Peter Schell, Muskoka Township

period, the aforementioned yacht *Spray* arrived at Gravenhurst from Toronto, later went to Orgill's Point, and ultimately (1910) became the hotel yacht at Gordon Bay House on Lake Joseph. All of the above vessels, except the *Sky Pilot*, which burned in 1916, and perhaps the *Fidelia*, had quite long lives, and most ended up as workboats.

Easily the most impressive pair of yachts yet seen on the Muskoka Lakes when they arrived in 1903-04 were the *Mildred* and her twin, the *Rambler*, both built by the Polson Works in 1903. Both were 70 feet in length by 10 in beam and registered 25.45 tons. Both had triple-expansion engines and elliptical sterns. The only difference between them was that the *Rambler* had an auxiliary steering position and a railing over the forward lounge, which the *Mildred* lacked. The *Mildred* was initially owned by the Canadian financier E.R. Wood, for whose daughter she was named, and was berthed at Mazengah Island, Lake Rosseau. Her sister belonged to the McKinnon family of Toronto, and afterwards to Edgar B. Whitcomb of Wistowe Island, Lake Rosseau and Detroit, Michigan. Sometimes parts were traded between the two vessels. Both still survive — as diesels — although the *Mildred* was rebuilt of steel after a fire in 1961. The *Rambler* is a wooden yacht with a steel frame, and is still kept in mint condition, retaining the stack and whistle from her days as a steamer.

The above tally does not exhaust the list of steam yachts on the Muskoka Lakes: dozens more soon followed. For now, however, let us leave the launches and take a look at other types of vessels on the waterway.

Steam Yacht "Mildred", on the Muskoka River.

Steam Yacht "Rambler", on the Muskoka River.

References have already been made to another category of steamboat: the supply boat. Such craft were used as "floating stores", to transport foodstuffs and other commodities around the lakes, stopping anywhere that was safe and selling provisions to campers, cottagers and the hotels . Supply steamers were very rare before 1882, but after that time, once the recreation industry had become a prominent feature on the local scene, they began to appear everywhere. For decades they were a familiar, and usually welcome, sight.

The owners of the supply boats can be grouped into two distinct categories: local farmers who used small steamers to distribute their own produce, and urban merchants, often organized into companies, to whom steamboats became floating adjuncts to their stores. Boats in the former category were usually converted launches with a canopy to protect the produce and the operator from the elements. Over half a dozen were used at various times over the years.

Perhaps the first individual to try peddling farm produce by boat in Muskoka was Frank Forge, a Yorkshireman who had been one of the three original settlers at Windermere in 1863. During the 1800s Mr. Forge began selling fruit and vegetables to campers and hotels on Lake Rosseau, starting out with a dugout canoe and then a rowboat. Encouraged by the response, Forge purchased a small 30-foot steam launch called the *Ethel May* (2.46 tons), which had previously been used on a tiny lake near Aurora, Ontario, and brought her to Windermere in 1888. He seems to have used her for three seasons, visiting all parts of Lake Rosseau and sometimes Lake Joseph as well, but in 1891 he sold her and resumed use of his rowboat. Four years later the *Ethel May*, now thirteen years old, became Captain Alfred Mortimer's tug. Sometimes the steamer *Edith May*, Captain Rogers' third vessel, was used to carry supplies from Port Sandfield during this period as well.

The first family to enter the supply boat business on Lake Muskoka was that of John James Beaumont, an East Anglian squire who had left England after an epidemic decimated his sheep flocks, and who eventually purchased the Muntz farm on the lower Muskoka River. The family worked hard, cutting logs and splitting tanbark during the winters, and soon had surpluses of lamb and vegetables for sale. In time they were employing over two dozen people as butchers, bakers and farm hands. As market gardeners before the advent of trucks, it was logical for them to acquire a steamboat, and after 1892 opportunity beckoned when the new steamer *Nymoca* (13 tons), having been rejected as a yacht by the cottagers at Monyca Island in 1892, became available to anyone who would take her. Apparently the unlovely vessel was left idle for a year or two, until the Beaumonts decided that, regardless of her aesthetic limitations she would make a good supply boat. Soon the little 52.5-foot craft was in regular service, towing in the spring and fall and taking produce in the summer to all corners of Lake Muskoka, usually under the command of Mr. Beaumont's son Frank. Every morning at 2:00 a.m. the butchers had to slaughter and dress lambs in order to have the meat in iceboxes by 7:00 a.m., when the *Nymoca* went out on her rounds. Fresh meat was something of a luxury during the days before electric refrigerators and much of what passed for "Muskoka lamb" in those days was actually venison! For over two decades the *Nymoca* sailed for the Beaumonts, and occasionally the Bracebridge newspapers carried stories of pleasure cruises taken aboard her.

The example of the Beaumonts was soon copied by William Packer and his family, who in 1877 began clearing and developing an extensive farm on East Bay, near Torrance. By the 1890s the farm featured cattle, sheep, an apple orchard and vegetable gardens, and soon the family was selling baked goods and dairy products as well as farm produce. They also built docks, cut ice in the winters, and took summer guests in their home. In 1897 William Packer purchased a small 32.8-foot steam launch called the *Devenish* (2.37 tons) from Toronto, for use as a supply boat, and kept her in service for about a dozen years, calling on campers, cottagers and hotels, usually on alternate days from the *Nymoca*. Tom Packer, one of William's sons, was captain. The *Devenish* is not mentioned after 1909, and about that time the Packers obtained the aging yacht *Onaganoh*, which had previously belonged to the Summit House at Port Cockburn. The *Onaganoh* seems to have lasted in her new role until about 1915, when she was dismantled and left to fall to pieces in East Bay. One further supply boat owner of this period was Frederick Mills of Milford Bay, who bought the little

Supply Steamer "Ethel May" 1896.
Aboard are the vessel's owner, Frank Forge; his captain, William Forge; his wife and the engineer.
Courtesy, Mrs. Dorothy Duke, Port Carling

Supply Steamer "Nymoca", from Alport.
Courtesy, Miss Ruth Tinkiss, Bracebridge

Manolia from Clevelands House in 1903 and used her to peddle produce until 1908, when he, too, acquired a larger vessel.

The urban supply boat owners, operating from such centres as Gravenhurst, Bracebridge, Bala, Port Carling and Rosseau, usually fitted out steamers that were much larger and more elaborate than those of the farming families. Their boats also tended to be more regular in their routes and far more varied in their stock. The owners were almost always settlers or sons of settlers who started out with tiny "bush-stores" during the pioneer period and ended up with thriving retail outlets, some of which, like the Hanna store at Port Carling and the Burgess store at Bala, are still in business today, though under different ownership. Generally, these early merchants branched out into supply boating in much the same way, always after their businesses were firmly rooted on dry land. Most of them started out during the "boom" years following 1896, though a few began as late as the 1910s. Only one firm, the Hanna Company of Port Carling, was seeking customers on the waves as early as 1887. Typically, the merchants started by renting a local steamboat to distribute groceries and dry goods, frequently hiring the vessel's owner to run it. By about the turn of the century, when business was thriving, they would decide to build or rent a larger, double-decked steamer with a high-pressure engine and a length of from 55 to 65 feet. Frequently, even this vessel would prove too small and too slow, and would usually be lengthened anywhere up to 70-85 feet and equipped with a new economical fore-and-aft compound engine. Then, as a rule, business would boom, and for a time a few operators even ran two steamers simultaneously. Considering that so many of their customers were cottagers without automobiles or private motorboats to take them into town to do their shopping, it is hardly surprising that floating food stores went calling on them at home. The cottagers would run up a white flag if they wanted the supply boat to stop, and any item not immediately available could be placed on order and delivered next time around.

The firm of William Hanna and Sons of Port Carling was the first to sense the new trend, and the only one to remain in the supply boat business for over half a century. William Hanna himself was one of Muskoka's foremost merchants. Born in 1848, he had settled with his family at South Falls in 1860. The next year his father was killed in the American Civil War, leaving young William, aged thirteen, to look after all the others. For some years he brought in the mail from Severn Bridge, regardless of the weather, and by 1870 he was working in a Bracebridge store. In 1883 he moved to Port Carling, where he opened a tiny store of his own. Despite setbacks, such as a fire in 1893, he developed and expanded the business until the summer of 1900, when he was able to transfer operations to a new store which was the largest in Port Carling. In 1887 we find him offering for sale "farm produce, bakery from our own ovens, boating hats, trolling lines, cork screws, cartridges and frying pans". He was now one of the most active and popular men in Port Carling.

It was in 1887, too, that Mr. Hanna first decided to try taking merchandise directly to his summertime customers by boat. He therefore rented a large 49.6-foot yacht called the *Lady of the Lake*[4], which had been built near Bala the year before by Arthur Thomas Lowe of Whiteside to ferry passengers around Acton Island and Bala Bay. Commanded by Captain William Kydd of Port Carling (no relation to the pirate!), and with Mr. Lowe himself as engineer, the *Lady of the Lake* modestly began carrying supplies of different kinds, which at the insistence of Mr. Hanna were unloaded from the boat every night and replaced the following morning. The vessel continued to take a few passengers as well. According to Captain Fraser, she was once taking a crowd from Whiteside to the fair at Rosseau when someone spotted a large black bear in the water near Acton Island. Not having a rifle on board, Captain Kydd went after the beast and tried to finish him off by running him down, but the bear only resurfaced and tried to climb aboard the steamer. Failing to do so, 'bruin' capsized a rowboat being taken in tow, then swam ashore and vented his indignation by killing a local farmer's lamb, while all the neighbours were away at the fair.

The *Lady of the Lake* was not used by the Hanna Company for long. Built to carry people rather than produce, she soon proved less than ideal as a supply boat, and as business expanded a larger vessel became necessary. Almost certainly in collaboration with the Hannas, A.T. Lowe built a larger, more suitable steamer at Port Carling in 1891, and once

Supply Steamer "Lady of the Lake".
The vessel is shown docked near the Port Carling House.

she was ready he sold the *Lady of the Lake* to Captain Marsh in 1892, while continuing to engineer on the new boat. Mr. Hanna rented the new steamer, which he christened the *Mink*.

The *Mink* was typical of the larger Muskoka supply steamers. She was originally 57.2 feet in length by 11 in beam, and was powered by a 2.15-hp. high-pressure engine. Having two full-length decks, she was far more commodious than the *Lady of the Lake*, and required a crew of four. (six on busy days). In 1896 Mr. Hanna bought the vessel outright from Mr. Lowe. Two years later, disaster struck the little craft on the evening of September 12, 1898, when she caught fire while returning to Port Carling. There was no loss of life, but all the stock on board was lost with the boat, and there was no insurance. The setback at least gave Mr. Hanna a chance to enlarge and re-engine his vessel, and when the *Mink* reappeared in 1899 it was with a new 8.16-hp. compound engine and a new length of 72 feet. She had to be registered anew at 38 tons. In 1904 the Hannas advertised her in the following words:

> . . The "Mink", a screw steamer . . is a general supply boat. She is fitted with compound engines and develops a speed of twelve miles an hour. Large refrigerators are on board, which keep provisions and meat in perfect condition. A specialty is made of catering to camps, and the prices are much lower than the tourist can bring in provisions himself, with the additional advantage of having everything always fresh.

While the Hannas were building up a good business with the *Mink*, two rival companies were trying their hand at it, with less success. One of them was the Burgess firm of Bala. In an earlier chapter, we saw how Thomas Burgess actually put the community of Bala on the map in 1868 by erecting the first store and sawmill at Musquash Falls. The mill was rotting away around the time of Mr. Burgess' death in 1901, though others had replaced it, but the family store was still going strong. By the late 1890s, Bala, hitherto a minor sawmill centre,

Supply Steamer "Mink"
Courtesy, Mr. Bill Gray, Port Sandfield

Crew of the S.S. "Mink".
Captain William Board stands second from the left.
Courtesy, Port Carling Pioneer Museum

was developing its share of summer hotels and becoming a prosperous resort community. In 1897 Donald Burgess, a son of Thomas, bought a 68-foot steam yacht called the *Gypsy* (13.63 tons) from Andrew Tait, one of the leading lumbermen of Orillia, and had her brought in from Lake Couchiching to serve as an adjunct to the family store. The *Gypsy* served as a supply boat for four years and proved a success — so much so that she was soon unable to cope with the expanding volume of trade and had to be replaced.[5]

Her successor was a larger, double-decked steamer optimistically named the *City of Bala*, which was built in 1901, at a time when the Bala community was reckoned to consist of barely 50 people: officially Bala was still just a post office. The *City of Bala* was a beautiful craft, similar to the *Mink* but larger, with a length of 76.3 feet, a beam of 12.7 feet, and a tonnage of 47.43. Her engine was a high-pressure Polson model, delivering 3.3 hp. The new steamer was launched at Bala with little fanfare and considerable difficulty: one of the Navigation Company ships[6] had to be called in to help her into the water. The *City of Bala* made a fine supply boat, but she was used in this role for only three seasons before she was sold to the Bracebridge "new tannery" to serve as a scowboat. She was not replaced. Familial rather than financial pressures seem to have dictated this move, since Donald Burgess, who had been in charge of the boat division of the business, decided to pull up stakes and seek his fortune out west at this time. The *City of Bala* meanwhile carried on scowing for the tannery and occasionally running excursions until 1911, when the Beaumonts of Alport took her over with the idea both of scowing and using her part-time in her old role as a supply boat, to relieve pressure on the *Nymoca*. The *City of Bala* was then drydocked at Gravenhurst for what were expected to be minor repairs. Unhappily, the vessel had been constructed of red oak, which, unlike the more usual white, tends to rot very rapidly in water, with the result that her ribs were found to be rotting out along the keel. Since repairs were out of the question the steamer had to be scrapped, and the Beaumonts were obliged to have another vessel built to replace her.

The third and last incorporated company to run supply boats on the Muskoka Lakes at this time was that of George Henry Homer, who ran a general department store in Gravenhurst. By 1890 this firm had become prosperous enough to open a branch store at Rosseau. Mr. Homer customarily despatched letter-order items, for his customers up the lakes, by way of the ships of the Navigation Company, of which he himself was a shareholder and director. In the spring of 1896 he and his partners bought the *Edith May*, Captain Rogers' former steamer, from the Prospect House at Port Sandfield, and used her to distribute commodities from Rosseau. The *Edith May* likewise proved too small for the purpose, and within two years the Company decided to scrap her and transfer her engines to a new and larger vessel, which was duly built at Gravenhurst in 1898. This craft was the *Constance*, an extremely serviceable boat that was to last for 40 years under fifteen successive owners. The *Constance* was originally 65 feet in length and listed at 28.53 tons, but as early as 1900 her owners, deciding that they needed a larger and faster vessel, replaced her old high-pressure engine with a fore-and-aft compound that gave her a speed of about ten miles per hour. At the same time her length was increased to 82 feet and her tonnage to 35.32. In 1904 the Homer Company advertised that "Our supply boat *Constance* calls at all Cottages, Camps and Hotels on Lakes Rosseau and Joseph, and is stocked with a complete assortment of fine 'Groceries, Fruits, Confectionery, Vegetables, Fresh Meats, etc'." Usually commanded by Captain William Giles of Rosseau, the "Connie" sailed for the Homer firm until 1905, when she was sold — perhaps with the store at Rosseau — to a local merchant, who continued to use her until 1908. She then went to a Bracebridge firm, before changing hands again and returning to Rosseau, but she remained a supply boat until 1921.

We shall have more to say about the supply steamers in subsequent chapters, but for now let us return to the affairs of the Navigation Company.

Steam Yacht "Gypsy".
The vessel appears above during her days at Orillia.

Supply Steamer "City of Bala"; Circa 1902.

Supply Steamer "Constance" (Original Version).

J.C.Little & Co's Supply Boat "Constance" Muskoka Lakes, Canada.

Supply Steamer "Constance" (Second Version).

Interior of the S.S. "Constance" Circa 1904.
Courtesy, Mr. Munroe Stephen

We left the Navigation Company in the mid-nineties, just nicely coming out of the red and starting to pay substantial dividends to its shareholders. The Company was then running six steamers, the *Nipissing, Medora, Muskoka, Kenozha, Oriole*, and (until 1896) the ill-fated tug *Lake Joseph*, which was sold in that year. Though most of "the Line's" profits were derived from freighting and taking passengers to the resorts, the Company was not quite ready to abandon the towing business to the local tugs. Some of the lumber companies, including the Rathbun firm, still had no tugs of their own and were willing to engage other boats to tow for them. Accordingly, the Navigation Company built a new tug at the Gravenhurst dockyards in 1896 to replace the *Lake Joseph*. This was the steamer *Ahmic* ("beaver"), a conventional 61-foot towboat with a single deck, a beam of 12.8 feet, and a 10.6-hp. compound engine. Registered at 29.10 tons, the *Ahmic* (fondly called the "Amy") was soon busy towing logs and scows for such firms as the Longford and Rathbun Lumber Companies. From the very start she was also advertised as being available for charter, or to substitute for her sister steamers whenever necessary. In August 1897, we find her taking a crowd of fans with foghorns from Beaumaris to Bracebridge for a baseball match (Beaumaris won, thirteen to five in seven innings), and in addition, the *Ahmic* was frequently engaged to tow the houseboat *Victoria*, which the Company had fitted out for fishing parties around 1896, to whatever corner of the lakes that patrons might desire. A roomy, cosy, ornate barge some 100 feet in length, the *Victoria* was still being chartered as late as 1908.

The *Ahmic* did not remain a towboat for long. Lumbering was now past its prime, the Longford Company soon left the scene, and in 1902 the Rathbun Company imported the *Comet* to do its towing. This left the *Ahmic* with little work to do in that line. Meanwhile, the passenger business was burgeoning, and the Company was busy building one new steamer after another to keep ahead of the rush. Finally, in 1902 it resolved to give up the towing trade for good. That winter the *Ahmic* was drydocked, strengthened and completely rebuilt. She was lengthened nearly twenty feet to 80.4 and re-registered at 48 tons. In addition, a promenade deck was added and her sides enclosed: henceforth the "Amy" was a passenger steamer. She now looked very much like some of the supply boats, such as the *Mink* and the *Constance*. So completely was she changed that the Company considered giving her a new name but this was never done, perhaps because seamen consider such a move bad luck!

The *Ahmic* was back in service by May of 1903. Unfortunately, she did not prove entirely satisfactory in her new role. She had no hurricane deck, which meant that passengers had to crowd down below on the freight deck whenever the weather was bad, and furthermore, all the additional superstructure made her somewhat unstable — which did not increase public confidence in her. As a result, she went back to the drydock in the winter of 1904-05, there to be given false sides, increasing her beam from 13 to 15 feet and her tonnage to 52. At the same time she received that badly-needed hurricane deck. The *Ahmic* still remained a trifle unsteady and tended to roll when heavily loaded, but she gave good service for the next 44 years.

We have already seen how the stubby old *Muskoka* was successively enlarged and remodelled between 1891 and 1898 to convert her into a passenger steamer. In 1897-98 the *Kenozha* had her turn: she too was drydocked and rebuilt, under the watchful eye of Captain Henry. First, she was cut in half amidships, stiffened by a new keelson, and lengthened nearly twenty feet, which made her, at 120 feet, almost as long as the *Medora* and *Nipissing*. Then, a new, oak-panelled lounge cabin was added to her promenade deck, while the hurricane deck was carried forward to shelter passengers at the bow. This entailed raising the pilothouse to the top deck and enlarging it at the rear to provide new berths for the captain and mate. When completed, the sturdy old *Kenozha* registered 225.29 tons, making her, for the moment, the largest ship in the fleet. She now had far more deck space and far more attractive appointments; only her dining saloon remained unaltered. In the spring of 1903 she was further improved by the installation of a new three-cylinder steeple-compound engine delivering 21 hp., plus a Fitzgibbon boiler capable of generating an extra 50 lbs. of steam pressure. This made the *Kenozha* the most efficient and economical steamer on the lakes. It is said that she could run 100 miles or one full day on just two cords of fuel wood. In 1905, she also received a second lounge cabin at the aft end of the promenade deck.

Str. "Ahmic" (Original Version) as a Tug.

Str. "Ahmic" & Yacht "Onaganoh" at Port Sandfield.
Photographed around 1898, the "Ahmic" is still a tug, but used sometimes to take passengers.

S.S. "Ahmic" (Third Version) as a passenger ship

S.S. "Kenozha" (Second-Version).
The vessel, painted in the black livery of the 1890s, is seen here next
to the Bala Falls Hotel.

S.S. "Kenozha" (Third Version), Circa 1899.

During the boom years, six steamers proved insufficient, and, needing a new auxiliary boat, the Company built the steamer *Islander* in 1900. A handsome little composite screw vessel officially registered at 76 tons, the *Islander* was 100 feet in keel, 17.4 feet in beam, and, for her size, drew a lot of water: 5.7 feet. This made her very steady and easy to steer on a straight course — a desirable characteristic in foggy or rainy weather. Sometimes the captain could simply attach a line to either side of the steering wheel between calls and leave the bridge for a time, letting the ship steer herself! On the other hand, she proved rather heavy and cumbersome to turn. The steel frame and machinery of the new steamer were built at Toronto, but assembled at Gravenhurst. Like her sister ships, the *Islander* was a double-decker, with a round, fantail stern and a small dining saloon. At first, she looked a little odd with her "floating" hurricane deck, but during the spring of 1904 she was improved with the addition of a much-needed lounge cabin on her upper deck. Unlike most of the other ships she was never lengthened or seriously altered. Commanded initially by the modest, obliging Captain William Henry Elder of Gravenhurst, the *Islander* plied for 51 consecutive seasons and greatly endeared herself to the travelling public during that time.

In the same year that the *Islander* was launched, the flagship *Nipissing* also came in for some extensive improvements. It was probably at this time that her paddle-wheels were lowered for better purchase in the water and the paddleboxes rebuilt. Later a new, enlarged pilothouse was built on her bridge, which was extended forward to provide a platform for it. The space below, formerly occupied by the old pilothouse and a cabin, was now turned into a handsome new lounge. The popular old sidewheeler was now better equipped than ever, and was sometimes known to carry crowds of 400 people.

The *Medora's* turn for renovations came in 1901-02. During that winter, the stately steamship was drydocked, cut in half, and lengthened by twenty feet, bringing her up to 142.6 feet in keel and her tonnage from 202.99 to 256.28, a record for the Muskoka Lakes. The enlarged *Medora* proved rather slow, still having the same single engine, and was very heavy to steer, since she was still equipped only with hand gears rather than steam powered steering, such as some of the later steamers were to have. She also had a pronounced tendency to vibrate. Her crews called her "the Moose", because of her size and her deep, booming whistle. She was popular and spacious, especially on the forward freight deck, and was sometimes known to take 350 passengers, though licensed for just 275, plus, it is said,

S.S. "Islander" (Original Version), Circa 1902.

S.S. "Islander" (Second Version).

S.S. "Islander" (Second Version)
Courtesy, Archives of Ontario S 15093, from the A.T. Brown Collection

enough iron wardrobe trunks to fill five railway baggage cars. The *Medora* was now so big that she would have been confined to Lake Muskoka, except that the locks at Port Carling were also enlarged in 1901-02 and rebuilt of stone, to be able to handle larger ships. When the *Medora* re-entered service in 1902, it was as flagship of the fleet, with Captain George Bailey, now "the Line's" senior skipper, still at the wheel.

She immediately had her capacity tested to the full. The newspapers of the day are full of accounts of Dominion Day cruises up to Rosseau on the *Medora*, or of sporting day events when trainloads of visitors flocked to Muskoka Wharf, crowded aboard the boats, and headed up to Bracebridge or some other destination for a picnic, a lacrosse match or a baseball game. People in those days cherished their holidays and were good at keeping themselves entertained.

One example of this took place on Labour Day, 1899. At that time the Spanish-American War, including the capture of Manila in the Philippines by Admiral George Dewey, was fresh in people's minds, and this gave the United Workmen of Gravenhurst an idea. They determined to requisition the steamer *Kenozha* and storm "Port Manila". Stocking the ship with food and ammunition, they set off in the afternoon, along with their wives and sweethearts and a band, and called at Port Sandfield. Some had supper at the Prospect House, while others cruised to Port Cockburn and back. By then it was getting dark, and the steamer headed off to attack "Port Manila", which was illuminated, and was soon seen to bear a striking ressemblance to Birch Point on Tobin Island, Lake Rosseau. The garrison, commanded by "General" W.L. Standish, was on full alert and ready for the impending assault. Sailing within range, the men on the *Kenozha* opened fire on the "Port", while the band encouraged them with stirring renditions of the march 'British Grenadiers'. The defenders, however, replied with a tremendous barrage of rockets and fireworks, lighting up the evening skies and making the shorelines echo with the din of battle. No direct hits were scored on the *Kenozha*, but apparently the reception proved too hot, and in time the ship and her stalwart troops were obliged to retire from the scene. "Port Manila" remained in enemy hands, but then . . no one really seemed to mind![7]

To return to more serious matters, the Muskoka and Georgian Bay Navigation Company was doing much more than remodelling its steamers and building new ones. It was becoming infected with some of the confident, vigorous optimism that was sweeping the nation after the revival of world trade in 1896. Ambitious schemes and dynamic ideas were in the air, replacing the cautious, pessimistic conservatism of the previous decade. Around 1900 a newcomer appeared on the scene in the person of E.L. Sawyer, a lawyer with the firm of Sawyer, Ross and Company of Toronto. Impressed by the seven fine steamships of the Navigation Company fleet, and by the annual dividends which rose to ten percent in 1901, Mr. Sawyer approached the Board of Directors and suggested the formation of a larger company, to embrace a combined navigation and hotel enterprise. He proposed to build one or more really first-class, thoroughly up-to-date summer hotels on Lake Rosseau or Lake Joseph, with the steamers to service them. The existing ships were to be taken over and new ones built. All should be equipped with electric lights, modernized plumbing and other improvements. Such proposals were very well received by the Board, and Mr. Sawyer succeeded in purchasing the stock of seven of the shareholders, including J.S. Playfair and A.P. Cockburn, to a value of about $41,000. This amounted to a controlling interest, although it was understood that Cockburn and Playfair were to receive large blocks of stock in the new company, and that Mr. Cockburn should continue to manage the steamship branch for the present. At first, all went well. With the unanimous approval of the old Board, a new company called the Muskoka Navigation Company was organized, a charter obtained on March 30, 1901, and Messrs. Cockburn, Playfair and Sawyer became provisional directors. Sawyer meanwhile strove to raise the necessary capital for a new hotel, and, after considering buying an existing one, such as the Monteith House at Rosseau, he plunged into the construction of a new hotel, known as the Royal Muskoka or Muskoka Royal. By the summer of 1901 the dining room, vestibule and one bedroom wing were complete.

S.S. "Medora" (Second Version), Drydocked.

S.S. "Medora" (Second Version).
The ship is seen leaving Muskoka Wharf around 1904. Note the American flag.

Dining Room, S.S. "Medora".

Crew Members, S.S. "Medora".
Captain George Bailey is seated left, among his female friends.

S.S. "Medora", with all decks full!

Captain George Bailey, Commodore of the Fleet.

S.S. "Kenozha", approaching a wharf.
Courtesy, Mrs. Joyce Schell, Barlochan

Captain Ben Dewey

At this point, enthusiasm began to give way to nervous apprehension. Stories about reckless expenditures and shady manoeuvres started to spread, until it seemed that E.L. Sawyer had embarked on a "wildcat" scheme that was ruining the Company. It was known, for example, that Sawyer had not succeeded in finding all the capital necessary for the Royal Muskoka, yet it was rapidly going up, at a cost of about $150,000. Finally Playfair decided that he had had enough of the whole affair and withdrew from his agreements with Sawyer. This apparently torpedoed the Toronto speculator's plans for good, and he was forced to bow out, leaving others to pick up the pieces as best they could.[8]

What followed next is obscure, but it is known that the Navigation Company put more stock on the market at this time and also issued bonds to complete the Royal Muskoka. Here A.P. Cockburn's long and friendly association with the Grand Trunk Railway paid off handsomely: the railway warmly supported the hotel project and offered to guarantee the bonds.

In March 1903, a "merger" was carried out between the Muskoka and Georgian Bay Navigation Company and the stillborn "Muskoka Navigation Company" (Sawyer's). The new firm was given the impressive title of the Muskoka Lakes Navigation and Hotel Company Ltd., and was authorized to issue stock to a total of $250,000, to be divided into 2,500 shares worth $100 each. Of these, some 1,736 shares, plus fragments of 31 more, had been allotted by 1905, representing a total of $173,634.89. This figure was never increased significantly. The terms of exchange for shares in both the old companies were spelled out exactly, and it was stipulated that the by-laws of the old Georgian Bay Company should be adopted by the amalgamated company "so far as applicable". At a meeting held on January 26, 1905, a new board of eight directors, including J.S. Playfair and A.P. Cockburn, was elected: Mr. Playfair remained President; Francis J. Phillips, President of the Phillips Manufacturing Company of Toronto was Vice-President; and Mr. Cockburn was Manager and Secretary. The other board members were mostly merchants and manufacturers from Toronto and Hamilton. A new figure appears as Treasurer of the amalgamated company in 1903: William F. Wasley of Gravenhurst. Wasley had first started to work for the Navigation Company in 1893, and had served on the boats in every capacity except that of captain. Although no one could have foreseen it in 1903, it was Wasley who would soon succeed A.P. Cockburn as Manager, and continue to direct its affairs for 36 years with a competence and dedication never surpassed even by Cockburn himself.

The Royal Muskoka, meanwhile, first opened for business in the summer of 1901 and was completed in 1902. Located on a lofty, sickle-shaped promontory jutting out into central Lake Rosseau, "The Royal" commanded a magnificent view and was by common consent the most splendid resort in Canada. It could accommodate between 300 and 350 guests at rates (in 1906) of $3.50 and up per day or $20.00 and up per week. Three storeys high, with picturesque red-roofed towers, stuccoed walls, electric lighting, steam heating, hot and cold running water and palatial staircases, the great hotel consisted of a vast rotunda overlooking the water, and two huge dormitory wings forming a 90-degree angle on either side. The grounds adjacent totalled 130 acres and featured — rare for Muskoka — a nine-hole watered golf course, plus bowling greens, tennis courts, riding stables, and miles of shaded walking trails. A carriage road ran from the rear of the rotunda down in a loop to the steamboat wharf, where there were two-storey boathouses with swimming platforms and every type of pleasure boat for hire. The Royal Muskoka also contained a post office, telegraph office, bar, billiard room, bake shop, newsstand, barber shop and beauty parlour. Many celebrities were attracted to it, starting with the new Governor General and his wife, Lord and Lady Minto, who stopped to pay a visit on June 3, 1903, during a cruise through the lakes on the *Medora*. "The Royal" was carefully managed and evidently well patronized: conventions, liked to meet there, and it also enjoyed the special friendship of the Grand Trunk Railway. It was, in short, the ultimate in the steady growth towards larger, more luxurious resorts catering to the very rich in the Ontario vacationlands. In fact, it may have taken those trends too far. The hotel required a large staff, and the tourist season was short. It is doubtful whether it ever really lived up to the hopes of those who sponsored it. Perhaps it did well during the prosperous Edwardian era, but most informed opinion today seems to

The Royal Muskoka Hotel, Lake Rosseau.
From a Lithograph produced around 1902.

Rear View, Royal Muskoka Hotel.

Golfing Green, Royal Muskoka Hotel.

S.S. "Nipissing" at Royal Muskoka Hotel Wharf.

agree that the Royal Muskoka became essentially a burden to the Navigation Company; sometimes consuming a good deal of the profits earned by the boats but doing little more in return than washing the steamers' linen.

The construction of the Royal Muskoka did not deter the Navigation Company from further expanding its fleet during those years, though all the steamers were mortgaged in 1903 and no further dividends were issued until 1913. As business continued to swell, the Company, as we have noted, rebuilt the *Ahmic* in 1903, and at the same time decided to acquire another auxiliary steamer. It therefore purchased a large yacht called the *Charlie M.*, which had been built at Gravenhurst six years earlier by Charles Mickle of Mickle and Dyment, who named the vessel after his popular son Charlie Mickle junior. The *Charlie M.* was 51.5 feet in length by 11 in beam, displaced 25.44 tons, and had, for her size, a powerful eight horse-power compound engine that gave her speeds of about fourteen miles per hour — not bad for the times. If necessary, she could be operated by a crew of two, a captain and an engineer. The Navigation Company used her primarily for special parties, and in 1907 it lengthened her to 74 feet, extended the cabin forward, and added a canopy over the aft cabins, which were henceforth entered through a gangway like the other steamers, instead of over the railing. Despite these adaptations, the *Charlie M.* did not make an especially good passenger boat, and was seldom used except in July and August.

During the spring of 1904, the steamer *Oriole* was also remodelled, but for somewhat different reasons. This little 75-foot craft had been used successfully since 1886, usually on the Bracebridge run, but she had never proved popular with the public on account of her relative narrowness and consequent tendency to roll. As it happened, those apprehensions proved justified. The *Oriole* was the first steamer to enter service in 1904, having spent the winter in drydock where $1,000 worth of work was done on her hull. On May 2nd., shortly after the ice went out, she made her first trip of the season to Bracebridge. Aboard was a crew of six, commanded by Captain Andrew Thomas Corbett, who had joined the Navigation Company in 1896. The snows had just melted, the river was high, and the roads were a nightmare; consequently, orders for provisions were flooding into Bracebridge, and upon arrival, the steamer's crew found teamsters delivering large consignments of freight, including hay, lumber and oats, to the wharf. The captain advised some of the merchants to hold off for a few days; many insisted that their cargoes could not wait, and by the time they were loaded the vessel was rolling more than usual, even at dock. There were also 37 passengers on hand, many of whom added purchases of their own, which they did not wish to leave behind. They did not like the looks of things, but the crew felt confident that everything would be all right.

Shortly before 3:00 p.m. the *Oriole* tooted her whistle, cast off her lines, and set off dubiously down the river. She did not get far. The current was very strong, and upon rounding the bend opposite the new tannery, the captain swung away from the scows that were tethered there. The steamer drunkenly started to roll over. The passengers, apparently none too surprised, kept cool and moved over to the upper side, catching the railings and stanchions. Seeing what was happening, Captain Corbett turned the bow towards the shore; the engine, still throbbing, ran her over to the bank opposite Andy Boyd's house. The captain then ran along the side, smashing windows to help those inside climb out. Some were able to step right off the bow onto the bank without even getting their feet wet; others got a ducking and a few had to swim. Mr. Boyd came out to help, as did a number of boats, and soon everyone was safely off except Captain Corbett and John Bibby, the mate. Buoyed up by the lumber and hay, the wallowing steamer remained afloat, but she drifted downstream on her side for nearly a mile before a line was finally secured to a tree.

The *Oriole* was raised six days later, with the help of two scows and a local tug. The following afternoon she managed to return to Gravenhurst under her own power, undamaged but full of mud. The official inquiry that followed concluded that the vessel careened because she was overloaded. No blame was imputed to Captain Corbett, who had done all that was reasonably possible under the circumstances. Most of the freight on board was a complete loss and the embarrassed Mr. Cockburn invited the merchants to make out duplicate orders at the expense of the Navigation Company. Meanwhile, he put the larger

Str. "Charlie M." (Original Version)
at Port Carling

Str. "Charlie M." (Second Version).
The big launch is seen docked at Port Sandfield. The steamer at right seems to be the
"Florence Main".
Courtesy, Archives of Ontario Acc. 14777-15

SS ORIOLE

S.S. "Oriole" on the Muskoka River.
Cruising near the Devil's Elbow, the little steamer appears above in her final, post-1904 version.

S.S. "Oriole", sunk in the Muskoka River, 1904.
Lending a helping hand are the tug "Gravenhurst" and her scow.

S.S. "Oriole", remodelled after the mishap of 1904.
The ship from which this picture was taken has not been identified.

S.S. "Oriole", capsized on a shoal.
The date and setting of this incident have not been established. The picture may have been taken near Gravenhurst. The steamer is in her post-1904 version.

Pilothouse, S.S. "Oriole"
Captain C.W. Henshaw
is at the wheel.

S.S. "Oriole" (Second Version) at Port Carling.
Behind her appears the bow of the yacht "Naiad".
From the Collection of the late Mr. Lester Turnbull, Dundas.

steamer *Islander* on the Muskoka River run. Since the *Muskoka* was then in drydock having her hull replanked, the *Oriole* was given towing duties for the rest of the spring; then, as soon as the cradles were vacant she went back on the ways. Determined that she should henceforth remain upright, the Company gave her a massive refit, adding false sides to make her three feet wider. Her sidewalls above the main deck were also rebuilt, eliminating many of the windows, while the hurricane deck was lengthened aft to the end of the stern. As a result, the *Oriole* looked very different when she re-emerged, with little of her former ornateness remaining except the domed octagonal pilothouse. To restore confidence in the vessel, Messrs. Cockburn and Wasley entertained the Gravenhurst town band aboard her when she re-entered service on July 18th., and the following evening the Bracebridge band plus a boatload of people accepted a free excursion to Beaumaris for a dance. Mr. Wasley was on board serving ice-cold beverages, and all seemed forgiven.[9]

On the evening of July 7, 1904, the Navigation Company nearly lost the *Nipissing*. She was cruising past Juddhaven on her way to Rosseau with about 40 passengers aboard, when smoke was discovered in the forward lounge cabin beneath the bridge. Then, flames broke out and the passengers became alarmed. The crew, however, went to work with pails of water and a fire hose, and the blaze was out soon. An investigation showed that the fire apparently started when someone dropped a match or cigar down behind a cushion inside the "box" formed by a low settee built around the asbestos covering of the stack.

By the season of 1904, the Muskoka Navigation Company was entering its heyday, with eight passenger steamers in regular service on the Muskoka Lakes, plus two more on the Magnetawan. Already it was laying plans for one or two steel hulled palace steamships. In general, the routes of the larger steamers remained unchanged around this time: the flagship *Medora* continued to ply daily from Port Cockburn every morning, and the *Nipissing* from Rosseau, and the old *Muskoka* from Whiteside; all arriving at Muskoka Wharf at 11:50 to meet the noon trains. All three set off at 3:00 p.m.; the *Muskoka* to do the rounds on Lake Muskoka, the *Nipissing* to Lake Rosseau, and the *Medora* back to Lake Joseph. All three called at Beaumaris twice a day at roughly the same time to connect with the *Oriole* (or another steamer) from Bracebridge. The *Kenozha* docked overnight at Muskoka Wharf and provided a morning service on all three lakes, arriving at Port Cockburn at 1:00 p.m. and meeting some of her sister ships at Beaumaris and Port Carling. The *Charlie M.* sailed every morning from Bala, the *Islander* from Gordon Bay on Lake Joseph, and the *Ahmic* from Royal Muskoka. All three called at Port Carling; then, depending on the numbers of passengers bound for the various ports, one would head up to Rosseau and back, while a second made a return trip to Bala. The smaller ships, excepting the *Charlie M.*, also had the longest seasons. Being cheaper to operate, they were the first out in the spring, and the last to be laid up for the winter.

Several times each summer, the steamers had to shake up their schedules when one community or another held one of the monster boating regattas which were becoming so popular. These allowed for plenty of animation and plain good fellowship, followed by a dance in the evenings, while all the wealthy cottagers could enjoy displaying and racing their yachts. Beaumaris, Windermere and Port Sandfield invariably held a regatta every season, while Port Carling used to specialize in Venetian-style water carnivals featuring boat races of every type and climaxing with a sail-past of illuminated steam launches in the evening amid coloured lights on the shores and subdued airs by the bands; altogether a dazzling spectacle.

On August 1, 1904, the first gala regatta was held at the Royal Muskoka Hotel. Perfect weather brought out huge crowds arriving on board the *Medora*, *Nipissing*, *Islander*, and *Oriole*. The *Kenozha* was along with the town band from Gravenhurst, while the *Muskoka* and the *City of Bala* arrived from Bracebridge with another band. Scores of yachts, steam launches, canoes and sailboats were out, and the wharf and hill slopes were black with people. A grand ball in the hotel rotunda brought the day to its close. Tourism in Muskoka had truly arrived in all its finery.

The Muskoka Lakes Navigation and Hotel Company was the culmination of the work of Alexander Peter Cockburn, but as it happened he did not long survive its inception. The Company manager had suffered some heart trouble since his bout with influenza in 1891, though he seemed in the best of health when he returned to his home in Toronto after a trip to Juddhaven on June 2, 1905. That evening, however, he was in the middle of a conversation with his wife, when suddenly she noticed that he was breathing very heavily. Alarmed, she roused the house and sent for a doctor, but before help arrived Mr. Cockburn had expired from a heart attack. Thus, quite unexpectedly, Muskoka's Grand Old Man passed away at the age of 68, leaving a widow, four daughters and a son to mourn his loss.

By and large, one feels, A.P. Cockburn's last years had been a period of frustration and anticlimax. He had been forced to contend with sniping and belittling by members of his own Company, aimed at undermining his prestige or prejudicing his reputation for integrity. He had spent many days and nights of worry and anxiety during his 24 years as manager. The success of his steamboat venture had never made him wealthy — he described himself as "one of the hardest worked and worst paid transportation managers upon the continent" — and his estate was found to be worth a rather modest $38,300. After his death, Mrs. Cockburn was obliged to sell her Rosedale home, plus all her shares in the Navigation Company, and move to downtown Toronto, where she died in 1922. Her husband's thorough dedication to the enterprise he had founded, and his unceasing interest in his Company's welfare, had never left him much time to brood over matters of salary.

Indeed, he had met with disappointments in several endeavours. He had been defeated in politics, both provincially and federally. Around the turn of the century, there was a widespread expectation that his services to the Liberal Party would be rewarded with a seat in the Senate, and indeed there was no lack of friends in high places to testify to the Prime Minister of Mr. Cockburn's merits to that distinction. But it turned out that there were others more deserving still — or perhaps, in the pitiless game of politics there was no place for losers, even after five electoral wins. A vacancy occasioned by the death of Dr. George Landerkin of North Grey in 1903 was awarded instead to Mr. Cockburn's old desk mate in Parliament, Sir Richard Cartwright of Kingston, who had been a cabinet minister in both the Mackenzie and Laurier governments. By this time Mr. Cockburn had also ceased to be the chief shareholder in the Navigation Company, and by 1905 it also seemed that he would soon be replaced as General Manager: one C.H. Nicholson was being groomed as his successor. The business which had been his life work was shifting into other hands. In 1904

S.S. "Medora" and "Nipissing" at Muskoka Wharf, Circa 1904.

S.S. "Medora" and "Nipissing" appear with a Grand Trunk Railway train at Muskoka Wharf, Circa 1904.
Courtesy Public Archives of Canada; PA68436.

Away they Go!
Packed to the gills, the S.S. "Medora", "Muskoka" and "Nipissing" leave Muskoka Wharf in concert around 1904.

Steamboat time at Beaumaris!
Lined up to exchange passengers are the S.S. "Muskoka" (left), "Oriole", "Islander" and "Nipissing", around 1905.

Boarding the S.S. "Medora" at Port Carling, around 1905.

Boats gathered at Royal Muskoka.
In the background can be glimpsed the steamers "Rosseau", "Charlie M." and "Islander"
The vessels in the foreground are not identified.

Regatta at Port Carling.
S.S. "Kenozha" is in attendance at left.

Boating Regatta at Port Sandfield.

— almost pathetically, one feels — he had written to Prime Minister Laurier, asking to be considered as one of the government directors of the new Grand Trunk Pacific Railway, both because he needed the money, and because he felt entitled to some sort of "consolation prize" after the senatorship disappointment. Although his qualifications were excellent and he had always been on good terms with the Grand Trunk executives, once again his hopes were dashed. It seemed as if the old man had been left out in the cold by the advance of time.

To Muskoka, he had never ceased to be the genial, popular A.P. Cockburn; founder of the Navigation Company, father of the Muskoka tourist trade, unwavering supporter of the District's development and projects for community betterment. Many a time during the 40 years he had identified himself with Muskoka's welfare, he had been the recipient of appreciative testimonials, banquets and awards, some of which were of considerable cash value. In the light of such occasions, and of the great success of his steamboat venture, it is likely that he considered his life to have been, on the whole, well spent. Probably to no other single individual has Muskoka ever owed so much.

Certainly the news of his death came as a shock to many in Muskoka and Toronto alike. For a week the *Nipissing* flew her flags at half-mast. On the afternoon of his funeral at Mount Pleasant Cemetery in Toronto, on June 6, 1905, a special train arrived in the city from the north, bearing many of the leading citizens of Muskoka. Dr. D.F. Howland of Huntsville, Sheriff Henry Bridgland of Bracebridge, and many Gravenhurst residents including Charles Mickle, George Homer, Frank Wasley (father of W.F.), former postmaster Alex Cockburn (A.P.'s nephew), and Thomas Robinson, who had been aboard the *Wenonah* during her maiden cruise, were all among the mourners, as were Captain Bailey, Captain McAlpine, Captain Ross Hansen of the *Kenozha*, and old John MacKenzie, Chief Engineer with the fleet. A convention of Canadian Passenger Agents meeting in Toronto was adjourned to permit its members to attend. Many floral tributes were deposited on the casket. Even the 'Muskoka Herald', which had so often assailed Mr. Cockburn, as much for his political affiliations as anything else, gave him the following tribute:

> Muskoka loses one of its best friends, one who, believing in its possibilities, invested his money here when the District was a wilderness and who, conscientiously, in Parliament and out of it, sought to advance its best interests. We think he did not receive a just recognition of his services to the District and the country at large, and on several occasions The Herald advocated his receiving a seat in the Senate. He was well and favourably known throughout the entire District and his death will be regretted by many friends.

Perhaps Mr. Cockburn's life did not close entirely on an anticlimatic note.

Steam navigation in Muskoka had almost reached its zenith at the time of A.P. Cockburn's death, and indeed it still had over half a century of life ahead of it. There were probably over eighty steam driven vessels on the Lakes around 1905, not counting those on the Huntsville lakes, with eight — soon to be ten — belonging to the Navigation Company. 'The Line' still had its problems, but never were its prospects better than at the beginning of the 20th. century. The Golden Age of the Muskoka steamships was now at hand.

Alexander Peter Cockburn (1837-1905).
Father of the Muskoka Steamships. Photograph taken shortly before his death.

FOOTNOTES

[1] Beechgrove Island, Lake Muskoka.

[2] The *Avon* was said to have been the first steamer built at Bracebridge.

[3] Possibly imported from Rice Lake.

[4] The same *Lady of the Lake* afterwards used by Captain Marsh on the Huntsville lakes.

[5] Her later history is a bit muddled: she may have been taken below the falls at Bala to run cruises on the Moon River for a few years after 1901, and in 1905 we hear of a workboat called the "Gipsy" on the Muskoka Lakes, but in 1907 the registry office was informed that the *Gypsy* was no longer in existence.

[6] The S.S. *Islander*

[7] One of the junior officers with the Navigation Company at that time was Captain Ben Dewey of Gravenhurst. It is not known that he took part in the "Battle of Manila", but he was not left unaffected by it: sometime around 1900, we are told, Captain Dewey managed to put the steamer *Oriole* on a shoal near Beaumaris; so tightly that it took two other steamers to pull her off. To commemorate this event, the captain was henceforth known to his shipmates as "Admiral Dewey".

[8] This was regretted by A.P. Cockburn, who considered Sawyer a most unselfish man who had sincerely desired to place the Company's affairs in good hands.

[9] Regrettably, the *Oriole* did misbehave again. Sometime around 1906 she tipped over once more, apparently as a result of piling up on another shoal, but the details and whereabouts of this episode are not known.

Str. "Queen of the Isles", scowing tanbark at Port Carling.
Courtesy, Mr. Gerald Leeder, Kearney

Captain George Parlett and friends enjoying a lunch beside the "City of Bala" at Picnic Island.
Courtesy, Mrs. Joyce Schell, Barlochan.

Steam Launches approaching Windermere Circa 1895.
Behind the (unidentified) launch is the Str. "Edith May" of Port Sandfield.

MAP SECTION

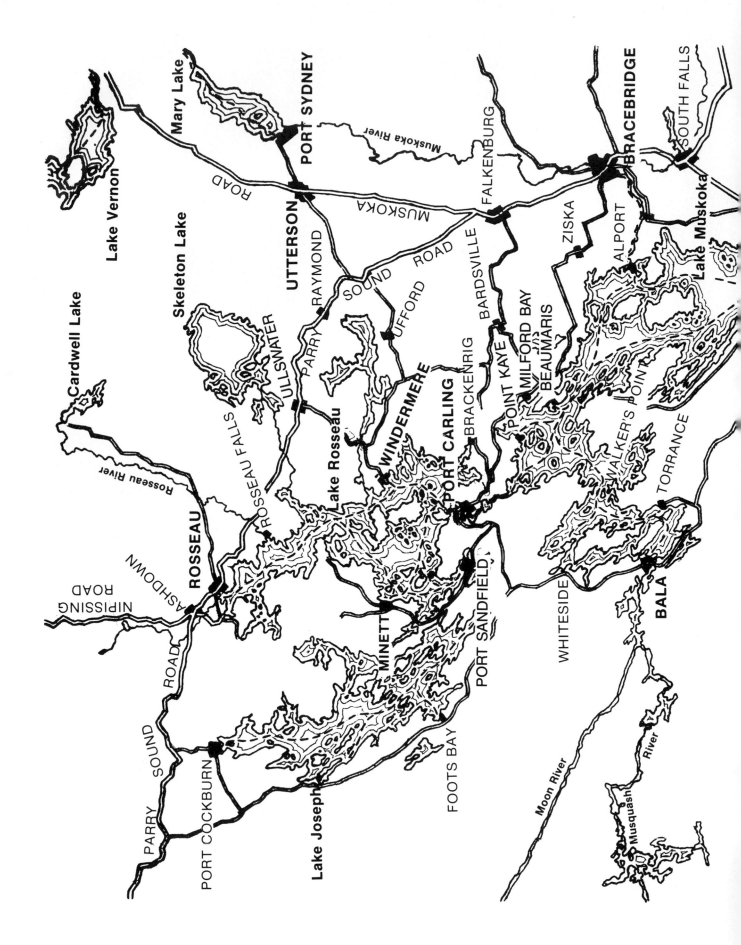

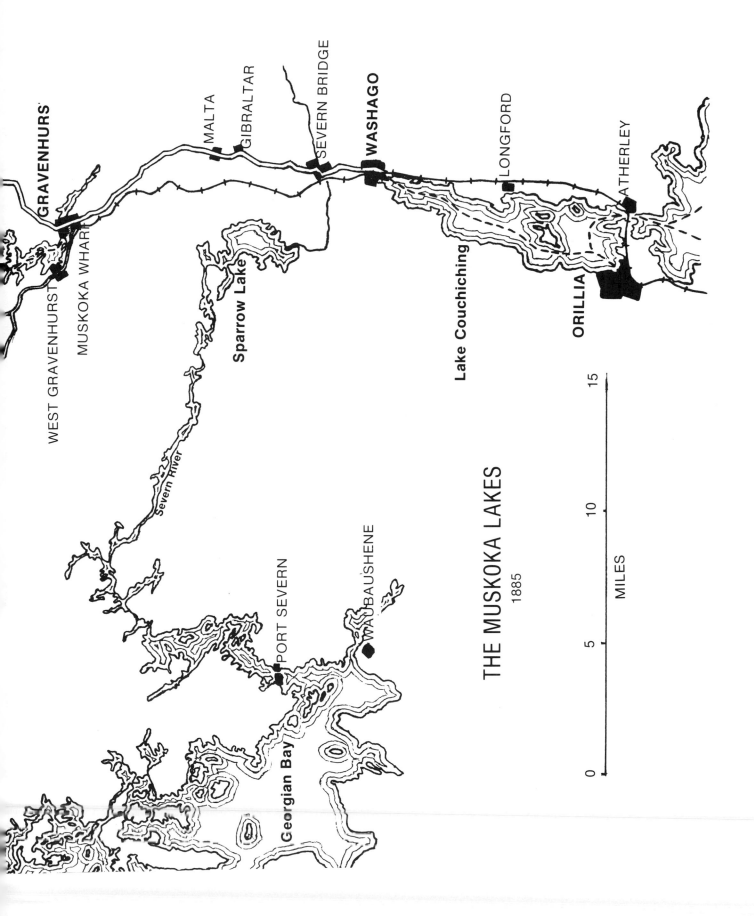

GRAVENHURST

WEST GRAVENHURST

MUSKOKA WHARF

MALTA

GIBRALTAR

SEVERN BRIDGE

WASHAGO

LONGFORD

ATHERLEY

Lake Couchiching

ORILLIA

Sparrow Lake

Severn River

PORT SEVERN

WAUBAUSHENE

Georgian Bay

THE MUSKOKA LAKES

1885

0   5   10   15

MILES

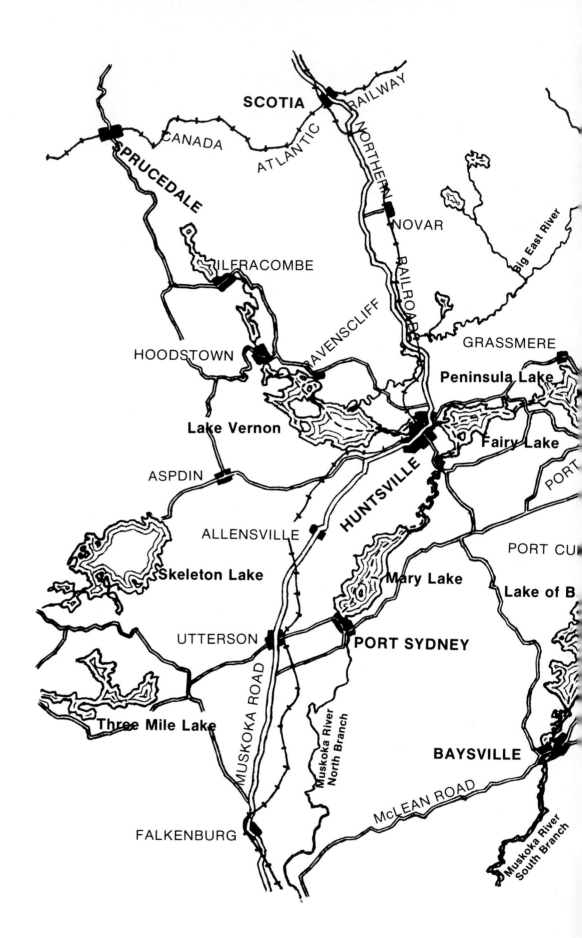

SCOTIA

CANADA

ATLANTIC

NORTHERN

RAILWAY

RAILROAD

NOVAR

Big East River

PRUCEDALE

ILFRACOMBE

HOODSTOWN

RAVENSCLIFF

GRASSMERE

Peninsula Lake

Lake Vernon

Fairy Lake

ASPDIN

HUNTSVILLE

PORT

ALLENSVILLE

PORT CU

Skeleton Lake

Mary Lake

Lake of B

UTTERSON

PORT SYDNEY

Muskoka River
North Branch

Three Mile Lake

MUSKOKA ROAD

BAYSVILLE

McLEAN ROAD

FALKENBURG

Muskoka River
South Branch

NORTH MUSKOKA LAKES

1886

```
0          5          10          15
|----------|----------|----------|
                MILES
```

HILLSIDE

ANAL

DWIGHT

Oxtongue River

Kawagama Lake

BIRKENDALE

Hollow River

NGTON

DORSET

GLENMOUNT

BOBCAYGEON ROAD

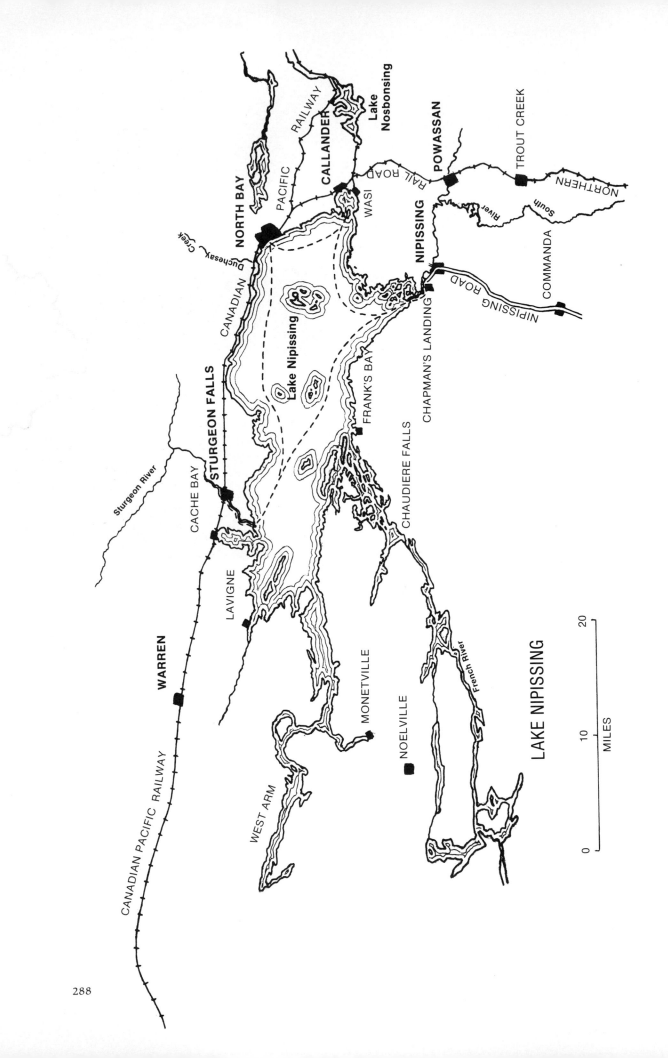

LAKE NIPISSING

0   10   20

MILES

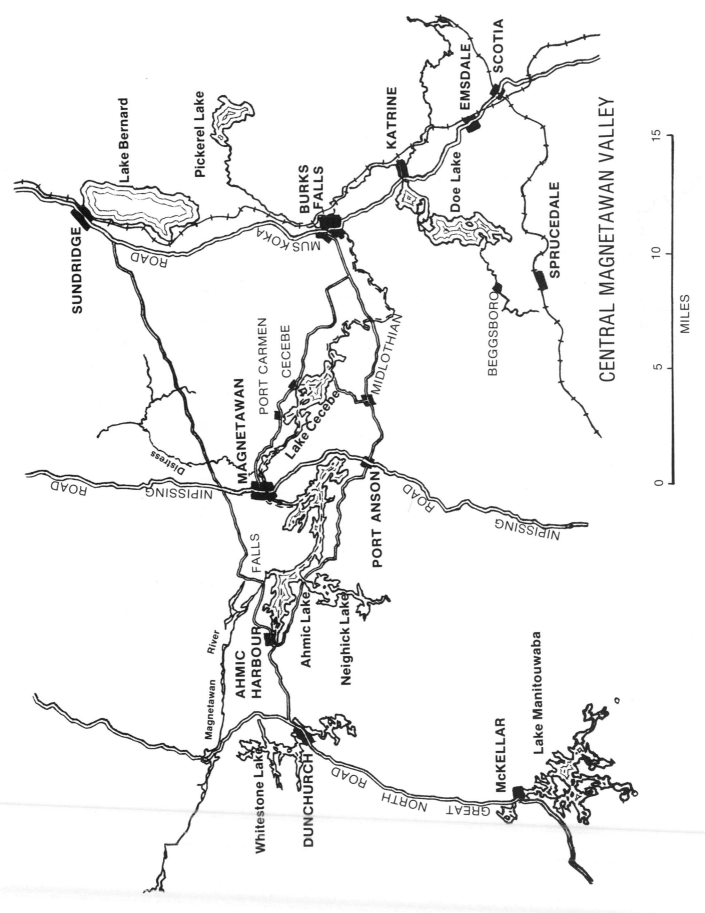

CENTRAL MAGNETAWAN VALLEY

Lake Bernard

Pickerel Lake

SUNDRIDGE

BURKS FALLS

KATRINE

EMSDALE

SCOTIA

Doe Lake

SPRUCEDALE

BEGGSBORO

MUSKOKA ROAD

PORT CARMEN

CECEBE

MAGNETAWAN

Lake Cecebe

MIDLOTHIAN

Distress

NIPISSING ROAD

FALLS

PORT ANSON

NIPISSING ROAD

Ahmic Lake

Neighick Lake

AHMIC HARBOUR

Magnetawan River

Whitestone Lake

DUNCHURCH

McKELLAR

Lake Manitouwaba

GREAT NORTH ROAD

MILES

0   5   10   15

289

S.S. "Nipissing" at a Regatta at Beaumaris Circa 1895.

Windermere, Lake Rosseau.
This picture, taken about 1895, shows the S.S. "Muskoka" at the wharf. The small steamer
in front is probably the yacht "Onaganoh" from Port Cockburn.

S.S. "Nipissing" (Final Version), on the Lake Rosseau run.

S.S. "Oriole" and S.S. "Kenozha" (rear) at Port Carling, around 1895.
Photograph taken from aboard the S.S. "Nipissing"

BIBLIOGRAPHY

PRIMARY SOURCES:
Atlases:
Atlas of the Province of Ontario by Counties
   Toronto, 1879
Guide Book and Atlas of Muskoka and Parry Sound
   Districts (edited by W.E. Hamilton) Toronto,
   1879

Directories:
The Union Publishing Company's Farmers and
   Business Directory for the Counties of Durham,
   Haliburton, Northumberland, Peterboro and
   Victoria, — and Districts of Muskoka, Nipissing,
   Parry Sound, Algoma, Rainy River and Thunder
   Bay, for 1899 (Volume XI) Ingersoll, 1899

Government Reports:
Canada: (Dominion):
Census, 1871 and 1881
Department of Marine and Fisheries:
   Steamship Inspection Reports, 1868-1905
Department of Marine and Fisheries: *List of*
   Vessels on the Registry Books of the Dominion of
   Canada, Volumes for 1871, 1874, 1877, 1880,
   1883, 1907, 1908
Department of Railways and Canals: *Shipping*
   Registers (Kingston, Montreal, Toronto etc.)
Powell-Sirois Report: Economic Background on
   Dominion-Provincial Relations, Volume I, 1939

Canada: (Province):
Bureau of Agriculture: *Reports*, 1858-1865
Department of Crown Lands: *Reports*,
   1859-1866
Legislative Assembly: *Journals*, 1857-1866
Legislative Assembly: *Sessional Papers*,
   1860-1866
Statutes, 1853-1866

Ontario:
Legislative Assembly: *Sessional Papers*
Legislative Assembly: *Sessional Papers: Petitions*
Department of Crown Lands: *Reports of*
   Commissioners, 1867-1878
Department of Public Records and Archives:
   Immigration Papers, 1868, & *Colonization Roads*
   Papers
Department of Public Works: *Annual Reports*,
   1886
Department of Public Works: *Reports of*
   Engineers, 1867-1881
Office of the Provincial Secretary: *Annual*
   Statements, Huntsville & Lake of Bays
   Navigation Company Ltd., Muskoka &
   Nipissing Navigation Company Ltd.,
   Muskoka & Georgian Bay Navigation
   Company Ltd., Muskoka Lakes Navigation
   & Hotel Company Ltd.

County of Simcoe: Municipal Council,
   Minutes, June 1865
District of Muskoka: *Land Patent Books*
District of Parry Sound: *Land Patent Books*

Manuscripts:
James Bain *Papers*
George Brown *Papers*
Alexander Campbell *Papers*
Casey, Frank, & Lillie, James, & Gillehand,
   L.J.: *A History of Sturgeon Falls*
Sir Wilfrid Laurier *Papers*
MacKenzie, Norman Hall: *The Economic and*
   Social Development of Muskoka, 1855-1888
   (M.A. Thesis) 1944
Mills, John M: World Ship Society *Compilation*
Murray, Wanda (editor): *Shipping on Lake*
   Nipissing: From Dugouts to Diesels 1979
Muskoka Papers: (Collection of Mr. Harry
   Linney)
Robinson, Thomas M: *A Voyage in Search of*
   Free Grant Lands
Smith, Ronald: *The History of the Newspapers in*
   Muskoka, 1869-1970 (Thesis)
Redmond Thomas *Papers*
Tweedsmuir Women's Institute: *History of*
   Baysville
Tweedsmuir Women's Institute: *History of*
   McKellar Township
Tweedsmuir Women's Institute: *History of*
   Washago and Severn Bridge

Maps and Charts:
Rogers' New Chart of Lakes Joseph and Rosseau:
   (John Rogers, compiler) Toronto, 1890
Rogers' Chart of the Muskoka Lakes: (John
   Rogers, compiler) Toronto, 1899

Newspapers:
Bracebridge *Gazette*
Bracebridge *Herald*
Bracebridge *Herald-Gazette*
Bracebridge *Muskoka Sun*
Bracebridge *Northern Advocate*
Burks Falls *Almaguin News*
Gravenhurst *Banner*
Gravenhurst *Muskoka News Magazine*
Huntsville *Forester*
Lindsay *Canadian Post*
North Bay *Nugget*
Orillia *Expositor*
Orillia *Northern Light*
Orillia *Packet and Times*
Orillia *Times*
Toronto *Evening Telegram*
Toronto *Weekly Globe*
Toronto *Mail*
Toronto *Daily Star*
Toronto *World*

Published Diaries, Journals, Reminiscences, etc.:

Aberdeen, Lady Ishbel: *The Canadian Journal of Lady Aberdeen 1893-1898* Toronto, 1960

Adam, Graeme Mercer: *Muskoka Illustrated, with Descriptive Narrative of this Picturesque Region* Toronto, 1888

Adams, E. Herbert: *Toronto and Adjacent Summer Resorts* Toronto, 1894

Bell, Robert: *Field Notes* Ontario: Department of Lands and Forests 1848

Cockburn, Alexander Peter: *To the Shareholders of the Muskoka and Georgian Bay Navigation Company* 1902

Cumberland, F. Barlow: *The Northern Lakes of Canada, the Niagara River & Toronto, the Lakes of Muskoka, Lake Nipissing, Georgian Bay, Great Manitoulin Channel, Mackinac, Sault Ste. Marie, Lake Superior* (Second edition) Toronto, 1886

Dale, Joseph: *Canadian Land Grants in 1874* London, 1875

Dufferin and Ava, Hariot Georgina Hamilton-Temple-Blackwood, Marchioness of: *My Canadian Journal, 1872-8; Extracts from my Letters Home, Written while Lord Dufferin was Governor-General* New York, 1891

Grant, George Munro: *Picturesque Spots of the North; Historical and Descriptive Sketches of the Scenery and Life in the Vicinity of Georgian Bay, the Muskoka Lakes, the Upper Lakes, in Central and Eastern Ontario, and in the Niagara District* Chicago, 1899

Hamilton, W.E.: *Muskoka Sketch* Dresden, Ont. 1884

Hathaway, Ann: [pseud. for Mrs. Fannie Cox] *Muskoka Memories: Sketches from Real Life* Toronto, 1904

King, Mrs. Harriet Barbara: *Letters from Muskoka, by an Emigrant Lady (1871-1875)* London, 1878

Kirkwood, Alexander & Murphy, J.J.: *The Undeveloped Lands in Northern and Western Ontario* Toronto, 1878

McAdam, J.T.: *The Lakes of Muskoka and the Georgian Bay, by Captain Mac* Toronto, 1884

McMurray, Thomas: *The Free Land Grants of Canada, from Practical Experience of Bush Farming in the Free Grant Districts of Muskoka and Parry Sound* Bracebridge, 1871

Podmore, Percy St. Michael: *A Sporting Paradise, with Stories of Adventure in America and the Backwoods of Muskoka* London, 1904

Roper, Edward: *Muskoka: Picturesque Playground of Canada* Toronto, 1883

Walker, W.W.: *By Northern Lakes; Reminiscences of Life in Ontario Mission Fields* Toronto, 1896

Watson, Dr. B.A.: *The Sportsman's Paradise, or the Lake Lands of Canada* Philadelphia, 1887

Periodicals and Brochures:

The Canadian Men and Women of the Time 1898

Map Chart: Muskoka Lakes (brochure) 1896

Lakes of Muskoka (brochure) 1883

Monetary Times

Muskoka Lakes: Highlands of Ontario (brochures) 1903 & 1909 editions

Official Guide: Huntsville & Lake of Bays Navigation Company Ltd. 1905

Railroad Magazine Nov. 1951

The Railway and Shipping World

Silver Anniversary: Bigwin Inn, Lake of Bays, Muskoka, Canada 1944

Secondary Sources:

Avery, Sid: *Reflections: Muskoka and Lake of Bays of Yesteryears* Bracebridge 1974

Barry, Larry J. (editor): *Memories of Burks Falls and District, 1835-1978* Burks Falls, 1978

Boyer, Robert J.: *A Good Town Grew Here* Bracebridge, 1978

Conway, Abbott: *The Tanning Industry in Muskoka* 1974

Cope, Mrs. Leila M.: *A History of the Village of Port Carling* Bracebridge 1956

De la Fosse, Frederick M.: *Early Days in Muskoka; Ontario History*, Volume XXXIII, 1939

De la Fosse, Frederick M.: [pseud. Vardon, Roger]: *English Bloods* Ottawa, 1930

Fraser, Captain Levi R.: *History of Muskoka* Bracebridge, 1946

Higginson, T.B.: *A Sportsman's Paradise: Historical Notes on the Burks Falls District, 1835-1890, and the Village of Burks Falls, 1890-1965* Burks Falls, 1965

Hunter, Andrew Frederick: *A History of Simcoe County* (Two Volumes, 1909) Revised edition Barrie, 1948

Jestin, Mrs. G.R.: *The Early History of Torrance* Bracebridge, 1938

Johnson, George H.: *Port Sydney Past* Cheltenham, 1980 (Boston Mills)

Kennedy, W.K.P.: *North Bay: Past-Present-Prospectives* 1961

Lavallée, Omer: *Narrow Gauge Railways of Canada* Montreal, 1972

Lower, Arthur R.M.: *The North American Assault on the Canadian Forest: A History of the Lumber Trade Between Canada and the United States* Toronto, 1938

Lower, Arthur R.M.: *Settlement and the Forest Frontier in Eastern Canada* Toronto, 1936

Mason, D.H.C.: *Muskoka: The First Islanders* Bracebridge, 1957

McLean, Fleetwood K.: *Early Parry Sound Ontario History*, Volume LVI, 1964

Murray, Miss Florence B.: *Muskoka and Haliburton, 1615-1875: A Collection of Documents* Toronto, 1963

Porter, Cecil: *The Light of Other Days* Gravenhurst, 1967

Scarfe, W. Lucien (editor): *John A. Brashear, the Autobiography of a Man Who Loved the Stars* New York, 1924

Schell, Mrs. Joyce I.: *Through the Narrows of Lake Muskoka* Bracebridge, 1974

Schell, Mrs. Joyce I.: *The Years Gone By: A History of Walker's Point and Barlochan, Muskoka, 1870-1970*

Scott, Harley E.: *Steam Yachts of Muskoka* Bracebridge, 1975

Spragge, George W.: *Colonization Roads in Canada West, 1850-1867; Ontario History,* Volume XLIX 1957

Stevens, G.R.: *The Canadian National Railways,* Volume I "Sixty Years of Trial and Error" Toronto, 1960

Sutton, Frederick W.: *Early History of Bala* Bracebridge 1970

Thomas, Redmond, Q.C.: *The Beginning of Navigation and the Tourist Industry in Muskoka; Ontario History,* Volume XLII, 1950

Thomas, Redmond, Q.C.: *Bracebridge, Muskoka: Reminiscences* Bracebridge, 1969

Wallace, W.S.: *The Early History of Muskoka; Queen's Quarterly,* Volume 49, 1942

Wolfe, Roy I.: *The Summer Resorts of Ontario in the Nineteenth Century; Ontario History,* Volume LIV, 1961

The Author is also enormously indebted to a great many private persons who very kindly supplied him with a host of valuable pictures and priceless information. In particular, he wishes to acknowledge the assistance and co-operation of the following people, all of whom helped make this volume possible:

Miss Mary Elizabeth Aitken of Windermere
Mr. Charles Allair of Katrine
Mr. Carl Ames of Gregory
Mrs. M. Anderson of Woodington
Mr. Wilbur Archer of Muskoka Township
Mrs. Jean Ariss of Rosseau
Mr. William J. Armstrong of Bear Creek (near Callander)
Mr. John Baker of Rockwynn and Toronto
Mr. Joe Barrio of North Bay
Mr. Max Beaumont of Alport
Mr. Alfred William Berry of Walker's Point
Mrs. Mildred Bird of Huntsville
Mr. Bill Boettger of Magnetawan
Mr. and Mrs. Charles Bonnis of Gravenhurst
Mr. Hilton Brown of Port Sydney
Mr. Ted Bunt of Burks Falls
Miss Ruth Burritt of Weston
Mr. Norman Campbell of Huntsville
Mr. Peter B. Campbell of Campbell's Landing (near Gravenhurst)
Ms. E. Casselman of Port Sydney
Mr. Ernest Chenai of North Bay
Mr. Norman Chevalier of Dwight
Mr. Fred Clairmont of Gravenhurst
Mr. Victor Clarke of Port Sydney
Mr. Wilfred Clarke of Port Sydney
Miss Dorothy Coate of Rosseau
Mr. Joe Cookson of Grassmere
Mr. Clarence Coons of Kemptville
Mrs. Leila Cope of Port Carling
Mr. Ted Corbett of Bala
Mr. Robert E. Cornell of Minett
Mr. Sid Cowan of Port Carling
Mr. Enoch Buell Cox of Port Sandfield
Mr. Guy Croswell of Burks Falls
Mr. and Mrs. J. Harry Croucher of Bracebridge
Miss Marjorie Demaine of Hoodstown
Mr. Charles Dillon of Birkendale
Mrs. Albert Dixon of Monck Township
Mr. Alex Dufresne of Callander
Mrs. Dorothy Duke of Port Carling
Mr. William Ray Fife of Windermere
Miss Mary Fowler of Beaverton

Mrs. Allan Fraser of Bracebridge
Miss Edna Fraser of Port Cockburn and Toronto
Mr. Thomas Norman Giles of Peterborough
Mr. Cecil Goodwin of Gravenhurst
Mr. Bill Gray of Port Sandfield and Toronto
Captain Donald Green of Callander
Mr. Arnold Groh of Gravenhurst
Mr. Albert Hallett of Magnetawan
Mr. Rufus Harris of McKellar Township
Mr. A. Ernest Hatherley of Gordon Bay
Miss Marie Henry of Huntsville
Captain Wesley D. Hill of Gravenhurst
Mr. Frank Hutcheson of Huntsville
Mr. George Hutcheson of Huntsville
Mr. Floyd Ireland of Bala
Mr. Robert Ireland of London
Mr. Claude Jackson of McKellar Township
Mr. Harry Jackson of Monck Township
Mr. Harwell Jackson of Bracebridge
Mr. John Jackson of Gravenhurst
Mr. Rod Jenkins of Ahmic Harbour
Ms. Margaret and Tillie Jestin of Torrance
Mr. George Johnson of Port Sydney
Mr. Bill Johnston of Nipissing Township
Mr. Bernie Judd of Juddhaven
Mrs. Mary Kennedy of South River
Mr. Colin Keppy of Spence Township
Mr. Herbert Knapp of Callander
Mr. Ronald Langford of Huntsville
Mrs. A.P. Larson of Gravenhurst
Mr. John Laycock of Huntsville
Mr. Gerald Leeder of Kearney
Captan and Mrs. Reg F. Leeder of Orillia
Mr. Henry Longhurst of Windermere
Mr. J. Lydan of Pinelands
Mr. Andrew D. MacLean of Gravenhurst
Captain Neil MacNaughton of Parry Sound
Ms. Pearl May of Huntsville
Mr. Ernest I. McCulley of St. Catharines
Mr. William McEwen of McKellar
Mrs. Dick McGibbon of Mimico
Mr. Norman McNeice of Bala
Mr. Fred Mills of Milford Bay
Mr. Luther Mills of Parkersville

Mrs. Rita Moon of Sturgeon Falls
Mrs. George Morris of Magnetawan
Mr. and Mrs. Eddy Mortimer of Mortimer's
  Point
Mr. Bernie Moulton of Parry Sound
Mr. D. Murdoch of Orono
Mrs. Anna Myers of Gravenhurst
Mr. Murray Neal of Torrance
Mr. Edgar Olan of Huntsville
Messrs. Cecil and Levi Porter of
  Gravenhurst
Miss Winnifred Prowse of Bracebridge
Mr. Charles Readman of West Gravenhurst
Ms. Dorothy Robson of Fox Point
Mr. Enoch Rogers of Port Sandfield
Mrs. Tilly Rowe of The Locks (near
  Huntsville)
Captain William Rowe of North Bay
Mr. and Mrs. Alvin H. Saulter of
  Gravenhurst
MNrs. Joyce Schell of Barlochan
Mr. Peter Schell of Muskoka Township
Mr. Harley E. Scott of Minett
Mrs. Edythe Scriver of Huntsville
Mr. Arthur Silverwood of Huntsville

Mr. Gordon Sloan of Gravenhurst
Mr. Ron Smith of Calgary
Mr. Claude Snider of Gravenhurst
Mr. Tomas Stanton of Port Stanton
Mr. Ralph Stephen of Port Carling
Mr. Reg Stephen of Port Carling
Mr. Dave Stewart of Burks Falls
Mr. Fred W. Sutton of Bala
Mr. Owen Swann of Huntsville
Mr. Redmond Thomas of Bracebridge
Mr. Gilbert Thompson of South Portage
Mr. Lester Turnbull of Dundas
Mrs. Viola Van Clief of Baysville
Mr. Aubrey Walton of Christian Valley
Mrs. Edgar Walton of Port Loring
Mr. Claude Wardell of Huntsville
Mr. James St. Clair Wardell of Huntsville
Mr. Dan Watson of Baysville
Mr. Brian Westhouse of Parry Sound
Mr. Hector Whitehead of Gravenhurst
Mr. John Whitehead of Parker's Point
Mrs. Dorothy Wilmot of Midlothian
Mrs. M. Wittick of Burks Falls
Mr. Victor Woodcock of Huntsville

In addition, the Author owes a special
word of thanks to the Magnetawan Museum
of Magnetawan Village, the Muskoka
Pioneer Village of Huntsville, the North
Himsworth Museum of Callander, the Port
Carling Pioneer Museum, the Segwun
Steamship Museum of Gravenhurst, and the
Woodwinds Museum of Barlochan; besides
the Central Reference Library of Toronto,
the University of Toronto library, and most
of the libraries from Orillia to North Bay;
for all their splendid co-operation and
assistance. He is also immensely indebted to
the Public Archives of Canada, and to the
Provincial Archives of Ontario. Also, a word
of grateful appreciation is due the
Explorations Branch of the Canada Council
for providing the Author with a substantial
grant for continued research.

    Furthermore, there are three people to
whom the Author owes a particular word of
thanks: his sister, Mrs. Mary E. Logan of
Ottawa, for kindly proof-reading his
manuscript, arranging to have it retyped, and
recommending a great many beneficial
changes; his friend Professor Gordon C.
Shaw of Thornhill, for all his encouragement
and criticisms; and finally, his father, Mr. L.
David Tatley of Brampton, for once again
patiently harbouring and humouring the
writer throughout the many months of
preparation and compilation required for this
book.

Index "A"
of the Steamboats that appear in this book

Asterisk (*) Indicates Photograph

Captain George Bailey, in front of the pilothouse of the S.S. "Nipissing".
(Note the carved wooden phoenix.)

Index "B"
of the People, Places and Enterprises that appear
in this book

302

S.S. "Medora (Original Version), locking through at Port Carling.
Courtesy, Mrs. Dorothy Duke, Port Carling